Surviving Persecution

SURVIVING
PERSECUTION

How to Understand, Prepare, and Respond

Vernon J. Sterk
foreword by Charles E. Van Engen

WIPF & STOCK · Eugene, Oregon

SURVIVING PERSECUTION
How to Understand, Prepare, and Respond

Wipf & Stock
An Imprint of Wipf and Stock Publishers
199 W. 8th Ave., Suite 3
Eugene, OR 97401

www.wipfandstock.com

PAPERBACK ISBN: 978-1-5326-3858-9
HARDCOVER ISBN: 978-1-5326-3859-6
EBOOK ISBN: 978-1-5326-3860-2

Manufactured in the U.S.A.   DECEMBER 9, 2019

All scripture has been taken from the New International Version (NIV) of the Bible.

All Spanish materials have been translated to English by the author.

Dedication

To my wife, Carla, who has faithfully accompanied me throughout all of the experiences and struggles that have been a part of our lives as missionaries in facing the challenge of persecution in Chiapas, Mexico. Her unselfish love for me and our family, her undying commitment to the Tzotzil people and cause of Christ in Chiapas, and her unfailing courage and insight as my missionary companion have formed the basis of our team ministry. With great appreciation and love I dedicate this study to Carla, for it is as much hers as mine.

To our daughter, Michele, and to our son, Shane, for their valuable part in our family's mission to the Tzotzil people, especially during the years of village living and throughout the most difficult years of persecution.

Contents

List of Illustrations and Photos

Foreword

JESUS TOLD HIS DISCIPLES, "Blessed are those who are persecuted because of righteousness, for theirs is the kingdom of heaven . . . Rejoice and be glad . . . for in the same way they persecuted the prophets who were before you." (Matt 5:10–12 NIV).

Being blessed in the midst of persecution does not mean the persecution is any less wrong, horrific, and unacceptable. Religious persecution is destructive, disruptive, and disastrous.

Although choice in faith-expression should be recognized as an inalienable human right, religious persecution has increased around the world. It is prevalent in many countries and growing. Rulers, governments, religious fundamentalist groups, and many rebel groups want to control religious expression. Religious persecution is a fact of life for adherents of many religions.

In a recent summary article, Associated Press national writer David Crary wrote,

> Government restrictions on religion have increased markedly in many places around the world, not only in authoritarian countries, but also in many of Europe's democracies, according to a report surveying 198 countries that was released Monday (July 15, 2019).
>
> The report released by the Pew Research Center, covering developments through 2017 . . . seeks to document the scope of religion-based harassment and violence. Regarding the world's two largest religions, it said Christians were harassed in 143 countries and Muslims in 140. This was Pew's 10th annual Report of Global Restriction on Religion. It said 52 governments, including those in Russia and China, impose high levels of restrictions on religion, up from 40 governments in 2007. It said

> 56 countries in 2017 were experiencing social hostilities involv-
> ing religion, up from 29 in 2007 . . . Globally, among the 25 most
> populous countries, those with the highest level of government
> restrictions were China, Iran, Russia, Egypt and Indonesia.[1]

The Pew study to which Crary is referring highlights government restrictions on religious expression. If one added persecution by one religious
group of other religious groups, the list would be much longer. Religious
persecution is a fact of life for adherents of many religions. Although we
acknowledge that religious persecution is also perpetrated by Christians on
adherents of other faiths, this book has to do with the religious persecution
of Christians by anti-Christian forces, people, groups, and governments.

More Christians are persecuted today because of their faith than ever
before in the history of the church. This fact of our day makes this book even
more necessary and urgent. This outstanding book has to do with Christian
response to persecution.

We often think of "religious persecution" as physical oppression or
suffering. This is very real and too prevalent. We know that during the
twentieth century more Christians died because they confessed their faith
in Jesus Christ than the sum-total of all Christians killed because of their
faith during the previous nineteen centuries combined.

But persecution may also include restrictions like articles of clothing
being prohibited, houses of worship being destroyed, restrictions on Christians meeting for worship, Christian teachers in public schools not being
allowed to speak of their faith while teaching, restrictions on voting, or dis-
allowing civil liberties, or restricting business or property ownership. When
we understand persecution in this broader sense, we begin to realize that
persecution impacts a large percentage of Christians on every continent.

Vern and Carla Sterk spent a lifetime career in Chiapas, Mexico, living
among a Mayan tribal group where all forms of persecution were exercised
by the local ruling leaders, especially against anyone professing to be a fol-
lower of Jesus Christ, as presented in the Bible. Vern's life experience and
academic reflection/analysis as an ordained pastor, theologian, Bible translator, anthropologist, and missiologist (PhD at Fuller School of World Mission) make Vern Sterk eminently qualified to teach us all how the Christian
church can see positive results from appropriate and wise preparation for
and response to persecution. Vern has been there, lived it, seen it, done it,
and learned from his ministry in a context of severe persecution.

There are many news items, articles, and books that report about religious persecution of Christians globally. But, to my knowledge, there is

1. Crary, "Government Restrictions."

no book like this one that analyzes the multiplicity of dynamics involved in persecution and then offers concrete, candid, doable, and very helpful suggestions as to how Christians and Christian churches may respond to persecution in ways that will enhance the spread of the gospel and the health and growth of the church: spiritually, theologically, organizationally and numerically.

This book is a must read for Christian leaders on all six continents who want to guide the church and its members toward a vibrant, healthy, impactful, and transforming presence in their local and global contexts, in spite of the persecution they suffer. Here we have a guide to Christian living that enables us, no matter the circumstances we face as followers of Jesus, to "give an answer to everyone who asks [us] to give a reason for the hope that [we] have," as the apostle Peter wrote to the persecuted Christians of his day (1 Pet 3:15 NIV).

Charles E. Van Engen
Holland, Michigan
August, 2019

Acknowledgments

I AM DEEPLY GRATEFUL to God for the following people and organizations:

The Reformed Church in America, for giving me its support for more than forty years of our mission work in Chiapas, Mexico.

The Tzotzil Presbyteries of Chiapas with their pastors and leaders, who have courageously dedicated their lives and hearts to the Lord's work in Chiapas, and who have guided me as I learned to walk the slippery paths of persecution with them.

My wife, Carla, for sacrificing many hours at the computer in proofreading, correcting, and editing to make this book a reality.

Charles Van Engen, close friend and former missionary colleague, whose practical help and expertise in completing the final stages of this book have been invaluable.

Marlene Braunius, who did the initial editing of this book.

Ruggles Church, who read the manuscript and offered his suggestions.

Judi Folkert, who spent many hours in formatting and typing in corrections after my bicycle accident left me unable to use my hands.

And thanks be to God for his protection and sustaining power during the many years in which I was involved with persecuted Christians.

Definition of Terms

THE FOLLOWING TERMS ARE defined in order to help the reader understand their use in the context of this book. Some of the terms are of Spanish derivation and will be translated in this section, even though they will be used in Spanish throughout the text.

Believer, or **believer in Christ**—is another term used for Christian. It is the word that the indigenous Christians use to refer to themselves in their indigenous languages, with which they differentiate themselves from those who maintain their traditional animistic folk religion.

Cacique—(pronounced "kah-See-kays") is a Spanish term that is extensively employed in this book to mean a political mafia boss in a tribal area. The original Spanish meaning of this term was a powerful leader, without implying the negative use of that power in domination and oppression. However, I will be using the term in the negative sense since this is its present usage in Chiapas.

Cargo—is a religious office or charge which the traditional indigenous Tzotzils serve on a rotating basis for one year. *Evangélicos* often refuse to serve in these animistic religious ceremonies, since they involve worship and service to tribal images.

Christian—is a term that will be used as one who believes in or professes belief in Jesus as the Christ. It is inclusive of both Protestant and Roman Catholic believers and will be used when it is meant to have the inclusive meaning. The Tzotzil Mayans do not use the Spanish term *cristiano* for a Christian because in the Tzotzil language *cristiano* is the word for person.

Evangélico—is a Spanish word used by Mayan Protestants for those who believe in the *evangélio*, which means the gospel. In this book the Spanish word *evangélico* is not synonymous with the English term "evangelical," which often implies right-wing fundamentalist.

Gospel—is used in its lower case to mean the good news or teachings of Jesus Christ as found in the New Testament of the Bible.

Indigenous—describes a member of the aboriginal races of Mexico, Central and South America, and the West Indies. In most cases the term will be used to describe the Mayan people of Chiapas and Guatemala.

Mestizo—is a term used in Mexico and Latin America to refer to a person of mixed race, one that has both Spanish and indigenous descent.

National Church—when used in the upper-case form will indicate the National Presbyterian Church of Mexico. It will be used only to avoid the repetition of the full name.

Persecution—is defined in this book as the negative reaction to the communication and acceptance of the gospel. It is the denial of basic human rights and the infliction of suffering because of religious commitment or belief. It has social and economic consequences and includes intimidation, coercion, public harassment, civil disabilities, expulsions, and violence.

Power Healing—is used to mean a restoring to health and wholeness through the divine intervention of God. It is a healing that results from prayer and the power of God, but it does not exclude the use of medical treatment.

Presbyterians—will be used for *evangélicos* who are affiliated with the National Presbyterian Church of Mexico. The reader should not assume that this term implies strict correspondence with the Presbyterian denominations in other parts of the world.

Presbytery, General Assembly, consistory—are all judicatory structures of the national Presbyterian Church of Mexico. General Assembly applies to the national level organization; Presbytery applies to district or regional levels; consistory applies to the local church level.

Protestant—has been avoided in this book as much as possible since it has negative connotations in Mexico and much of Latin America where it implies one who opposes and protests against Roman Catholics. When the term is used in this study it will carry the meaning of a Christian who is distinguished from a Roman Catholic.

Shaman—is a religious practitioner or spiritual medium whose principle role is exorcism and communication with the tribal deities. Tzotzil shamans perform curing ceremonies in an attempt to restore physical and spiritual wholeness.

Traditionalist—refers to an indigenous leader who adheres to or defends the ancient Mayan customs and religious practices.

Tzotzil—is the specific Mayan language of the people in the central highlands of Chiapas, Mexico, with whom I worked. See their tribal area on the Chiapas map.

Worldview—is defined, in the words of Paul Hiebert, as "the basic assumptions about reality which lie behind the beliefs and behavior of a culture."[2]

2. Hiebert, *Anthropological Insights*, 45.

Introduction

THIS BOOK IS WRITTEN from my perspective as a missionary who entered an unevangelized Mayan tribe in Chiapas, the southern-most state of Mexico. During my forty years of working with indigenous people who were resistant to the gospel, I closely observed the phenomena called persecution. As I attempted to counsel and encourage new Christians who faced opposition and persecution, I was frustrated by the lack of any thorough analysis or study that could help the church in hostile situations.

This study describes, analyzes, and gives guidelines for preparation and response to persecution. It begins with historical, worldview, and biblical perspectives; moves to the origins, stages, and results; and finally suggests responses at the local, national, and international level.

Persecution can damage the church when it is violent and long-lasting. Under the onslaught of persecution, the church can be obliterated. However, my experience as a missionary among the Mayans has shown that a clear understanding, an adequate preparation, and the proper response to persecution can help the church survive and grow.

Persecuted Christians often do not comprehend the complexity of why suffering has been thrust upon them. Throughout the history of the Christian church, there has been little analysis of the causes and effects of persecution. Many volumes and hundreds of articles have been written about specific acts of persecution and oppression carried out against those who identify themselves as Christians. Yet, even though most of these writings contain detailed descriptions of the suffering and horror of persecution, there is a lack of guidelines for those living in an environment of opposition to the gospel.

As I attempted to communicate the good news of Jesus Christ in a resistant culture in a way that would not incite persecution, I found that it was necessary for me to gain an in-depth understanding of this phenomena.

From my experience and observations comes the thesis of this book: when the gospel is introduced into hostile cultures, persecution is inevitable and will negatively affect the growth of the church, but the damaging effects can be minimized through an adequate preparation for and proper response to persecution. Out of this thesis emerges the necessity of projecting models for the anthropological approach to resistant cultures and suggesting guidelines that could be helpful in surviving persecution.

A complicating factor in dealing with the problem of persecution is the common assumption that persecution, in itself, is a positive element in causing the growth of the church. This seems to be based on Tertullian's well-known statement that "the blood of the martyrs is indeed the seed of the church."[3]

Many authors and contemporary church leaders continue to assume that persecution will inevitably be followed by church growth. My experience in working with persecuted Christians in the Mayan tribes caused me to question this assumption and motivated me to move on to an analysis of persecution.

The purpose of this book is to help the persecuted church survive the damaging effects of premature persecution and enable the church to understand, prepare, and respond in a way that will encourage maximum growth both before and after the inevitable confrontation of the gospel. This study is intended to share my observations and principles with those who are presenting the gospel in hostile environments. To assist the reader, my notes can be found in observation boxes throughout each chapter. It is my hope and prayer that this book will be a blessing to those confronted with persecution.

3. Tertullian, *Apol.* 50.

Chapter 1

The Historical Context of Persecution in Chiapas

THE GROWTH OF THE Protestant churches in Chiapas, whose members are known as *evangélicos*,[1] is well known. Less well known is the story of severe, cruel, systematic, physical persecution that was the environment in which the Protestant churches in Chiapas not only survived, but also grew dramatically. For us to understand the dynamics of Christian responses to persecution, it is first necessary to grasp what persecution is all about. What does it look like? In this chapter, I have included numerous specific, authenticated stories of persecution that form the historical context of persecution in Chiapas. The stories shared in this chapter are only a few of hundreds. This chapter serves to set the scene of persecution in Chiapas, and offers a preliminary description of the type of persecution that has been most common there, specifically among the indigenous tribes. The stories from Chiapas have their counterparts in the history of persecution in early Christianity, in medieval Europe, and later in the colonial histories of peoples in Asia and Africa. In this volume, we are focusing our attention on Chiapas as a case study of persecution.

Persecution is not new to the highlands of Chiapas, Mexico. It certainly did not have its beginnings when the first *evangélicos* crossed the

---

1. *Evangélico* is a Spanish word used to describe those who are followers of Jesus Christ and place an emphasis on the gospel as revealed in the Bible. In Mexico and most of Latin America the term Protestant is avoided because it can imply anti-Catholic. The English term "Evangelical" has certain difficult connotations in some areas of the world where the term implies extreme right-wing fundamentalists.

border of Chiapas from Guatemala in 1901 and 1902. Prior to the arrival of the Spaniards, there had been major armed conflict between Mayan groups, but not systematic religious persecution. That began with the coming of the Spaniards in the early sixteenth century. Hugo Esponda records the first persecution in Chiapas carried out by the Spanish conquerors against the Mayan culture and religion only a few years after the successful invasion in 1518 and 1519 led by Juan de Grijalva and Hernán Cortéz.[2]

Centuries before Columbus's arrival in the New World, the Mayan civilization had developed one of the world's most remarkable cultures.[3] Mayan religious systems were also highly developed, evidenced by elaborate pyramids, palaces, and artifacts that still stand. Into that pre-Columbian Mayan world, the Spanish soldiers and Roman Catholic priests introduced violent oppression and persecution. They smashed most of the Mayan gods and temples in their path of destruction, and the Catholic faith was imposed on the indigenous people at sword point. The conquest and the persecution were cruel and devastating. In 1542 Fray Bartolomé de Las Casas begins his *Brief Account of the Devastation of the Indies* with this description of the treatment of the indigenous:

> And Spaniards have behaved like ravening beasts, killing, terrorizing, afflicting, torturing, and destroying the native peoples. We can estimate very surely and truthfully that in the forty years that have passed, with the infernal actions of the Christians, there have been unjustly slain more than twelve million men, women and children. In truth, I believe without trying to deceive myself that the number of the slain is more like fifteen million.[4]

Although Las Casas was most likely describing the killing of indigenous peoples all over Mexico and Central America prior to 1542, he offers an excruciating view of the devastation of the indigenous tribes in places like Chiapas.[5]

The conquest of Mexico may be better described as a military invasion than as religious persecution. However, it was carried out in the name of God and the king of Spain. The violent form of persecution used in

2. Esponda, *Historia de la Iglesia*, 26–27.

3. Von Hagen, *World of the Maya*, 11.

4. Las Casas, *Devastation*, 4.

5. The indigenous populations of Mexico were nearly decimated between 1532 and 1608. In a chart shown in Dussel (*History of the Church*, 42) statistics reveal that the indigenous populations in Mexico fell from a total of 16,871,408 in 1532 to a total of only 2,649,573 by the year 1658. That means that in just twenty-six years more than 14,000,000 indigenous people had perished, resulting in only 1,069,255 remaining.

attempting to obliterate the Mayan religion and culture sought to force the indigenous of the Americas to change their traditional religious worldview. Las Casas described the method for bringing them to Roman Catholicism:

> Nothing was done to *incline* the indigenous to embrace the one true Faith, they were rounded up and in large numbers *forced* to do so. Inasmuch as the conversion of the indigenous to Christianity was stated to be the principal aim of the Spanish conquerors, they have dissimulated the fact that only with blood and fire have indigenous been brought to embrace the Faith and to swear obedience to the kings of Castile or by threats of being slain or taken into captivity.[6]

Enrique Dussel explains how the Spanish conquest also became persecution by the Roman Catholic Church. Spanish Christendom had

> entered the eighth century locked in a desperate struggle against Islam, a conflict that continued for eight centuries and which produced in the Spanish people a spirit of the "crusades" . . . But it was not until 1492, the same year that Columbus discovered some of the islands of the Caribbean, that the Moors were finally expelled from Granada . . . In Spain there existed, therefore, something akin to a "temporal messianism" in which the destiny of the nation and the destiny of the Church were believed to be united. Hispanic Christianity, it was believed, was unique in that the nation had been elected by God to be the instrument for the salvation of the world.[7]

The idea that the Spanish had been elected by God was given full backing by the Roman pontiffs during the period. As Dussel says: "This was the first time in history that the Papacy gave to a nation the twofold authority to colonize and evangelize, that is, temporal and eternal, political and ecclesiastical, economic and evangelistic authority."[8]

Instead of evangelizing the indigenous cultures of Mexico, the Roman Catholic Church set out to destroy what they saw as pagan. Instead of seeking to transform the Indian practices, the Spaniards were scandalized by such things as the offerings of human sacrifices. Because they were unable to understand or appreciate any part of the Indian worldview or cultural forms, they "sought to obliterate every vestige of pre-Hispanic American civilization."[9]

6. Las Casas, *Devastation*, 18.

7. Dussel, *History of the Church*, 37–38.

8. Dussel, *History of the Church*, 38.

9. Dussel, *History of the Church*, 42.

Fray Bartolomé de Las Casas was the first to attempt to defend Latin America's indigenous against persecution and annihilation by the Spanish conquerors. He had joined Father Antonio de Montesinos of the Caribbean island of Hispaniola in condemning the Spanish colonists for their exploitation and persecution. Bartolomé de Las Casas had undergone a major conversion in his view of the Indian persecution. In Santo Domingo in April 1514, he admitted that as a priest and *encomendero* (land/slave holder) he himself was inflicting injustice and persecution against the indigenous people. In August 1514 he made formal charges against Governor Velazquez and began a lifelong campaign of defending the Indian cause in the Americas by writing many treatises.[10] By the time this Dominican priest was named bishop of Chiapas in 1543 and arrived in San Cristóbal during Lent of 1545,[11] he had carried out a long and fierce battle against the Spanish injustices and persecution from which he did not deviate until his death in 1566. He attempted to overturn the *encomienda* (land- and slave-holding) system in Chiapas, which he felt was nothing more than enslavement of the indigenous people. However, most of the local priests and the Spanish colonists immediately opposed him.[12] Las Casas was only able to remain as bishop of Chiapas for six months before he was violently expelled and forced to return to Spain. There he continued to fight for Indian rights, but he was never able to return to Chiapas or San Cristóbal de Las Casas, which now bears his name as the great "Universal Protector of the indigenous."[13]

> *Observation: Those who oppose the forces of persecution and attempt to defend the rights of the persecuted risk facing violent opposition from the established powers.*

Thus, the imposition of Christianity was forced on the cultures of Mexico and Latin America through violent persecution. Las Casas's valiant battle to convince the Spaniards that evangelization could not occur by force of arms was ultimately rejected. Even when the Spanish Crown was convinced that "New Laws of the Indies"[14] were indispensable to halt the

10. Fray Bartolomé de Las Casas wrote extensive documents like *History of the Indies*, *Brief Account of the Devastation of the Indies* (1542), *Plan for Reformation of the Indies*, and *Petition in Defense of the Indian*.

11. Dussel, *History of the Church*, 52.

12. Dussel, *History of the Church*, 52.

13. Dussel, *History and the Theology of Liberation*, 83.

14. The full name of the edict was "New Laws of the Indies for the Good Treatment and Preservation of the indigenous." One of the principal statements included was: "The Indian is henceforth free. To enslave them or to mistreat them in any way is a misdemeanor punishable by law" (McHenry, *Short History*, 63).

persecution, those laws were never applied by the governors and colonists in the Americas. When Spain sent Francisco Tello de Sandoval to enforce the New Laws, the colonists and land/slave owners mounted a major rebellion and finally convinced the emperor to repeal the laws.[15]

> Observation: Laws against persecution and oppression are useless if those in power only enforce them when it is to their advantage.

The attempt to violently impose Christianity on the indigenous cultures of Latin America was never successful. As Enrique Dussel says: "Latin American culture is still in a pre-Christian stage, although it has been affected in many respects by Christianity."[16] The first effect of the imposition of Christianity was that indigenous cultures and worldviews were forcibly submerged. Much of the Indian population was annihilated, and while this disintegrated the Mayan worldview, it did not destroy it. The second effect was that a people was victimized but never evangelized. Dussel describes them as "a people who long for the completion of evangelization."[17] Roman Catholic Christendom never succeeded in evangelizing the indigenous people of Mexico. Instead, the church and its priests became a part of the force of domination and political control over these indigenous people.

When the Hispanic colonial empire began to collapse in the late 1800s and early 1900s, Roman Catholic Christendom had to yield much of its power to growing nationalism. In the Mexican Revolution of 1917, the Catholic Church lost most of its wealth and land, and the separation of church and state cost the Catholic Church much of its legal and political power. The doors were opened to the Protestant *evangélicos* in Mexico, and in Chiapas the Presbyterians accepted the task of evangelization. Thus began a new period in the historical context of persecution in Chiapas.

Persecution in the Indigenous Areas of Chiapas

The history of the Protestant church in Chiapas is a story of persecution. Since the first contacts with the gospel through lay missionaries from Guatemala in 1901,[18] opposition to *evangélicos*, and notably to the Presbyterians, has been constant. When persecution abated in the Spanish-speaking areas of Chiapas, the growth of the church in the Indian tribes brought on a new wave of persecution.

15. Parkes, *History of Mexico*, 94.
16. Dussel, *History of the Church*, 21.
17. Dussel, *History of the Church*, 71.
18. Esponda, *Historia de la Iglesia*, 26.

The most persistent and violent persecution has taken place in the indigenous and tribal areas of the state of Chiapas. At the entrance of the gospel in each tribal area, some form of persecution has been evident. The tribal areas of Ch'ol, Tzeltal, Tojolabal, and Tzotzil have struggled with the problems of persecution for many years. Pauses in this persecution have allowed the church to grow, just as waves of persecution, with their time of relief, allowed for growth in the early church.[19] All of the Mayan Indigenous tribes of Chiapas have experienced such waves. In what follows are short documented accounts of persecution in Chiapas.

Ch'ol Persecution

As early as 1935, relatively weak and sporadic persecution against groups of Presbyterians in the Ch'ol tribe broke out. However, as late as 1953, four Presbyterian Ch'ols from Tumbalá were jailed for almost five years in the Chiapan capital of Tuxtla Gutiérrez for the false accusation of having burned the Roman Catholic Church in Tumbalá.

In the 1950s several itinerant evangelists were jailed briefly in Ch'ol villages, but the gospel spread rapidly, and no further major persecution incidents or expulsions have occurred. The lack of organized persecution can be attributed to fact that the Ch'ol tribe had no strong central organization controlled by a group of tribal chiefs or *caciques*.[20] When the Roman Catholic Church failed to promote persecution in the area, the scattered villages in the Ch'ol area could not sustain persecution against the *evangélicos*, and opposition faded. The Presbyterian membership in the Ch'ol area grew to nearly thirty thousand believers in Christ by 1990.

Persecution did not break out again in the Ch'ol area until February 1990 when a local Roman Catholic priest, Gerónimo Hernandez Gómez, stirred up traditionalists in the village of La Arena, a jungle village near the Guatemalan border. He told the growing number of Presbyterians there that since they did not comprise the majority, they would be expelled. When the *evangélicos* refused to leave after being threatened, the village leaders proceeded to burn two of the believers' houses. Word spread around that all *evangélicos'* houses would be burned if they did not leave.

19. Lesbaupin, *Blessed are the Persecuted*, xii–xiii.

20. *Cacique* is a Spanish term that will be extensively employed in this book. In Chiapas, it has come to mean a political mafia-like boss in a tribal area. The original Spanish meaning of this term is "Indian chief." It traditionally meant a powerful leader, and did not imply domination and oppression.

> *Observation: Persecution begins with threats and warnings as persecutors hope they can scare evangélicos into leaving their homes without having to risk illegal physical expulsions.*

The indigenous people in this village did leave voluntarily to avoid the burning of their homes and continued violence. However, the Ch'ol Presbytery and the National Presbyterian Church of Mexico convinced them to return to their homes in the village of La Arena, though government officials failed to grant them any legal guarantees. The persecution ended when a show of National Church and Ch'ol Presbytery support convinced the persecutors that they could not intimidate the Presbyterian *evangélicos*.

Tzeltal Persecution

In 1949, shortly after the first Protestant *evangélicos* appeared in the Tzeltal area, tribal authorities presented formal accusations against the *evangélicos* and the two women missionaries, Marianna Slocum and Florence Gerdel. Lic. Guillermo Sozaya, the director of the Departamento de Asuntos Indígenas, the Department of Indigenous Affairs of the Mexican government, heard the following allegations:

> That these women, as well as the other followers of that "protestant" doctrine, were preparing to burn the temple saints located in the Oxchuc Catholic Church; That those women are in reality men in disguise; That they wear rubber breasts to make themselves look like women; That as men which they really are, they are sexually abusing the best young Tzeltal girls; That they eat dead people, bodies of persons that they have kidnapped alive and then have boiled them in large pots in order to later eat them.[21]

When the first Tzeltal Protestant evangelicals exposed the preposterous accusations to the government lawyer, he told them that as long as they did not obligate anyone to become an *evangélico*, they were not breaking any law in Mexico. This simple statement of religious freedom rapidly spread throughout the Tzeltal tribe and encouraged the early growth of the Tzeltal Protestant evangelical church during in the years of 1951–1953.

---

21. Esponda, *Historia de la Iglesia*, 262.

> *Observation: An official statement of the law by government au-*
> *thorities regarding religious freedom can be effective in slowing*
> *persecution.*

As the Tzeltal Protestant evangelicals realized rapid church growth and organized the first Presbyterian congregation, the persecution against the *evangélicos* reemerged. In 1954 Wycliffe Bible translators, Slocum and Gerdel, reported that an *evangélico* from the Cancuc area had been persecuted:

> Suddenly one night, shortly after he believed, he discovered that there was a group of 15 indigenous and Mexicans outside his hut armed with guns, intent on killing him for having dared to depart from the religion of his forefathers. They fired several shots, but he tore a hole in the bamboo wall in the back of the hut and escaped into the darkness.[22]

This Tzeltal man, Juan Espinosa later returned to his village, and the gospel began to spread rapidly in that area. The following year, however, the houses of all of these new Protestant evangelicals were burned, which slowed the growth of the church in the Cancuc area.[23]

> *Observation: Persecution emerges or reemerges as a result of the*
> *growth of the church, not the other way around.*

Threats against the Protestant evangelicals became commonplace, especially death threats. When the Roman Catholic priests working in the Tzeltal area stirred up persecutors against the *evangélicos*, the grass-roofed church in Corralito where the first congregation had been organized was nearly completely burned. Except in a few isolated occasions, this persecution did not go beyond the stage of threats and warnings against individual *evangélicos*. While there were several years of intimidation against preachers and members of the Presbyterian Church, the persecution rarely took the form of physical attacks and expulsions.[24]

However, when the gospel was carried by Tzeltal evangelists to other municipalities, some violent persecution did occur. In Tenango, one of the early Presbyterian evangelicals, Sebastian Ts'ul, was shot to death. In 1956

22. Marianna Slocum, second letter from her Tzeltal diary, unpublished, in author's files (Apr 1955).

23. Esponda, *Historia de la Iglesia*, 267.

24. Esponda, *Historia de la Iglesia*, 266.

the first congregation of Presbyterians in the municipality of Bachajón was attacked during a worship service by a group of twenty-five armed assassins backed by the local Roman Catholic priest, Eleazar Mandujano.

> *Observation: Persecution usually becomes violent only after some external source lends its authority to an internal source.*

These assassins planned to kill a well-known leader of the Protestant evangelicals, but when the armed group found the Presbyterians singing hymns in his home, they opened fire on the entire group. When one of the *evangélicos* went out to see what was happening, he was killed instantly by the blasts from a double-barreled shotgun. Two women in the house were wounded before they, along with other *evangélicos* gathered, escaped into the mountains and watched the assassins burn the house in which they had been worshiping.

These Bachajón Protestant evangelicals escaped by walking to the distant Corralito church, where they received help and counsel from the highland Tzeltal *evangélicos*. A local schoolteacher there wrote an official complaint to municipal authorities in Yajalón, demanding justice in this murder and expulsion. The authorities acted by ordering the capture and the imprisonment of the killers and their accomplices. One received a prison sentence. History notes that

> this just intervention by the authorities worked as a brake, and there was never again any similar attempt against the Protestants in that place, and because of this, those who had been expelled from their places returned to their respective villages with the full protection of the law and they were able to continue to preach the gospel.[25]

> *Observation: Enforcement of the law in cases of violent persecution often brings a halt to persecution and allows the return of expelled Protestant evangelicals.*

In the Tzeltal tribal area, the Presbyterian Church spread rapidly. Scattered incidents of violence and expulsions of Protestant evangelicals continued, but government intervention effectively halted the persecution. By 1991 the Tzeltal Presbyterian Church had grown to two full presbyteries with more than fifty thousand members and about 350 congregations.

25. Esponda, *Historia de la Iglesia*, 288.

Tojolabal Persecution

Persecution first broke out among the Tojolabal tribe as early as 1958. The Tojolabal Mayans, who are located to the south and east of the central highlands of Chiapas, had expelled Julia Supple, a Wycliffe Bible translator, along with four families of new Protestant evangelicals from the village of Jotoná. The expelled believers moved into the Spanish town of Las Margaritas where there was an active Presbyterian church. A short time later, two other families were asked to leave the village of Jotaná. This core of six families represented the first evangelical breakthrough in the Tojolabal tribe. They returned to the Tojolabal area to do evangelism work in the San Pedro valley. Although they were jailed and put out of that area, these first *evangélicos* in the Tojolabal tribe did not give up. By 1977, most of the people in the village of San Pedro had become Presbyterian evangelicals.

The gospel slowly spread to a few other villages in the Tojolabal area, but the village of Jotoná, where all of the Protestant evangelicals had been expelled in the initial persecution, never again responded to the gospel and remains very closed and resistant.

In the fall of 1988 when nine families in the village of Saltillo became Presbyterian *evangélicos*, organized persecution reappeared among the Tojolabal tribe. There had been threats against individual families for several years, but in November 1988 the persecution turned violent. When four *evangélicos* from the village of San Pedro visited Saltillo's Presbyterians, they were jailed overnight and told to never again return. A few days later three of them were jailed and beaten and their houses were torn down.

When the elders of the consistory of the large Presbyterian church in Las Margaritas managed to get an arrest warrant for the land commissioner in the village of Saltillo, villagers blockaded the road and would not let the police vehicle enter the village. The angered villagers retaliated against police intervention by vowing to jail all nine of Saltillo's Presbyterian families, but all of them escaped to Las Margaritas, where they were housed by church deacons.

The persecutors sought out and kidnapped three *evangélicos* in the town of Las Margaritas, who were taken back to Saltillo to suffer a week of mistreatment and torture. Municipal and state authorities finally arranged a settlement that did little more than secure the release of the kidnapped men and did nothing to prevent the expulsion of the Presbyterians from the village.[26]

---

26. Personal letter from Samuel Hofman to the author, Jan 1990.

In another Tojolabal village, La Libertad, in 1988, the Presbyterians were beaten and forced to sign a document in which they promised to pay their dues to the local Catholic church. They could remain *evangélicos*, but "no one else in the village could be converted."[27] However, in August 1989 three young men from the village were seized and put in jail for attending an evangelistic campaign in a nearby Spanish town. These three and their extended families were gathered with the other twenty families of *evangélicos* in the village, and they were all told by a mob with clubs that they must "sign a new document that said they were voluntarily leaving the village and promised to move out before April 1990. They were told that their blood would flow if they didn't. They signed."[28] The Spanish church in Las Margaritas helped the twenty-three expelled families to form a relocation village on land purchased with the help of the National Presbyterian Church of Mexico.

Amatenango Persecution

For over three years the Presbyterians in the Tzeltal sub-dialect group of Amatenango had been subjected to threats and harassment. In 1988 and 1989 several small groups of *evangélicos* had left their tribal villages in the Amatenango area because of the persecution pressure and gone to live near the large Chamula relocation village of Betania.

As the church continued to grow in Amatenango, the tribal *caciques* increased the threats and in January 1991 told all of the Presbyterians that they were going to be expelled. When they did not leave voluntarily, as some of the *evangélicos* before them had, the tribal president called a mass meeting in the tribal center on February 24, 1991. They called seventeen families of Presbyterian evangelicals to stand trial, and the tribal president gave them official expulsion notice. However, when the Presbyterian group leaders answered that they refused to leave unless they had an official document from the state governor supporting the expulsion, the tribal *caciques* reacted with violence. They severely beat the Presbyterian leaders and put all seventeen men in jail. In the meantime, a mob of persecutors proceeded to destroy the believers' houses. Three houses were burned while the others were badly damaged. To ensure that the Presbyterians would leave, the mob stole their food and possessions. Later in the afternoon, tribal leaders released the Presbyterians from jail and told them that since they no longer had houses, they must accept expulsion from Amatenango.

27. Personal letter from Samuel Hofman to the author, Jan 1990.
28. Hofman, "Liberty," 3.

The battered group of Presbyterians did not leave the village. They salvaged materials from their demolished houses and made makeshift shelters.
They had previously decided that they were not going to leave their village
or give up their religious freedom.

Persecution among the Tzotzil Tribes of Chiapas

The story of persecution among the Tzotzil tribes has been long and unend-
ing. From 1957 until 1997, there has been recurring and systematic persecution that has shown only temporary signs of respite.

Since it is impossible to recount all incidents of persecution in the
Tzotzil tribes, the intent of this chapter is to cite some principal cases in
Huixtán, Chenalhó, Chamula, Santa Marta, Zinacantán, and Mitontic tribal
areas to give an overview as a basis for analysis.

Map of Chiapas tribal areas

Huixteco Persecution

In May 1968, when the small group of new Huixteco *evangélicos* began to evangelize neighboring Huixteco villages, they were told that the leaders of those villages did not want to hear the Word of God. The itinerant preachers were told to stop visiting villages and preaching "or something may happen to you on the trail."[29]

The lay evangelists continued their visits to other villages in June. One Sunday afternoon in July, two Protestant evangelicals were shot at. Sebastian was hit twice. One bullet passed through his left hand, and the other hit just left of his heart. He recovered in a few months.[30]

The Huixteco *evangélicos* reported the incident to authorities in the Bureau of Indigenous Affairs. A man from the village of Chijton was arrested and jailed. This ended violent persecution in the Huixteco tribe, and no expulsions or major incidents occurred for almost twenty years.

The gospel, however, did not spread rapidly. When a new evangelistic effort brought renewed growth in 1986, persecutors destroyed the small church building in the village of Lopez Mateos and expelled a few families of new believers from the village of Shuncala'. Persecution stopped the short spurt of growth in the Huixteco tribe.

> *Observation: Violent persecution can effectively discourage evangelism and the growth of the church.*

Chenalhó Persecution

In 1957, when the small group of new Protestant evangelicals in the village of Chibtic had grown to more than ten people, the first persecution against the Chenalhó *evangélicos* broke out. Although there had been individual attacks against the first Protestant evangelicals in the village of Chibtic, the tribal leaders' fury was turned against these *evangélicos* when they preached openly that Catholic images worshiped as tribal deities were nothing more than idols without any power, that the Bible prohibits worshiping them, citing Exodus 20 and Psalm 115.[31] The tribal president and leaders planned to kill these men who had no respect for the tribal customs.

29. Copy of letter from Marian Cowan to Frank Cowan. San Cristóbal de Las Casas, Chiapas, July 16, 1968.

30. Copy of letter from Marian Cowan to Frank Cowan. San Cristóbal de Las Casas, Chiapas, July 16, 1968.

31. Esponda, *Historia de la Iglesia*, 316.

> *Observation: Persecution can be prematurely invited through an offensive attack by Protestant evangelicals on some traditional forms or values.*

When the Protestant evangelicals were called to public trial for their statements about the Catholic images, they presented a booklet of the Mexican Constitution, reading Articles 24 and 16 to demand their rights of freedom of religious belief. But the tribal president tore the booklet to shreds. Soon after this confrontation, the tribal leaders plotted to exterminate the Protestant evangelicals in Chibtic. The attempt was carried out by dividing the killers into two groups that would approach the village from opposite directions where the *evangélicos* lived and allow none of them to escape.

Two former tribal presidents headed these two groups and were heavily armed. However, they hit obstacles: the doors of each house that they tried to attack were barred so well that they could not enter, and dogs barked so loudly that the attackers retreated. When the killers later reported that they had not been able to open the heavily barred doors, the *evangélicos* realized that God's protection had saved them, for none of them had secured their doors with more than the traditional piece of thin twine.[32]

Although there were other attempts to ambush *evangélicos*, none were successful. These courageous early believers used prayer as their principal defense, and were encouraged when they saw evidence of answers through examples of miraculous protection. By 1961, groups of Protestant evangelicals sprang up in two other villages: Pechiquil and Ajteal.

> *Observation: When people perceive that persecution is halted by a demonstration of the power of God, the result can be rapid church growth.*

When the growth of the Protestant evangelical church in the Chenalhó tribe accelerated, the tribal leaders angrily accused the *evangélicos* of disrupting tribal unity and of refusing to allow their children to attend the government schools. Since the accusations were made before the judicial authorities in the city of San Cristóbal de Las Casas, the *evangélicos* were in constant prayer during the all-day trek. When they reached the outskirts of the city, they took a special time for prayer that God would give them words to speak before the authorities.

---

32. Esponda, *Historia de la Iglesia*, 32.

After hearing the testimony of both the Protestant evangelicals and the accusers, attorney Manuel Castellanos charged the accusers of false allegations against those whose only crime was to study the Word of God. He threatened to throw all of the tribal leaders in jail, but finally let them go after levying them stiff fines and warning them to stop bothering the Protestant evangelicals. Most of the people in the Chenalhó tribe attributed this unexpected turnabout to the spiritual power of God and to the prayers of the evangelicals.

The persecutors' next attempt to impede the growth of the church was through witchcraft and casting of curses. Since these animistic people believed that the spiritual power of their tribal deities and shamans would defeat the power of the *evangélicos*, they chose to initiate a spiritual battle. However, when the witchcraft and curses failed to affect the Protestant evangelicals, the word began to spread that their God was more powerful than the tribal gods. And when some of the persecutors decided to take matters into their own hands, their planned assassination was foiled by a torrential storm, which allowed the potential victims to escape unharmed. Even in the face of continual persecution threats, the growth of the church in the Chenalhó tribe increased rapidly because the tribal people were hearing the stories of the demonstration of God's power in protecting the *evangélicos*.

During this time of severe threats and persecution, the Chenalhó church began ongoing twenty-four-hour prayer vigils, asking that God use his power to protect their church leaders and to break the power of the tribal persecutors. Because of continued assassination threats, the *evangélicos* asked the tribal president to intervene. Due to energetic warnings from Castellanos to the president of Chenalhó that he would be held personally responsible for any killings in Chenalhó, the tribal president called in all of the enemies of the Protestant evangelicals and told them that they would be jailed if any further violent acts were carried out against them. The Protestant *evangélicos* in Chenalhó perceived this miraculous declaration on the part of the tribal president as a clear act of God in answer to their unceasing prayer vigils.

A few months later, when a group of persecutors did ambush and kill an *evangélico* named Amporox Pasciencia near the village of Chimix, the tribal president gave orders for the capture and imprisonment of the killers. The killers were apprehended and sentenced to long prison terms in the state penitentiary. As a result of this tribal action against the persecution, the opposition in the Chenalhó tribe diminished and almost ceased, and the church experienced explosive growth.[33]

33. Esponda, *Historia de la Iglesia*, 320–22.

> *Observation: Enforcement of religious freedom laws is only effective*
> *when carried out at the local and tribal level.*

Chamula Persecution

The year 1963 marks the conversion of the first two Protestant evangelicals in the Chamula tribe. In 1964, the first house church services were held in the home of Tumin Nachij, located in the tribal center of San Juan Chamula. Four members of the Caxtuli' family were the first to attend.

Personal evangelism spread the gospel to the village of Joltsemen where, in 1965, during a nighttime attack on the home of a Protestant evangelical, three small girls were burned to death and two others escaped with nearly fatal machete and gunshot wounds.[34] This persecution by means of burning houses at night spread to almost all of the villages containing Protestant *evangélicos*. *Evangélicos* spent most nights hiding in the caves and mountains during that year.

By 1966 the gospel had spread to several other villages in spite of the house burnings and killings. The tribal leaders attempted to stamp out the new beliefs of the Protestant *evangélicos* by assigning them traditional *cargo* (religious charge in the animistic folk religion positions), but this didn't stifle their growth. After public warnings to the *evangélicos*, the tribal leaders attacked and burned the houses of recognized *evangélicos* in three villages. These Protestant *evangélicos* fled to San Cristóbal, where the district attorney promised legal guarantees if they went back to their villages. They returned and continued to meet in the home of an *evangélico* in San Juan Chamula.

When tribal *caciques* realized that the gospel continued to spread rapidly in spite of the persecution, they issued a formal expulsion decree for all Protestant *evangélicos*. In that same year of 1967, the Chamula authorities and *caciques* made a public declaration that they would not respect the legal documents explaining the rights of Protestant *evangélicos*, and they formally expelled all known *evangélicos*. They pronounced death sentences for any who tried to remain.

> *Observation: A strong cacique system will eventually nullify national*
> *law guarantees and eliminate legal options.*

---

34. The story of the killings of Chamula Protestant evangelicals was written under the title "Night of the long knives" by Hugh Steven.

For a total of nine years (1966–75), the *evangélico* leaders from Chamula tried every legal and governmental approach in their search for justice and human rights, obtaining legal guarantees even from federal authorities. During this time, recurring expulsions and numerous incidents of violence occurred against the *evangélicos*.

For three of these nine years (1969–71), due to the able help of lawyer Manuel Castellanos Cancino from the government's National Indigenous Institute (INI), there were no expulsions, and the government orders against persecution were respected in Chamula. However, when a new government office of the Bureau of Indigenous Affairs was formed, two new lawyers took the place of Castellanos. Angel Robles and Pablo Ramírez reversed the policies that had been so effectively carried out by Manuel Castellanos, and when a new tribal president was named in 1972 by the Chamula *caciques*, they began to carry out massive expulsions of Protestant *evangélicos*, along with severe beatings and violence. In one week more than six hundred Chamula *evangélicos* were forcibly trucked out of Chamula and dumped in San Cristóbal de Las Casas.[35] With the same ferocity, the Chamula *caciques* continued to expel all Protestant *evangélicos*. By 1985 the estimated number of Chamula *evangélicos* evicted from the Chamula tribal area was about eight thousand people.

To handle the influx of expelled Protestant evangelicals from Chamula, the National Presbyterian Church of Mexico helped purchase land. In 1975 sixteen acres were purchased on the outskirts of San Cristóbal to form a colony called Nueva Esperanza. That became the first relocation settlement. During the next fifteen years, more than twenty relocation communities were formed in the municipal areas of San Cristóbal and Teopisca in the attempt to accommodate the thousands of Protestant *evangélicos* who were violently expelled as a result of the persecution in the Chamula tribe.

After 1972 the Mexican governmental and the justice systems were unwilling to confront the Chamula *caciques* by enforcing constitutional law; thus, violence and expulsions continued in waves. On July 24, 1981, Mol Miguel Cashlan was kidnapped, brutally tortured, and killed by Chamula *cacique* leaders.[36] In 1990, there were expulsions of more than fifty families from two Chamula communities.

35. Esponda, *Historia de la Iglesia*, 335.
36. Steven, *They Dared*, 211.

Santa Marta Persecution

Beginning in May 1980, only a few months after the first Protestant evangelicals appeared in the Santa Marta tribe, nine of them were called before the town mayor. When they refused to reject their new faith in Christ, they were jailed for two days, warned, and released. In May 1981, after the group of *evangélicos* had almost doubled, fourteen of these Protestant evangelicals were jailed for refusing to serve the expensive religious *cargo* (religious charge in the animistic folk religion) positions of *alférez* and *mayordomo*. The hostilities increased during the next year with threats and beatings at the hands of the local authorities. The *evangélicos'* homes were accosted by armed groups who surrounded and fired upon their houses at night.

In May 1982 all twenty-two male family heads from the Protestant evangelical community were arrested, beaten, and jailed without food and water for three days and nights. The tribal leaders then elaborated a document that declared their expulsion and the loss of all their possessions and land in the Santa Marta area.

Under threats of further beatings and more days in jail, the tribal leaders forced the twenty-two Protestant evangelical men to sign their agreement to the expulsion notice. Upon their release, the *evangélicos* took their families and fled to the Chenalhó tribal center where they found assistance from Presbyterian families.[37]

Zinacanteco Persecution

On Sunday, January 25, 1981, after a short meeting in a house church in the village of Pajal-ch'ixte' (previous to this the Zinacanteco *evangélicos* had been rotating meeting places to avoid persecution), the small group of worshipers was arrested and taken to the tribal center where they were forced to sign a legal document in which they promised to stop being Protestant evangelicals.

> *Observation: Regular worship meetings with increased attendance pose a threat to ethnic cohesion, thus triggering persecution.*

In January 1982, after the Protestant evangelicals had continued to meet for worship and had almost doubled in size, their attempt to secretly build a small church brought opposition in the village of Tojtic. Village leaders tore down its walls before the *evangélicos* could finish the construction.

37. *Avante*, "Denuncia," 3.

When the Protestant *evangélicos* tried to rebuild it, the tribal leaders responded by making plans to expel all Protestant evangelicals from the Zinacanteco tribal area.

> *Observation: Construction of a church building symbolizes a foothold in tribal areas; thus, persecution often begins or reemerges at any attempt to build a place of worship.*

On February 20, 1982, in the village of Nabenchauc, where we had lived for almost a decade, the first two families of Protestant evangelicals were arrested and trucked off to the tribal ceremonial center to be jailed. On Sunday, February 21, the tribal *caciques* rounded up the remaining thirteen families of known Protestant evangelicals from other Zinacanteco villages. When these Zinacanteco *evangélicos* were put on trial before the tribal leaders and refused to renounce their faith, the tribal president gave the order to have them taken away to be killed. When the assassinations were thwarted by the intervention of other Christians, the tribal *caciques* severely beat some of these new believers.

Shune, the first Zinacanteco believer, was severely beaten.

A few suffered serious injuries, but none were killed. Later that Sunday, all fifteen families were expelled from Zinacanteco tribal land. These fifteen families of expelled Zinacanteco *evangélicos* later started the relocation village that they named Vida Nueva (New Life).

As the gospel continued to spread through family lines to other villages in the Zinacanteco tribe, the expulsion of Protestant evangelicals steadily continued, although less violently, since the new *evangélicos* simply left their villages when served expulsion notices. In June 1985 three families were expelled from the village of Tzequemtic, and the following year several families were put out of the villages of Apas and Nachij.

In September 1990, however, a new wave of violent persecution hit the area around the village of Tzequemtic. In the five years since the first three families had been expelled from this village, the number of Protestant evangelical believers had rapidly increased. From January to October 1990, these *evangélicos* held worship services in house churches and chose several leaders. Also, growing groups of Protestant evangelicals existed in several of the surrounding villages, including the nearby village of Granadia. However, when four previously expelled Zinacanteco Presbyterians went to visit new Protestant evangelical families and show the *Jesus* film in Granadia, the *caciques* from the area villages captured them and confiscated the movie equipment. After a harrowing weekend of being beaten, having their hair cut with knives, and being tied tightly with ropes around their necks and shoulders, the four Zinacanteco Presbyterians were released.

These four Zinacantecos were ridiculed by having pieces of their hair chopped off.

The leaders of the Tzequemtic Christians were beaten and forty-four Protestant *evangélicos* agreed to sign a document that they would either cease being *evangélicos* or voluntarily leave the tribal area.[38] Through the local Bureau of Indigenous Affairs, the expelled families were later granted permission and protection to remove their personal possessions and livestock from their homes.

38. Henríquez Tobar, "44 Personas."

Leaders of the Tzequemtic Christians were beaten and bloodied.

Mitontic Persecution

In 1987, after more than twenty years since the first violent persecution of
Mitontic Protestant evangélicos, the group of Presbyterians had grown to
over six hundred people in several villages. The tribal leaders decided to
attempt to discourage the renewed growth of the Protestant *evangélicos* by
arresting and jailing all of the men, women, and children from the village of
Suyalo, where the gospel had first taken root. With hands tied behind their
backs, the believers were force-marched the three-hour trek to the tribal
center of Mitontic, where they were locked up in a tin-roofed coffee stor-
age building. In the windowless and cramped building, the *evangélicos* were
subjected to extremely hot daytime temperatures and were given no food,
water, or bathroom facilities for three full days and nights. At midnight of
the third night, after intimidating the women and girls with daily threats of
drowning and rape, the tribal *caciques* forced the Presbyterian men to sign
a document acknowledging their agreement to expulsion from the tribe.

Mitontic men were forced to sign an expulsion document.

On July 14, 1987, these Presbyterians signed an agreement before a representative of the state governor and the president of Mitontic that guaranteed their return to their tribal villages. However, they were also obligated to serve the traditional *cargo* (religious charge in the animistic folk religion) positions. The entire Mitontic *evangélico* community agreed to return to their tribal homes.

On June 28, 1989, the tribal *caciques* called thirty of the *evangélico* men to a meeting in the Mitontic tribal center and accused them of not living up to the agreement signed in Tuxtla Gutiérrez, the capital of the state of Chiapas, in 1987. The tribal president, however, actually spoke at the municipal meeting about the fact that something had to be done because there were "too many" *evangélicos* in the community.[39] After the tribal leaders incited the angry mob, the thirty Presbyterians were seized, and bands of persecutors were sent off to round up their families from the surrounding community. The president then ordered them loaded onto trucks and transported several hours away to San Cristóbal de Las Casas, where they were dumped off at the Bureau of Indigenous Affairs. On the next day, the tribal mafia leaders sent a mob to the villages of Suyalo and Chib Uc'um where they destroyed the Presbyterian church buildings and several houses of *evangélicos*.

39. Woehr, "Mexican Governor Pledges," 8.

Destroyed Suyalo Presbyterian Church

This prompted all Presbyterians in the Mitontic tribal area to flee to San Cristóbal de Las Casas.

On July 14, 1989, another government meeting was called, at which time fifteen demands were presented by the tribal leaders. After agreeing to some of the points in this new demand, the Presbyterians were again supposedly given permission to return to their tribal homes.

> *Observation: When tribal caciques are superficially pressured by external authorities to respect the law, they will use torture and violence to force compliance with tribal norms or coerced withdrawal.*

However, since the tribal leaders had not succeeded in forcing the Presbyterian evangelicals to meet all of the fifteen demands, it was only a week after the return of some of the *evangélicos* that the tribal *caciques* began a systematic and violent harassment of individual Protestant evangelical leaders, using mobs to beat them and issue death threats. When two of the *evangélicos* were nearly killed by a mob action, the Presbyterians again decided to abandon their plans to remain in their tribal homes.

Summary

Oppression and injustice have long filled the history of the indigenous tribes of Chiapas, from the time of the Spanish conquest until today. However,

It is the challenge to worldview assumptions that initiates persecution both for the missionary and for any person in the receptor culture that might, by his or her acceptance of the gospel, present a threat to the cultural norms. When the worldview assumptions are questioned, that challenge will inevitably bring on a vehement defensive response or attack that I am calling persecution.

In his well-known textbook, *Christianity in Culture*, Charles H. Kraft pictures worldview as the "central control box" of a culture that has been imposed upon the youth of that culture by its own means of teaching and learning.[3] Kraft points out that worldview is composed of four basic structures: Religious Structure with values, beliefs, rituals, mythology; Linguistic Structure with semantics, grammar, phonology; Social Structure with family, economics, politics, education; and Technological Structure with tools and techniques.[4] Thus, worldview is the organizer and controller of the cultural system and governs the conception of reality and expectations of behavior of the participants in a culture.

A common, but faulty, explanation for initial persecution, even by anthropologists and especially by political leaders, is that persecution is the result of a threat to the religion of a culture. They judge that a Christian missionary threatens to replace the religion of a culture with the religion of his or her own cultural background. It is important for us to see that this explanation of persecution is very simplistic and completely inadequate. If we understand worldview being composed of at least four basic structures, religion (as it is commonly understood) is only one aspect of worldview. Thus religion, as we will see in succeeding chapters, is only one of the factors that must be taken into account in the study of persecution. Worldview is the more comprehensive and useful concept with which we can more readily understand and analyze the multiple facets of persecution.

> *Observation: Threats to any of the worldview structures, not only religious conflicts, may initiate persecution reactions.*

Functions of Worldview

Worldview functions also provide keys to understanding the multiple facets of persecution. In a given culture, the worldview serves a number of essential functions. Kraft describes the functions of worldview using five

3. Kraft, *Christianity in Culture*, 53.
4. Kraft, *Christianity in Culture*, 54.

major categories: explanation, evaluation, reinforcement, integration and interpretation, and adaptation.[5]

Explanation

The explanation function answers the *why* and *how* questions in a culture. This function defines the basic assumptions of a people for how and why things got to be the way they are and how and why any changes might take place. If any change agent or missionary proposes innovations that do not fit into the culture's perception of the worldview function of explanation, the reaction will most likely be that things don't happen that way. In an animistic society, the why question will be answered by naming the spiritual forces that control the behavior and actions of a culture's people.

In the Zinacanteco tribe, the *q'uin cruz* (fiesta of the cross) ritual performed on the first day of May each year determines the arrival of the spring rains. If that tribal fiesta is not carried out in proper fashion, then the tribal gods will not send the rains necessary for crops to grow. In the Zinacanteco worldview, the function of explanation is clear. Why do they fail to have enough rain in certain years? Because not enough sacrifices were offered during the May rain fiesta. If the reason for that failure to offer sufficient sacrifices can be attributed to Protestant evangelicals who refuse to participate in the rain ceremony, those who must be punished are the *evangélicos*. In the Tzotzil cultures, the explanation for the fact that no change of religious allegiance can be allowed in their cultures is that the tribal deities control all behavior and events in their society. Thus, a lack of respect for that control could bring tragic results upon the entire community or tribe. Persecution is then justified as a defensive reaction to protect the community and culture from such a tragedy.

Evaluation

Worldview also functions to judge and validate a culture's way of life and its view of reality. Most cultures believe that their worldview is superior to others, or at least that other worldviews would not work for them. Thus, they develop concepts that function to validate their way of life.

The Tzotzil tribes of Chiapas call themselves the *bats'i crischano*, which literally means the real people. They have developed worldview concepts that identify their tribal areas as the *shmishic balamil*, the navel of the earth.

5. Kraft, *Christianity in Culture*, 54–57.

The Tzotzils believe themselves to be the central core around which the rest of the world revolves, and this worldview concept is then confirmed by their deities and gods. The patron saint for each tribal area has the specific task of being the guardian for and giving sanction to that specific area. As Charles Kraft says: "For most of the cultures of the world the ultimate ground for these sanctions is supernatural. It is by their God or gods that most people understand their worldview and their culture as a whole to be validated. He/they are seen to value these customs more than those of any other peoples."[6]

Persecution is thus justifiable and valid to the Tzotzil Mayans of Chiapas because they see any challenge to their tribal deities or ancestral religion as a threat to the validity of their entire culture. The most common reason given for persecution among the Tzotzils is that the *evangélicos* are out to undermine and destroy their customs and culture. Thus, a challenge or threat to any accepted behavior in a culture will be seen as justification for persecution, even if that accepted behavior is not a part of the cultural ideal. For instance, the excessive drinking of *posh*, the tribal hard liquor, is not seen as an ideal behavior. However, if an *evangélico* refuses to participate in the drinking ceremonies, he is told that he cannot be a *bats'i cristiano*, real tribesman, if he doesn't drink *posh*. Persecution would be a means of pressuring such a person to behave in the culturally accepted ways, according to patterns that have received approval in the cultural evaluation.

Reinforcement

Worldview also functions to give psychological reinforcement to a particular group or tribe. The way certain crisis events and transition times in life are handled reinforces a culture's understanding that its worldview is functioning well. Often this reinforcement takes the form of a ritual or ceremony in which many people participate, such as funerals, harvest celebrations, and initiation or graduation ceremonies.[7]

The shamanistic practices and prayers in the Zinacanteco tribe clearly serve to reinforce a way of life. When the shaman performs a curing ceremony for a sick person, and that person regains his or her health, the whole system is reinforced. For example, in her first months of pregnancy, one Zinacanteco woman was told by the shaman that the fetus she carried was a deformed, animal-like being. However, after the shaman had offered the appropriate sacrifices to the gods and carried out the proper ceremonies, the fetus was transformed into a healthy baby. The woman did not question

6. Kraft, *Christianity in Culture*, 55.
7. Kraft, *Christianity in Culture*, 55.

whether the baby would have been born normal and healthy without the shamanistic ceremonies, for her worldview was reinforced by the events that had taken place.

Persecution often strikes when an insider in a culture no longer participates or cooperates in the tribal reinforcement ceremonies. A Christian who no longer calls on the services of a shaman in the Tzotzil tribes is an immediate candidate for persecution since he or she is threatening the entire reinforcement function of the worldview.

Integration and Interpretation

Worldview helps the people of a culture to understand their world, to give their conception of reality some kind of system and order. In the Tzotzil tribes, this function is realized through the ceremonies and rituals carried on in the regular cycle of tribal fiestas. All of the dramas that are carried out in these fiestas serve to interpret and systematize the worldview concepts.

The well-structured *cargo* system, which organizes all religious service or charges for the members of specific Tzotzil tribes, is another model for bridging the gap between people's worldview and their practical understanding of it. The *cargo* system required expensive involvement in service to the tribal deities at religious festivals and in the daily rituals of caring for the saints in the main tribal shrines. Every adult male was included in the list for the various levels of *cargo* positions, and any refusal to serve in these costly roles would be met with ostracism and jailing. This *cargo* system serves not only to integrate every person in the tribe through required involvement, it also provides hands-on service in which tribal values and traditions were clearly interpreted and taught. So, when an *evangélico* refuses to participate in this *cargo* system, that person rejects an important worldview function and threatens the whole tribal structure with disintegration.

Adaptation

A fifth function of worldview is to set the rules for what can and can't be changed in a particular culture. Since all cultures are in a process of some degree of cultural change and adaptation, worldview determines how and at what speed concepts and perceptions can be adapted. This function of worldview is especially important when new concepts or new technology invades that worldview.

When the Roman Catholic missionaries, who came with the Spanish conquerors, brought images of their saints as symbols of the Christian religion, the Tzotzil tribes were forced to adapt, and they adopted these Roman Catholic images as replacements for many of their animistic spirits and deities. The concept of an image that could house the spirit of one of the tribal deities fit well into their adaptational tolerances.

However, other invasions stretch that adaptational ability of the worldview beyond its limits. The Tzotzil concept that the moon is the *ch'ul me'tic*, the mother god, was seriously threatened in 1969 when radio and television made it hard to ignore the fact that astronauts had landed and walked on the moon. This went far beyond the accepted worldview rules of acceptability. An even more disruptive event was the electrical fire in the large tribal shrine-church that housed most of the main tribal saints and deities. When most of these images were destroyed in the fire, many of the younger Zinacantecos begin to ask: "If the tribal gods are alive (as the worldview teaches), then why did they not escape when the church was on fire?" The tragic event was not within the worldview's adaptational limits, and it created several new fuzzy areas in the Zinacanteco tribal worldview.

Persecution often arises when cultural changes brought about by the gospel are allowed to take place at such a rapid rate or in such an unacceptable way that the adaptational function of worldview is threatened. In cultures in which decision-making patterns are basically multi-individual rather than individual, the decision of one young man to become a Christian is very disruptive, since it challenges the adaptational rules of the worldview. Persecution then results as much from the abuse of those rules as from the actual change of religious allegiance.

> *Observation: If we are to discover the underlying factors of persecution, and if we hope to avoid unnecessary and premature persecution, an understanding of worldview can lend valuable insights.*

Tzotzil Worldview

The Tzotzil Mayans of Chiapas have drawn on their prehistoric past, four centuries under Spanish conquerors, and current confrontation with the modern world in fashioning their present way of life. Their culture represents a highly integrated and complex system based on an animistic worldview. There are variations in worldview in the different tribal areas of the Tzotzil-speaking people.

The Tzotzil world is visualized as a large cube, with the tribal ceremonial center seen as the "navel" of the world. Above the cubical world is the sky, which is the realm of the *ch'ul totic* (holy father sun), *ch'ul me'tic* (holy mother moon), and the stars. Under the influence of Spanish Catholicism, the Tzotzils have come to associate the sun with God and the moon with the Virgin Mary.

Below the visible, cubicle world is the *balamil* (underworld) which contains a complex layer of gods and spirits. The most important Tzotzil deities are the ancestral gods that reside in the mountains around the various tribal centers. These deities provide the ideal for and have control of human life and are the jealous guardians of the Tzotzil way of life. Deviations are instantly noted, and guilty people are punished in a variety of ways. Much of a traditional Tzotzil's time and resources are taken up in attempting to sustain and appease the ancestral gods with offerings of black chickens, candles, incense, and rum liquor.

Next to the ancestral gods, the most important deity is the *Yajval Balamil* (Earth Lord). Crosses, which were introduced by the Spanish conquerors and Catholic priests, marked the place of entry to the underworld where the Earth Lord resides and controls waterholes, rain, lightning, clouds, and everything that is produced by the earth.

Consequently, a Tzotzil Mayan cannot use land or any of its products without compensating this Earth Lord with appropriate offerings in a shamanistic ceremony. This god has come to be associated loosely with the Roman Catholic idea of Satan.

In the centuries since the Spanish conquest, the Tzotzils have acquired fifty-five sacred images they call saints. These are thought of as gods with extraordinary power, each with an inner soul that must be cared for. These saints are probably replacements for the indigenous idols that appeared in the aboriginal temples of the Mayans at the time of the conquest. The ancestral gods

Vern Sterk in tribal dress beside a sacred Tzotzil cross.

and saints are treated with complex ritual care, elaborate ceremonial fiestas, and prayer and sacrifices.

Interaction between the living Tzotzils and their gods takes place via two types of souls that are possessed by each human being: a *ch'ulel* and a *chanul*. The *ch'ulel* is an inner, personal soul located in the heart of a person and is composed of thirteen temporarily divisible parts. This inner soul is placed in the body by the ancestral deities and leaves the body at the point of death when it again joins the pool of inner souls that is kept by the ancestral gods. During life, *comel ta balamil* (soul loss) can be caused by punishment of the ancestral gods, or by witchcraft, in which one's inner soul might be sold to the Earth Lord. Without all thirteen parts of the inner soul intact, a person will feel or possess *chamel* or sickness. Then an *h'ilol* (shaman) must be called to diagnose the cause of the sickness and perform a ceremony to recover the missing parts of the soul. Not only people, but also everything that the Tzotzils consider important in life possesses an inner soul.

The second type of soul is the *chanul*, which is a kind of animal spirit companion. Each person and his or her animal spirit companion share the same inner soul. This means that when the ancestors install an inner soul in the embryo of a Zinacanteco, they simultaneously install the same inner soul in the embryo of an animal. Thus, if anything happens to one's animal spirit companion, it will also happen to that person. And anything that stirs up the anger of the ancestors will cause them to make that person's animal spirit companion wander alone and uncared for in the woods. This then serves as a means of social control for deviant behavior, since a shaman must immediately perform the proper ceremony that will bring that animal spirit companion back to safety, or both it and the person will die.

Death never results from purely natural, physiological causes, but is due to soul loss. The body of the deceased is then prepared and surrounded by various articles that will both aid the soul in its journey and protect the living relatives from having their souls taken by this deceased person. During the spiritual journey, the soul must pay in various ways for its sins; during this time, it may wander around the earth and expect care from its living descendants. When the journey is completed, the soul is then returned to the bank of souls from which the ancestral gods will reincarnate it into the body of another person.

The above description explains the complexity of communicating to another culture with its distinct worldview. Also, from this segment of Tzotzil worldview, it is clear that any intrusion from a very different worldview presents a serious threat. This threat causes fear of worldview change, which triggers persecution.

Fear of Worldview Change

One of the essential roles that worldview plays is to give a sense of validity, security, and stability. Anything that threatens to alter that sense by suggesting worldview change will produce fear. The reaction is a defensive move to get rid of the threat, which results in persecution.

In the Zinacanteco tribe of Chiapas, where I spent the first ten years in village evangelism, my first months of contact with these people was spent in trying to find a village where the people would allow us to live. This tribal group, like most Tzotzil-speaking Mayans in Chiapas, has a great distrust of any strangers or foreign influences that might threaten their world. Much of their fear and distrust is the result of centuries of conquest and oppression at the hands of Spanish foreigners who they call *hcashlan*. History had proven that people from other cultures threatened their worldview and sense of security. In reaction, they had formed an effective wall of defense against anything or anyone that did not fit their worldview categories. Our first task was finding a way to penetrate that defense and receive permission to live among them, to become incarnate as real human beings in their perception.

The Incarnational Approach

As most missionaries have found in attempting to begin communication with unreached peoples in any area of the world, one doesn't just go to a tribe or people group, sing "Jesus Loves Me," hand them a Bible, and expect them all to become Christians. Because most people are fairly sure that their worldview is the only one that is valid, for anyone to suggest that they might want to try something new and different is going to invite fear of worldview change, some immediate resistance, and probable persecution.

How can we avoid that immediate negative response to the gospel? Eugene A. Nida declares that good missionaries have always been good anthropologists: "Effective missionaries have always sought to immerse themselves in a profound knowledge of the ways of life of the people to whom they have sought to minister, since only by such an understanding of the indigenous culture could they possibly communicate a new way of life."[8]

Charles H. Kraft suggests some specific guidelines to help avoid immediate negative response to the gospel with his explanation of the "incarnational approach to cross-cultural communication."[9] Three principles

---

8. Nida, *Customs and Cultures*, xi.
9. Kraft, *Christianity in Culture*, 173–78.

in particular are helpful in avoiding premature persecution: identity, cred-ibility, and response to felt needs.

Identity

Much has been written about the importance of the missionary or change agent identifying with the host culture. The attempt to live like, dress like, talk like, and act like the people to whom one desires to communicate is essential in avoiding the immediate fear of worldview change reaction, es-pecially in so-called resistant or hostile situations.

Charles Kraft has pointed out that God is our ultimate example of identification within a cultural setting when he revealed himself in Jesus Christ. In the incarnation, "God not only came, he became. He, in Christ, identified himself with his receptors. God in Jesus became so much a part of a specific human context that many never recognized that he had come from somewhere else."[10]

While it may be impossible for us to identify in such a complete way with the host culture, it is critical for our approach in resistant situations that we, as communicators of the gospel, make every possible attempt to identify with the people. While identification does have certain limits—whites cannot hide their Caucasian features—a choice to establish identity with a culture is invaluable. We certainly cannot expect the receptor culture to identify with us to establish a common frame of reference. Thus, we must go at least ninety percent of the distance in adapting and identifying with the host culture's frame of reference, in hope that the receptors might come ten percent of the distance that is impossible for us to span, and in this way achieve real identity.

In resistant environments, this identification principle is basic to one's continued presence in a culture. It is also foundational for any future com-munication of the gospel message.

> *Observation: The more effectively missionaries are able to identify with the host culture, the less likelihood there will be of their causing persecution as a result of the fear of worldview change.*

---

10. Kraft, *Christianity in Culture*, 175.

Credibility

A second part of the incarnational approach is credibility, that of being seen as a real person by the receptors. We only gain this respect by participating in and respecting the worldview and worldview functions of the host culture. Again, this might be called the anthropological approach in that it is mainly participant-observational.

There are three principles of credibility that can help us be seen as real human beings by the host culture:

1. Show vital interest in learning about and understanding their worldview. One does this by attending ceremonies and rituals, observing, and asking questions.

2. Look for and emphasize all possible points of agreement: sin, prayer, sacrifice; pouring out of blood. The "affirm and fulfill model" in this chapter will discuss this point in detail.

3. Act out everything that a Christian conscience allows. This means taking part in shamanistic ceremonies, drinking rituals for greetings, and *Q'uin Santo* (Day of the Dead) for ancestral spirits.

The goal, of course, is not just to learn about the culture and worldview in a participatory way, but also to present ourselves so that the receptor culture begins to see us as credible human beings in the cultural perception of what a human being does and says. If this kind of credibility can be established in a resistant and hostile environment, it will accomplish two things.

First, it will destroy stereotypes of who we are as outsiders, which might be the basis of the fear that causes persecution. For example, when we moved to the village of Nabenchauc, many Zinacantecos believed that white-skinned people were cannibals, but when we lived among them, they could begin to see us as credible human beings who did not fit that stereotype.

Second, it can potentially demonstrate to the host culture that we are actually affirming instead of threatening to destroy their worldview concepts, which will reduce the motive for much persecution. The Zinacantecos feared that we might burn their saints, but by attending Mass and inviting the Catholic priest to our home, we communicated an appreciation for their religious forms.

> *Observation: By becoming a credible human being to the host culture, the missionary or change agent minimizes the amount of foreignness*

The Sterks learned about Tzotzil culture by living in it.

A final side benefit of the incarnational approach is that eventually people also share their basic physical and spiritual needs and ask questions such as: Can I pay you to talk to your God about my *c'ac'al o'onil* (anger)? Do you have medicine for *balamil* (soul loss)?

While missionaries or change agents are identifying with the people of a culture, gaining credibility, and meeting specific felt needs in a culture, they must at the same time be analyzing what they are communicating through their attitude toward that culture.

Attitudes Toward Culture

Charles H. Kraft approaches our attitude toward culture[12] by first looking at God's attitude toward culture: "We advance the theory that God's basic attitude toward culture is that which the apostle articulates in 1 Corinthians 9:9–22. That is, he views human culture primarily as a vehicle to be used by him and his people for Christian purposes, rather than as an enemy to be combated or shunned."[13]

---

12. Kraft, *Christianity in Culture*, 103–15.

13. Kraft, *Christianity in Culture*, 103.

David J. Hesselgrave, in his book *Communicating Christ Cross-Cultur-ally*, presents a similar discussion based on H. R. Niebuhr's five views of theologians on the relationship of Christ and culture.[14] This chapter formulates Kraft's position in the following five attitudes toward culture.

God against Culture

This first position views culture as evil, just as the world is evil. It is something that is, in itself, satanic and must be destroyed or replaced. Missionaries holding this view regard all cultural forms as evil and encourage the extraction of individual converts out of their culture. This attitude toward culture will immediately be perceived by a receptor culture as an imminent threat, which can ignite the first sparks of persecution. The missionary is viewed as one who is on a search-and-destroy mission in relation to the receptor's culture. Even when there is no immediate negative reaction against the missionary who might hold this view of culture, there will likely be a quick and violent response against any converts from that culture.

God in Culture

This view, which is often taken by secular anthropologists, says that God is simply something that man makes in his own cultural image. Out of the universal psychological need for a concept of deity, a kind of folk hero image is developed. It is interesting to note, however, that when this view is communicated by a certain advocate like an anthropologist or a government agent, it will often meet with a very defensive and negative response from the host culture because it is seen as atheistic, and thus a threat to that particular culture and its spiritual worldview.

God Endorses Certain Cultures

This position holds that there are only certain cultures that are ordained by God and are superior to all others. Some may refer to North American culture, or an ideal Christian culture, or even a biblical culture, while indicating that all cultures should be patterned after one of these cultural models for them to win God's approval. Although missionaries do not often openly espouse this kind of cultural imperialism, they are often perceived by the receptor as having a judgmental attitude toward the receptor's culture, which

14. Hesselgrave, *Communicating Christ*, 79–80.

implies that the missionary's own cultural forms or values are God's ideal in comparison to those of other cultures.

This position is similar to the God against culture position except that it is more subtle in its threat to other cultures. However, it will result in a similar persecution response as soon as people in a particular culture realize that its goal is the replacement of cultural forms and values with those of the missionary.

God above Culture

This attitude about culture believes that God is basically unconcerned about and disinterested in culture and all human affairs. Out of this deistic view come an emphasis on humanism and the idea that biblical faith is irrelevant and out of date. Culture is seen as perverted but redeemable through human effort.

God above but through Culture

This view believes that God is transcendent and outside of culture, but that he interacts with human beings through human culture and forms. God chooses to use cultural forms to communicate and interact with people of those cultures. This biblical view of culture should be the one held by missionaries. It yields important implications:

1. Culture is a vehicle that God uses for communication, so most forms of culture are valid for the communication of the gospel.

2. Christian forms in one culture are not superior to the forms in another culture.

3. The transformation of culture can come from within a particular culture through the work of God and his Word.

4. Both conversion and the function of the church can take place within cultural norms.

If the missionary's attitude is one of God working to transform culture, then the message of the Bible does not threaten to destroy or cause the disintegration of cultures. Rather, the Bible presents the acts of God in history within various cultural settings and forms. The work of God and the gospel are not limited to any one culture or cultural form, and the message can be adequately communicated in all cultures. As Paul G. Hiebert has pointed out,

> The failure to differentiate between the gospel and human cultures has been one of the great weaknesses of modern Christian missions. Missionaries too often have equated the Good News with their own cultural background. This has led them to condemn most native customs and to impose their own customs on converts. Consequently, the gospel has been seen as foreign in general and Western in particular. People have rejected it not because they reject the lordship of Christ, but because conversion often has meant a denial of their cultural heritage and social ties.[15]

Much persecution has been caused by the same failure.

Observation: Much persecution could be avoided if our attitude toward culture and worldview would reflect the conviction that God is actually working through a particular culture to transform it.

The Need for Non-Confrontational Communication

The incarnational approach and a proper attitude toward culture are essential in avoiding premature and unnecessary persecution. Some forms of persecution can result from a faulty approach in laying that foundation. However, persecution more often emerges when a threatening message is communicated. Persecution most often takes shape as a negative reaction to the communication of the gospel. However, the gospel must be communicated. It is not enough for the missionary to establish a valid presence in a culture or society. The missionary must communicate the gospel message, taking into account complex historical and cultural backgrounds. As Hesselgrave says, "The missionary task is fundamentally one of communication. Missionary communication is simple *and* it is complex. One can engage in it without studying it. But to study and analyze it is to greatly increase one's potential effectiveness."[16]

When this communication is perceived as presenting a possible confrontation with the worldview of the receptors, the probabilities of worldview clash and persecution are very high. If we are to avoid unnecessary and destructive persecution, we must be concerned with communication of

---

15. Hiebert, *Anthropological Insights*, 53.
16. Hesselgrave, *Communicating Christ*, 61.

Principles of the Affirm and Fulfill Model

The principles of the affirm and fulfill model are not new. Jesus emphasized them when he spoke in Matthew 5:17–18 of the fulfillment of the Law: "Do not think that I have come to abolish the Law or the Prophets; I have not come to abolish them but to fulfill them. I tell you the truth, until heaven and earth disappear, not the smallest letter, not the least stroke of a pen, will by any means disappear from the Law until everything is accomplished."

It is obvious that Jesus was not specifically discussing worldview transformation in his stated intention of fulfilling Jewish Law and traditions. However, his life and ministry demonstrated that he was not on a mission to abolish or destroy anything in the Jewish culture, but that he had come to fulfill it. It wasn't that Jesus could not identify many aspects of Jewish life and culture that needed transformation, but he knew that his Father's will for communication and transformation was not to destroy but rather to fulfill. The affirm and fulfill model for worldview transformation follows this same intention. Simply stated, the affirm and fulfill model intends to affirm everything in the culture's worldview that can be attested by the biblical record and example, and then fulfill those elements in the worldview that are not in accord with scriptural concepts.

The basic principles of the affirm and fulfill model are as follows: First, transformational change can best be brought about by affirming the worldview concepts of a culture that are not in direct conflict with biblical teaching. This must take place especially in the clear focus area of the worldview. This clear focus area is defined in the elaborate rituals of the specific culture. The Tzotzil ritual sacrifice of a chicken as a substitute for the soul of a person was a clear focus area that could be affirmed in both Old and New Testament instances. This is just one example of affirmation of cultural forms that indorse as valid the clear focus concepts of the culture. I believe that there are very few cultural forms that cannot be connected biblically.

When we are able to affirm a clear focus area of the culture, we build bridges as communicators so that we can discover redemptive analogies. My best example of such a discovery in the Tzotzil cultures came in the shamanistic ritual sacrifice of a chicken. The Tzotzils call the animal sacrifice for the wrongdoing or sin of a person a *"q'uexol"* which literally means "substitute." This concept can be affirmed as a part of God's plan as revealed in biblical history, first in the Old Testament sacrificial system and even more clearly in the "substitutionary sacrifice" of Christ on the cross. By affirming this clear-focus cultural form, the communicator or missionary is recognizing the cultural form and also making a direct connection with biblical theology. For the Tzotzils this was important because they could identify with the Bible as something mentioned by the Roman Catholic priests. However, they had never made any connection of biblical theology with their own animistic traditions and forms. The result is that the receptor culture not only shows interest in integrating these already-accepted cultural entities, but also the communicator gains trust because he/she is not seen as a threat to the cultural worldview and forms.

Second, in specific worldview concepts, there often exist some fuzzy areas—those that are not well defined or that have lost their clear focus in the culture's thinking and beliefs. We must look for these fuzzy areas and fulfill them with biblical teaching. When the apostle Paul addressed the men of Athens (Acts 17:22–23), he found a fuzzy area described in an inscription on the altar "to an unknown god." He immediately set out to fulfill the unclear area by proclaiming a clear biblical message (Acts 17:24–31) related to that unknown concept or object of worship.

Every culture struggles with many areas of their worldview that are unclear and which raise questions and doubts. It is in this ambiguous perception of reality in a culture that we have the possibility of introducing a message or idea that might fulfill or give some clarity to an existing cultural ideal or value. In the next section, I will share the example of the Tzotzil concept of time as a test of the model.

Third, change will take place in the whole worldview concept as time is allowed for the "ripple effect"[21] to transform the clear focus area of the worldview concept.

Fourth, the pressure for change is continued by concentrating on the communication of biblical meanings in the fuzzy areas. This is done by using the cultural forms that are well known through which we communicate the biblical meanings.

Finally, the insiders of the culture are the only ones who have the right to determine what the Bible has to say to both their worldview concepts and cultural forms.

In applying this model, the missionary begins with any affirmation that can be found through initial study and contacts. In very general terms, the missionary can begin by a biblical affirmation of historical and ethnic pride. In the Tzotzil tribes, this attempt to affirm their culture not only reveals a non-threatening attitude of the missionary toward the receptor culture, but it also communicates the idea that the Bible itself is not a confrontational enemy. To then affirm, by means of the Word of God, some of the specific parts of the Tzotzil cosmology and their concepts of deity and spirits serves

---

21. Hesselgrave, *Communicating Christ*, 347.

to deepen the perception of the receptor culture that the gospel and the missionary have not arrived to threaten or destroy their cultural worldview.

> *Observation: Many of the worldview concepts of any culture can be affirmed by the Bible, thus avoiding initial confrontation and persecution.*

In the Tzotzil worldview, I found that it was possible to affirm the existence and eternal nature of the inner soul of a person. As I observed other aspects of the Zinacanteco/Tzotzil worldview, I was amazed to find that much could be affirmed by the Bible and Christianity. This is our starting point in communication with the receptor culture.

> *Observation: It is important to affirm worldview concepts even though there are parts that are in need of eventual Biblical reinterpretation.*

The second step in the model is to search for the fuzzy areas in the worldview concepts, and fulfill these with what the Bible teaches. This means that fulfillment could be defined as a bringing to completion through reinterpretation a worldview concept or value that has previously been affirmed. But it is preferable to look at a specific worldview concept to better understand how the affirm and fulfill model might bring about deep worldview change without causing undue cultural dislocation and undesired persecution.

The Worldview Concept of Time as a Test of the Model

We can affirm the general cultural concept of time in the Zinacanteco worldview. First, we can affirm the Zinacanteco way of perceiving time as event. A biblical study of the concept of time, such as that done by Henri M. Yaker in *The Future of Time*,[22] reveals that the Zinacantecos' view of time as event is more biblical than the Euro-American view of time.

We can also affirm the Zinacanteco perception of time as divided into time as both sacred and ordinary. The Bible again affirms this perception of time in its use of *chronos* as opposed to *kairos*. As Yaker points out, "the term 'kairos' refers to a special time."[23] The Old Testament clearly exempli-

22. Yaker, *Future of Time*, 15–33.
23. Yaker, *Future of Time*, 18.

fies the importance of special or sacred time in Jewish cycles of yearly Jewish celebrations and ritual festivals and sacrifices. In Leviticus 23 the Israelites were commanded to observe several yearly sacred times. The list of special feasts is introduced with these words: "The Lord said to Moses, 'Speak to the Israelites and say to them: These are my appointed feasts, the appointed feasts of the Lord, which you are to proclaim as sacred assemblies . . . the sacred assemblies you are to proclaim at their appointed times'" (Lev 23:1, 2, 4).

The Old Testament books of Exodus, Leviticus, Numbers, and Esther enumerate twelve different sacred events, each with its own specific time designation during the year. Each of the feasts are set aside as sacred time as over against ordinary time. Clear instructions denote the sacred time quality with such phrases as: "Do no regular work . . . Hold a sacred assembly and deny yourselves, and present an offering made to the Lord" (see Lev 23:7, 8, 21, 27). Thus, in the Old Testament there is a clear affirmation of the concept of sacred ritual time. In the communication of the gospel to the Zinacantecos, it is extremely important to acknowledge the perception of sacred ritual time known as q'uin (fiesta). This affirmation can take place both on the family level and on the level of the important tribal ceremonies, and it must be expressed both before evangelism takes place as well as after the church is planted. This can be done by affirming the positive and biblical aspects, functions, and values exemplified in the tribal ceremonial q'uin, and by encouraging the Christians to replicate the functions and values of the q'uin in their special event Sunday q'uin celebrations.

Finally, we can affirm specific aspects of the Zinacanteco perception of time as cyclical. Even though this cyclical view of time leads the Zinacantecos to a belief in reincarnation, it is important to first affirm the cultural concept that is not in conflict with biblical teaching. Genesis 8:22 confirms a cyclical view of time in relation to the pattern of days and seasons:

> As long as the earth endures,
> seedtime and harvest,
> cold and heat,
> summer and winter,
> day and night
> will never cease.

The Bible assures us of God's creation of the cyclical patterns (Ps 74:16–17) as well as their continuation (Jer 5:24). Ecclesiastes 3:1–8 gives a poetic description of the cyclical view of life by indicating, "There is a time for everything, and a season for every activity under heaven" (Eccl 3:1).

Thus, we affirm the cyclical patterns of the solar cycles, yearly cycles, and life cycles. We can affirm their functions in giving order and meaning to life by encouraging sacred Christian events that mark these cycles. We can even affirm the Zinacanteco beliefs in ancestral deities and in other local gods and saints that are actors in the cyclical journey of the soul. After all, the Bible does not deny that there is a "great cloud of witnesses" (Heb 12:1), nor does it deny the existence of other gods and spirits.

We must also fulfill the concept with biblical meanings. The affirm and fulfill model suggests that this be done by approaching the fuzzy areas of a concept. In the Zinacanteco concept of time, the idea of reincarnation and the destination of the soul after death are very vague and unclear for almost everyone in the culture. The Zinacanteco cannot explain the time or process in which the soul makes its way from *c'otebal* (similar to purgatory), on to *htojob-mulil* (the place where sin is purged) or *vinajel* (heaven) and back to the pool of souls or ancestral control. This area of unclear focus in the worldview can be fulfilled biblically, and the people are often willing to discuss this area. Thus, biblical reinterpretation can clarify and fulfill the unclear area of time and reincarnation.

The apostle Paul was very intentional about using a kind of affirm and fulfill model in his approach to the men of Athens. He carefully affirmed the fact that they were very religious (Acts 17:22). He affirmed their objects of worship by showing intense interest in them and in even using one of them as the basis for his message, which was to fulfill with meaning what was previously "unknown" to them (Acts 23). Paul's message is a good example of how we can affirm specific aspects of the culture before we attempt to fulfill them with God's message.

After the biblical concept has penetrated the previously fuzzy area with Christian meaning, then the ripple effect will begin to transform the rest of the worldview concept that comes in conflict with the Bible. The advantage of the ripple effect is that it puts the biblical concept and teaching into the hands of the insiders of a culture and allows them to make the decisions that will lead to worldview transformation. In this way, the affirm and fulfill model has the potential of presenting a transformational message in a non-confrontational way.

Affirm and Fulfill in Other Worldview Areas

The affirm and fulfill model can be applied to all areas of worldview concept transformation. It is also useful in looking at cultural forms and rituals. Most of these forms and rituals are clear-focus elements that can be affirmed, but the meanings are often fuzzy or unclear, and they can be fulfilled with biblical communication and reinterpretation. This same model could apply to the Zinacanteco ancestral deities, gods, and saints. These constitute the clear area of the cosmology, and their existence can be affirmed. But the idea of a high God is very unclear and vague in the Zinacanteco worldview. By allowing the biblical message to fulfill that perception without challenging the clear-focus area of the worldview, transformational worldview change can begin to take place with a minimum of disruption.

> *Observation: By affirming and fulfilling a culture's worldview in the communication of the gospel, the receptor culture is less likely to perceive Biblical Christianity as threatening and destructive to its worldview.*

A Warning about the Affirm and Fulfill Model

The affirm and fulfill model is not a magic formula to prevent all persecution. In many cases, in spite of the intention of the communicator of transformational change to be perceived as both affirming and fulfilling in a particular culture, there will be a certain number of receptors who will inevitably perceive any attempt at reinterpretation of cultural meanings as a threat, and the result may still be persecution. However, the principles of the affirm and fulfill model are extremely important and useful in helping avoid the beginnings of persecution for the wrong reasons. One of the dangers of the affirm and fulfill model is that the missionary might be too careful and concentrate too heavily on the affirmation of the culture's worldview. This can lead to syncretism and/or no impact of the gospel message, and no conversion. However, if transformational change is guided by the faithful communication of biblical meanings in the fuzzy areas, through indigenous language and forms, the fulfillment of the worldview can take place through the work of the Holy Spirit.

A Sample Application of the Affirm and Fulfill Model

Every culture has ideals for behavior and ideas about what constitutes improper actions. The affirm and fulfill model would aim to initiate the communication of the gospel message by identifying certain cultural ideals and then linking them with a specific scriptural ideal. In a majority of cultures, most of the Ten Commandments can be clearly linked with already honored

tribal or cultural ideals. Many Old Testament stories and examples communicate ideals that can readily affirm the receptor culture.

An example in the Zinacanteco tribe might be the cultural ideal of
concern for one's own tribe. The Bible affirms that ideal in both the Old and
New Testaments, telling us to "love your neighbor as yourself" (Lev 19:18
and Matt 22:39). We can readily affirm the cultural ideal with the biblical
ideal. However, the Zinacantecos would be the first to admit that they are
not able to live up to the ideal since they are fearful and suspicious of most
of their fellow Zinacantecos. The Bible then can fulfill the cultural ideal by
teaching that it is not speaking of God's wrath in pronouncing judgment on
the Zinacanteco cultural ideal but rather of God's love that can cast out that
fear (1 John 4:18) and instill love in their hearts.

In this way, the Bible touches people where they are and shows them
the way to where they want to be, but without confrontation. By studying
the ethical system of a culture, one can discover a number of cultural ideals
that can serve as "points of contact"[24] to communicate the idea that the Bible
is indeed a positive resource to the receptor culture.

Persecution often arises from an evangelism approach that judges the
indigenous ideals as pagan or sinful and exhibits an attitude that God is
against the indigenous culture. A missionary may erroneously communicate that his or her own cultural ideals are actually outlined in Scripture
as God's ideals to which the indigenous ideals need to conform. This confrontation gives Christianity an image of foreign intrusion that can become
either a cause of, or a justification for, persecution. A practical application
of the non-confrontational affirm and fulfill model can eliminate much of
this unnecessary persecution.

Summary

An understanding of worldview and its functions can help us avoid persecution that is a result of fear of worldview change. The incarnational approach,
which also includes meeting felt needs, will reduce suspicion and fear that
can initiate persecution. Our attitude toward culture and worldview can
promote communication that is not perceived as a threat, thus reducing
confrontation.

I propose the affirm and fulfill model in an attempt to allow the receptor culture to perceive the communication of the gospel as non-confrontational. This model is used as a basis in this book for avoiding persecution in
the communication of the gospel.

24. Nida, *Message and Mission*, 213.

As ways are sought to minimize the negative effects of confrontation and persecution, biblical teaching about persecution must be explored. Chapter 3 will attempt to formulate a biblical perspective of persecution which must be considered before moving to an analysis of and response to persecution.

Chapter 3

A Biblical Perspective on Persecution

THE PERSECUTION OF THE church has been observed and documented since its founding. Some would claim that the persecution of the people of God can be traced back to the Old Testament sufferings of Israel in the midst of the nations and to the afflictions of the Old Testament prophets. Many volumes have been written describing the persecution and trials that both Jews and Christians have undergone, but very little has been done to actually formulate a biblical perspective that analyzes persecution.

This chapter will attempt to formulate an understanding of persecution that is based specifically on the New Testament passages that deal with persecution. It will not deal with the historic development of the subject beyond the scope of the New Testament. The persecution and suffering of Jesus, and of the Old Testament prophets and people of God, are also not a part of this reflection. I will not now deal with Satan's role in causing persecution, or the concept of spiritual warfare since both of these are discussed in chapter 4. This chapter concentrates on the church of Jesus Christ as revealed in the New Testament. The attempt will be made to answer such questions as: Are we to expect persecution as Christians? Is all persecution for our good? Are blessings derived from persecution? What is the proper reaction to persecution? Are there negative effects from persecution? How can we prepare for persecution?

Inevitability of Persecution

To follow Christ means that one should expect persecution and suffering. Three of the four Gospels clearly tell us that "anyone who does not take his cross and follow me is not worthy" (Matt 10:38). The same passages speak of giving up father or mother, or even being willing to lose one's life for the sake of Christ. It is obvious that Jesus required a deep commitment to him, but does that mean that we will be persecuted?

Persecution usually means the experience of being threatened or actually suffering for a cause. When Jesus taught his disciples, there was little doubt that he expected that they would be persecuted. In Mark 13:9–11 he said: "You must be on your guard. You will be handed over to the local councils and flogged in the synagogues . . . Whenever you are arrested and brought to trial . . ." (see also Matt 10:17). Jesus was not saying *if* you are persecuted; he was saying you *will* be persecuted. Jesus made this very clear in John 15:20 when he said: "If they persecuted me, they will persecute you also." Jesus warned the disciples that the world would hate them and persecute them (John 15:18–21).

Paul and Barnabas warned their new converts that they "must go through many hardships to enter the kingdom of God" (Acts 14:22). And the New Testament church soon found that those who openly confessed their new faith in Christ would face persecution. In Galatians 6:12, Paul warned the believers that they should not submit to circumcision if the "only reason they do this is to avoid being persecuted for the cross of Christ."

Jesus made the fact of conflict and confrontation clear when he said that he came to bring division, not peace. He even warned that this conflict would pit "father against son and son against father, mother against daughter and daughter against mother, mother-in-law against daughter-in-law, and daughter-in-law against mother-in-law" (Luke 12:53). In the book of Acts, we find that even when the sick were healed and evil spirits cast out in Jesus' name, the result was persecution (Acts 5:15–18). The fact is that when Christians become involved in spiritual warfare, they place themselves in the battle of the kingdom of God against the kingdom of Satan. Where there is battle, there is conflict and confrontation.

Western Christianity has been eager to preach an easy faith that brings with it the promise of a better and more prosperous life. Often missionaries have evangelized by holding out the carrot of "the good life in Christ," implying that Jesus will solve all needs and problems. However, Christians around the world, especially those who live in hostile situations, have come to realize that even if they try to avoid unnecessary persecution, the gospel will bring confrontation. In 2 Timothy 3:12, Paul warns that not only did he have to face persecution, but "everyone who wants to live a godly life in Christ Jesus will be persecuted." The demands of the gospel are so radical, and the change of allegiance from other gods to the living God is so threatening, that there is going to be strong opposition.

So, we are to expect persecution if we are a part of the kingdom of God in Jesus Christ. In 1 Peter 4:12–13 we read: "Dear friends, do not be surprised at the fiery ordeal that has come on you to test you, as though something strange were happening to you. But rejoice inasmuch as you participate in the sufferings of Christ." Thus, we should not be surprised that persecution is unavoidable in the life of a witnessing Christian. It is even considered a privilege to be persecuted and to suffer for Christ. Philippians 1:29 almost makes it sound like we are being given this privilege as a gift when we face persistent opposition: "For it has been granted to you on behalf of Christ not only to believe on him, but also to suffer for him."

> *Observation: No matter how successful we are in avoiding persecution, the radical demands of the gospel will bring inevitable opposition.*

Reasons for Persecution

So, we expect persecution, or at least we realize that persecution is in some sense unavoidable according to New Testament teaching. But does that mean that we should seek persecution? No, the Bible does not teach the doctrine of redemptive suffering, with the idea that suffering persecution carries with it saving or redemptive value in itself. As we have just seen, there may be some privilege in suffering persecution for Christ, and we will see later in this chapter that there are certain blessings promised when we are willing to stand the test of persecution. However, the New Testament is clear that persecution must be for the right reasons.

Wrong Actions That May Provoke Persecution

Before we determine what the right actions for being persecuted might be, we need to see what could be the wrong actions. In 1 Peter 4:15 we are told: "If you suffer, it should not be as a murderer or thief or any other kind of criminal, or even as a meddler." Not all suffering should be called persecution just because it happens to those who identify themselves as Christians. If we suffer for wrongdoing or even for well-intentioned mistakes in judgment, and if these are perceived by those who cause the persecution as social meddling or as culturally destructive, it may be that we are suffering for wrong reasons. If we are persecuted because we have failed to understand the worldview of a culture, or if we simply have projected an ethnocentric attitude toward a particular culture, we will be persecuted for the wrong reasons. At least, from the receptor culture's view the communication that has been projected is threatening and destructive.

Much of what we call persecution against Christians is the result of an unclear message that we ourselves present. We may be perceived by those who oppose us as representatives of another culture or as an economic or political threat, a perception that may well be the cause of persecution for the wrong reasons. Suffering resulting from such persecution cannot be assumed to serve any real purpose in the kingdom of God. At least, we should avoid all persecution that would proceed from misunderstandings and misconceptions. Matthew 5:10 tells us that "those who are persecuted because of righteousness" are to be blessed. But it is implied that if we are persecuted for reasons other than that, we will not receive that blessing.

The Reason for Enduring the Suffering of Persecution

Scripture indicates that God's blessings will be received in the midst of suffering and opposition if persecution is for the right reason. Matthew 5:11 states: "Blessed are you when people insult you, persecute you, and falsely say all kinds of evil against you because of me." The key, of course, is in the phrase "because of me." Jesus gives clear guidelines for the reason for persecution; it is because of him. He says it again in the parallel passage in Luke 6:22; here we read that we are blessed when persecuted "because of the Son of Man." And in Mark 10:29 he again says: "for me and the gospel." In other words, Jesus gives us only one good reason for suffering persecution: when it is actually for the sake of Jesus and the gospel.

This emphasis on suffering for the right reason is clearly affirmed in Acts 5:41: "The apostles left rejoicing because they had been counted worthy of suffering disgrace for the Name." It was for the name of Jesus that they were happy to suffer. First Peter 4:14 repeats the note: "If you are insulted because of the name of Christ, you are blessed." Paul adds the concept of "the cross of Christ" (Gal 6:12) to the motive behind persecution.

Thus, the only right reason for being persecuted is the name and the cross of Jesus Christ. First Peter 4 continues in verse 16: "If you suffer as a Christian, do not be ashamed, but praise God that you bear that name." In this way, the identity with the name of Christ and the cross of Christ is associated with the Christian. It is clear that this is the only reason that we would praise God for persecution. If the persecution is for reasons of cultural insensitivity, or for foolish approaches, or for a lack of proper preparation for presenting the gospel of Christ, then the receptors will not actually be persecuting us because of the cause of Christ, but rather for some other perceived cause, be it cultural, political, social, or other.

Charles E. Van Engen points out that an "essential aspect of the Church's nature" is "yearning for numerical growth."[1] It is clear in the New Testament and in the ensuing history of Christian missions that it is this "yearning" to advance and spread the name of Christ to others that is the reason for enduring persecution.

Possibly it needs to be clarified that there is only one way that blessing comes out of persecution. That is when the yearning for numerical growth is truly perceived to be because of the cause and name of Jesus Christ. This is only right reason.

> *Observation: There is only one right reason for persecution that will bring positive results—that is when it is truly perceived by the receptor culture to be because of belief in Jesus Christ.*

It may be that the right and wrong reasons cannot be so easily separated, especially when conversion to Christ has social and cultural effects. However, every attempt must be made to communicate our motives and reasons for being Christian, to separate ourselves from the wrong reasons, that the perception of the non-Christian receptor is not easily confused. This is not an easy task, especially when the church often arises out of such sociopolitical issues as injustice and oppression. Yet, our communication must constantly call attention back to the central issue: salvation in Jesus Christ.

Blessings of Persecution

If the gospel of Jesus Christ is clearly communicated so that Christians are actually persecuted for bearing the name of Christ, then there will be blessings that come out of persecution.

1. Van Engen, *Growth of the True Church*, 488.

Future Blessings

The New Testament promises eternal blessings to those who are suffering persecution for the cause of Christ. James 1:12 says: "Blessed is the one who perseveres under trial, having stood the test, that person will receive the crown of life that God has promised to those who love him." This seems like a future promise of eternal life for those who do not revert in the face of violent opposition. This same sense is given in Romans 8:17: "Now if we are children, then we are heirs, heirs of God and co-heirs with Christ, if indeed we share in his sufferings in order that we may also share in his glory."

Hebrews 11:35b–38 gives us a list of those who were faithful in persecution, and yet "none of them received what had been promised." (v. 39) Not all who had suffered and been faithful had experienced immediate triumph, but their victory would be in that they would "be made perfect" (v. 40), referring to their redemption being complete in Christ.

Romans 8:37 tells us that one of the blessings of persecution and hardship is that "we are more than conquerors through him who loved us." But Paul goes on to explain in verse 39 that this is because nothing "will be able to separate us from the love of God that is in Christ Jesus our Lord."

Present Blessings

We are not only promised future blessings when we are persecuted; we are also promised blessings both in the midst of the trials and as a result of them. In a way, some of the future blessings are also present blessings, since they have their beginnings and effects already working in this present world. Still, there are even more tangible promises that God has given to those who are willing to be faithful.

Miraculous Power of God

The suffering described in 1 Peter 1:6 is prefaced by telling the Christians that through faith they "are shielded by God's power until the coming of the salvation that is ready to be revealed in the last time." It is a tremendous encouragement and real blessing to know that Christians are "shielded by God's power." For this reason, followers of Christ can "greatly rejoice" in trials. Christians suffering persecution can often give witness to the miraculous power that God has shown to shield and protect his children in present trials. In chapter 1, I related the example of God's protection in the Chenalhó persecution, and other Tzotzil instances of God's miraculous power will be told in chapter 7. The apostle Paul describes his many persecutions in 2 Timothy 3:11 by saying: "Yet the Lord rescued me from all of them." During times of persecution God often reveals his power to rescue and protect. God sometimes intervenes to provide an escape from persecution.

Guidance of the Holy Spirit

The promise that Jesus gave his disciples when they were arrested and brought to trial was, "Do not worry beforehand what to say. Just say whatever is given you at the time, for it is not you speaking, but the Holy Spirit" (Mark 13:11). This is clearly an immediate and present kind of promise to those who face oppression and persecution and stand before governors and kings as witnesses.

Multiplication of Material Possessions

In Mark 10:29–30, Jesus offers a strange combination of the hundredfold return for those things that must be given up for the sake of the gospel. That promise is combined with yet another promise: that there will also be more persecution. It is most interesting that Jesus' promise of the hundredfold return is "in this present age." Again, those who have suffered persecution can witness to the fact that this actually takes place in many cases. Many Christians who have suffered persecution are blessed in real and tangible ways. Tzotzil Christians in Chiapas who have suffered expulsion and loss of all of their possessions due to persecution are clear witnesses to the fulfillment of this present promise of blessing.

Time of Relief

In 1 Peter 1:6–7, a time of relief from the present troubles is promised. God's justice will be revealed in its fullness in the day of the Lord's return, but also is a part of the promise for the present. Verse 6 says: "Though now for a little while you may have had to suffer grief in all kinds of trials." To be assured that suffering will be "for a little while" is tremendously encouraging to anyone being persecuted. First Peter 5:10 also gives some indication that the present sufferings will end "after you have suffered for a little while." Even in Chiapas where persecution has been quite persistent, *evangélicos* have experienced waves of persecution and times of reprieve.

Genuine Faith and Commitment

The great promise for the church of Jesus Christ is that God will work through the refiner's fire of persecution to produce genuine faith and commitment. First Peter 1:7 tells that persecution and trials "have come so that the proven genuineness of your faith—of greater worth than gold, which perishes even though refined by fire—may result in praise, glory and honor when Jesus Christ is revealed." James said: "Consider it pure joy, my brothers and sisters, whenever your face trials of many kinds, because you know that the testing of your faith produces perseverance" (Jas 1:2–3). That perseverance develops mature and complete Christians who are the key to the growth and maturing of the church. Romans 5:3–4 pursues the same emphasis on suffering as producing perseverance, character, and hope. First Peter 5:10 concludes that this time of suffering will be followed by Christ restoring the Christian to one who is "strong, firm and steadfast."

This promise of increasing faith is clearly the main contribution of persecution to the growth of the church in the face of persecution. It has been witnessed many times that the trials do produce Christians who are ready to stand firm for their faith and become mature witnesses and evangelists. It also unites local believers around a common cause for Christ. First Peter 5:9 encourages these Christians to stand united in the faith "because you know that your brothers throughout the world are undergoing the same kind of sufferings."

> *Observation: There are some clear blessings that are conferred by God to those who are persecuted.*

Reaction to Persecution

In some ways, the reaction of the persecuted Christian to those who are the persecutors is the most important scriptural teaching in this area. The New Testament guidelines are clear and must be taught to those who face persecution.

> *Observation: The results or blessings in the midst of persecution are dependent not only on the reasons, but also on the reaction to that persecution.*

Love and Forgiveness

Romans 12:14 provides the most concise and clear summary of what the reaction to persecution should be: "Bless those who persecute you; bless and do not curse." Of course, Jesus had set the pattern for what this means when he said: "Love your enemies and pray for those who persecute you" (Matt 5:44). Again, in Luke, we read Jesus' words: "Love your enemies, do good to those who hate you, bless those who curse you, pray for those who mistreat you" (Luke 6:28). In both passages, the emphasis is on love. Christians are to respond to persecutors in love. Jesus exemplified this kind of love in his prayer from the cross for those who persecuted him: "Father, forgive them for they do not know what they are doing" (Luke 23:34). And Stephen prayed: "Lord, do not hold this sin against them" (Acts 7:60), as his persecutors stoned him to death.

This reaction of love needs to be carried out in specific and practical situations. Therefore, 1 Corinthians 4:12–13 tells Christians that even if they are treated as "the scum of the earth, the refuse of the world," this must be their response: "When we are cursed, we bless; when we are persecuted, we endure it; when we are slandered, we answer kindly." This is a clear directive of how to answer in love, and not in revenge or violent self-protection. It is this kind of situation to which Jesus is referring when he counsels his followers to turn the other cheek (Matt 5:39).

> *Observation: The first and most important Christian reaction to persecution should be love and forgiveness to those who persecute us. There is no other single factor that is more essential or more basic than this teaching on persecution.*

Proclaiming and Witnessing

The apostles exemplify another essential reaction to persecution: "Day after day, in the temple courts and from house to house, they never stopped teaching and proclaiming the good news that Jesus is the Christ" (Acts 5:42). Even when the persecution became more violent and widespread and the Christians were forced to scatter throughout Judea and Samaria, we read, "Those who had been scattered preached the word wherever they went" (Acts 8:4).

Paul's response to persecution was "from morning till evening explaining about the kingdom of God . . . and tried to persuade them about Jesus" (Acts 28:23b), and he reminded others: "For the Spirit God gave us does not make us timid, but gives us power, love and self-discipline. So, do not be ashamed of the testimony about our Lord or of me his prisoner. Rather, join with me in suffering for the gospel, by the power of God" (2 Tim 1:7–8).

Teaching, preaching, and testifying to the love of Jesus Christ is the response to persecution that serves the role for which God ordained it: spreading the good news to others. It is often during persecution that the attention of many outsiders is drawn to the gospel; preaching and teaching and love can then bring them into the kingdom.

> Observation: Persecution causes the growth of the church only when the response of the persecuted is forgiving love and continued courageous proclaiming of the gospel.

Pain and Suffering of Persecution

Even though the Bible shows that positive effects can result from a proper reaction to persecution, there are many aspects of pain and suffering for those persecuted. This aspect of persecution cannot be ignored.

The pain of persecution extends to children.

Paul acknowledged the hardships of persecution on many occasions. In 2 Corinthians 6:3–10 he lists such sufferings as "troubles, hardships and distresses; in beatings, imprisonments and riots; in hard work, sleepless nights and hunger." He goes on to mention "dishonor . . . regarded as imposters . . . dying, and yet we live on; beaten, and yet not killed; sorrowful . . . poor . . . having nothing." The fact is that this was not only true for Paul, but for the majority of those who suffer persecution. The pain and suffering of persecution are not to be taken lightly. Hebrews 11:35–38 gives a graphic description of the horror of persecution: "They were put to death by stoning; they were sawed in two; they were killed by the sword."

We have already noted that persecution causes people to be scattered and disrupted socially and culturally. Jesus warned that this would be true and even extend to family disruption. In Luke 12:51–52, he says: "Do you think I came to bring peace on earth? No, I tell you, but division. From now on there will be five in one family divided against each other, three against two and two against three."

It is also necessary to recognize the disruption that can be caused in the church. The division that was just noted in families often takes place as well in the family of believers and causes division and factionalism (1 Cor 1:10–12). Also, not all remain faithful under persecution and threats. In the parable of the sower, Jesus tells of those who fall away "when trouble and persecution comes because of the word" (Matt 13:21). In such cases, persecution certainly does not result in a stronger church or in the growth of the church.

> Observation: Some of the negative results of persecution indicated in the New Testament are: human pain and suffering; social, cultural and family disruption; division and factionalism in the church; reversion of Christians. These do not result in a stronger church or in the growth of the church.

The death, disruption, and destruction that are part of persecution must be taken seriously and should call the church to look closely at the reasons for and the response to persecution. Attention also should be given to the importance of teaching Christians and those who are new converts about persecution as it is presented in the New Testament.

Preparation for Persecution

Paul was very aware of this need to prepare Christians for the trials that they would be facing. In 1 Thessalonians 3:3–4, he tells that he sent Timothy to strengthen and encourage the believers "so that no one would be unsettled by these trials." He continues to say that he had warned them before: "In

fact, when we were with you, we kept telling you that we would be persecuted. And it turned out that way, as you well know."

Paul was very concerned that the church be prepared for persecution,
not only in knowing how to react to the persecutors, but also in knowing
how to support the persecuted among themselves. In 1 Corinthians 12:25–
26, there is the concern expressed "that there be no division in the body, but
that its parts should have equal concern for each other. If one part suffers,
every part suffers with it." Hebrews 13:3 reminds Christians not to forget
their brothers who were imprisoned and abused for the sake of Christ:
"Continue to remember those in prison as if you were together with them
in prison, and those who are mistreated as if you yourselves were suffering."
This clearly directs Christians and the church to not forget the persecuted.

Summary

It is clear from the biblical perspective that Christians are to expect persecution. Being involved in spiritual warfare means that conflict and confrontation will be inevitable. Persecution was presented to the New Testament
church as something that should come as no surprise. However, the New
Testament makes it clear that if one suffers for reasons other than the cause
and name of Christ, it will serve no real purpose.

To those suffering persecution for the cause of Christ, it is encouraging
to know that not only are there eternal promises awaiting them, but that
there are also immediate blessings that are promised. The five assurances
of present blessings are more than an encouragement; they also set foundations for church growth and unity.

The importance of a Christian reaction to persecution cannot be overemphasized. To react in love and forgiveness to the persecutors is the basis
of the growth of the church in times of persecution. Persistent preaching
and witnessing, in spite of opposition, will spread the gospel to many others.

Chapter 4

The Origins of Persecution

PERSECUTION IS NOT CONCEIVED in a vacuum, nor is it instigated for no real reason. Persecution is initiated by a threat or a challenge which, when encountered by a person or group, turns into confrontation. Such confrontation can be healthy and positive in that it allows for the comparison and choosing of options for change. But it can also trigger a defiant reaction that, in religious confrontation, can activate persecution. Thus, to discover the primary origins of persecution, one must consider the confrontational nature of the gospel.

The Confrontational Nature of the Gospel

When the gospel message comes face to face with any people or culture, it will be confrontational. As David J. Bosch claims, "The Gospel is foreign to every culture."[1] Because its claims are new and radical, it brings the potential for defiant confrontation. As Kenneth Scott Latourette says: "So radical are the claims of the Gospel, so sweeping are its demands on the faithful, so uncompromising does it render those who yield themselves fully to it, that opposition and even persecution are to be expected."[2]

> *Observation: When the gospel message begins to transform people in any culture, there is going to be some kind of confrontation.*

1. Bosch, "Mission in the 1990s," 150.
2. Latourette, *History of Christianity*, 81.

This, of course, is not a new discovery. Jesus said, "Do not suppose that I have come to bring peace to the earth. I did not come to bring peace, but a sword" (Matt 10.34). He clearly warned his disciples about the opposition and confrontation they would encounter. Hostility and antagonism would be something they could expect, but to which they should not respond with the sword. Jesus said, "In the world you will have trouble" (John 16:33b). Jesus knew very well that the human heart would not always react positively to the good news because "men loved darkness instead of light because their deeds were evil. Everyone who does evil hates the light and will not come to the light for fear that his deeds will be exposed" (John 3:19–20).

Ivo Lesbaupin, in his chapter "A Theology of Persecution," notes that in the early church the Christians had "done no evil, and committed no crimes." Many of them emphasized all of the cultural virtues and placed clear emphasis on obedience to the law. Yet Lesbaupin concludes with what the Christians themselves concluded: "Confrontation is inevitable."[3]

The Tzotzil Protestant evangelicals in Chiapas found that even though they had attempted to follow the pattern of the early church, that even though they had been very careful to avoid persecution, it would in some form eventually be a part of their experience. Even those *evangélico* groups that had made well-planned efforts to avoid persecution discovered that when the group of new believers in Christ expanded beyond the extended family there would be some kind of persecution reaction.

Santa Marta is an area of Tzotzil-speaking Mayans bordering on the northern edge of the Chenalhó tribe. When the gospel spread to this new area from the witness of Chenalhó *evangélicos*, the new Protestant evangelicals in Santa Marta were warned of probable persecution, so they agreed to do all they could to keep the tribal leaders from taking a negative view of the *evangélicos*. The tribal *cooperaciones*, assessments for the fiestas to the saints and ancestral deities, were paid by all of the *evangélicos*. When the tribal leaders demanded that the Christians serve in the tribal *cargo* positions, the Christians reluctantly decided to try to keep good relations with their own tribal people by complying. However, when the original small group of Protestant evangelicals began to grow and spread to other areas of the tribe, and when those who served in some of the *cargo* positions continued to be witnessing *evangélicos*, a severe persecution broke out against all of the Protestant evangelicals.

It was clear to these *evangélicos* that they were not able to avoid the persecution, in spite of sincere attempts to satisfy tribal requirements and demands. These Protestant evangelicals noted that the motivation behind

---

3. Lesbaupin, *Blessed are the Persecuted*, 44–47.

the demands was to coerce them to deny their new belief in Jesus Christ and conform completely with tribal and animistic tradition and practice.

> Observation: *The principal aim of all persecution is to force Christians to revert to the traditional worldview.*

The apostle John wrote from exile on the island of Patmos that he was persecuted "because of the word of God and the testimony of Jesus" (Rev 1:9). Protestant evangelicals in Santa Marta as well as Chamula, Zinacantán, Mitontic, and others have found that as long as they maintained their belief in the Word of God and their faith in Jesus Christ, the confrontation would yield the defiant reaction of persecution.

Even if the affirm and fulfill model (chapter 2) is carefully and diligently applied in the communication of the gospel, the transformational nature of the Christian faith will cause some receptors to perceive life-changing "fulfillments" more as a threat to the receptor culture than as a fulfillment. It should be noted that the affirm and fulfill model is intended to reduce or delay persecution, but the revolutionary character of the message will be perceived as confrontational by certain types of receptors in a particular culture.

> Observation: *Persecution originates from the confrontational nature of the gospel message.*

Sources of Persecution

When persecution breaks out, the first questions we ask are: Who are the persecutors? Why did they react this way? We want to know the sources and reasons behind the persecution.

It is important to realize that persecution usually comes from two different sources. As in the first century, Christians first face persecution from an internal source and later from an external source. The internal source is often cultural or tribal. It may vary from family members to village and tribal leaders and authorities. The external source is often governmental, legal, or institutional. It is a broad-based, organizational type of pressure exerted against Christianity and exemplifies itself in state and national structures.

Internal Sources of Persecution

The first Christians described in the Book of the Acts encountered initial opposition from a very internal source: their own people. We find many examples in the New Testament of persecution stemming from their own people. Jesus was not only rejected at Nazareth by his own hometown people, but this persecution was reflected in a violent change of attitude that resulted in Jesus' own people being ready to use physical violence. Peter and John were put in jail and then threatened by the Sanhedrin (Acts 4:1–21). The apostles were jailed and put on public trial (Acts 5:18). Saul's attempt to destroy the church was yet another interior source of persecution. When Paul and others went out on missionary journeys, they continued to face local persecution in places like Philippi, Thessalonica, and Corinth. It continued to be the Jews, an internal source, who were stirring the opposition (Acts 18:12; 19:13), and the conflict was induced by local groups.

Historian Kenneth Scott Latourette has noted that early persecution is usually internal or, as he calls it, "local": "But until the second half of the third century, persecutions were mainly local. Some of the educated scorned Christianity as a superstition and as untenable by intelligent men. More widespread was popular antagonism. Christians were regarded as separated from society and therefore destructive of the Greco-Roman way of life."[4]

> Observation: Most persecution is initiated by local or internal sources.

Internal persecution sources are often family or neighbors, and include local religious and/or political leaders. As the hostilities in persecution escalate, the family appeals to village leaders; and the village leaders go to the tribal or municipal leaders, but the opposition is still within the homogeneous unit group. It is still internal.

When Shune Tontic, the first Zinacanteco young man interested in the gospel, told his family that he had started to read God's Word and wanted to become an *evangélico*, his entire extended family group turned against him. His father soon reported to a few of the village shamans and later to the local political leaders that his son was in danger of angering the ancestral deities by what he was learning. The local tribal leaders reacted swiftly by standing Shune up before the whole town council and threatening his life if he persisted in this religion brought by the foreigners. The source of the persecution was clearly family and local tribal leaders.

4. Latourette, *Christianity through the Ages*, 34.

Since Shune Tontic found support and encouragement from my wife and me, he was able to withstand the ostracism and local pressure. However, when a second man decided to become an *evangélico*, and my wife and I were on a short furlough, the local leaders appealed to the tribal-municipal leaders for help in discouraging the continued growth of this Protestant religion. The tribal president responded by confiscating all of their biblical materials and cassette tapes and threatening the two young men with jail terms and even death if they didn't abandon their new beliefs.

**Shune Terratol, the second Zinacanteco evangélico believer,
was expelled along with his family by local leaders.**

In this case, the persecution continued to be internal. It was not until some years later, when the number of Protestant evangelicals in the Zinacanteco tribe had increased to more than twenty families and had spread to several other villages, that the internal sources appealed to some external religious and political sources.

External Sources of Persecution

The external sources of persecution usually do not become involved in the confrontation until the internal source or sources become frustrated at not being able to handle the threat themselves. The external source is usually a political or religious institution that represents a higher power or authority than the internal source. In many instances, it has taken the form of government or government agencies. In others, especially where one church is dominant, another church or religious institution is the source of external persecution.

The early church was first persecuted by the Jews. It was not until the burning of Rome in the year 64 that there was any external persecution of the Christians. When Paul made his appeal to Rome in the year 60, there was no real hostility on the part of the Roman Empire against Christians. Paul obviously felt confident that he would be treated favorably. The external source of persecution began with Nero's legal decree: "Let there not be Christians."[5] From then until the year 313, the source of persecution, which brought wave upon wave of violent oppression, was external. It was the empire, the state.

Tzotzil persecution typically has begun with local, internal conflict. It was usually intensified by the local politicians or *caciques* making concerted efforts to rid their tribal areas of the Protestant evangelical witness. However, it has always moved to the higher level or source of opposition when the local political leaders solicited the support of external political or religious forces. In the Zinacanteco case, the tribal leaders felt that they needed endorsement from a higher level of political authority in order to carry out a more effective form of persecution against the growing number of Protestant evangelicals. Thus, they went to the next level in the government structure, the state level. There they appealed for legal and governmental authority and action to halt what they saw as a threat to their control. In doing this, the persecution was carried from the internal level to the external level. The village and tribal leaders asked for the help of an external source, the Spanish-speaking Latino society.

Since this is such a clear and common pattern in most persecution, it will not be necessary to illustrate this more fully. However, the reason that it is important to be aware of the two main sources of persecution is so that we can better prepare Christians and the grassroots church for how to react to such conflict. It is essential to recognize the source of persecution, since this will significantly alter the reaction and response. The dynamics of persecution are very different when it begins with an external source such as the Roman Catholic Church rather than when it originates from an internal source such as the family or tribe.

> *Observation: The response to persecution from an internal source should differ significantly from the response to persecution from an external source.*

5. Lesbaupin, *Blessed are the Persecuted*, 7.

In analyzing the sources of persecution, it is also important to determine from which of the two sources the persecution had its inception. In instances in which national governments initiate the persecution of Christians without the impetus coming from local and tribal groups, the original source of the persecution is obviously external. An example of this kind of external persecution apart from the internal sources would be the communist takeover in China. The point is that the response to such purely external persecution must differ from the response to internally initiated persecution.

Causes of Persecution

Charles H. Kraft has stated: "Worldview is what makes a culture tick. Social control sets its limits."[6] Every culture and every organization have its own set of worldview assumptions or perceptions of how things should be. To ensure that these assumptions are maintained, every culture and organization sets its limits or has its forms of social control. We can best perceive persecution as the exertion of social control by a group or society who perceive some threat to their power.

General Cause of Persecution: A Threat to Power

The general cause of all persecution is the threat to some existing power or powerful group. When a member of a society confronts those who hold the power of control over that society, the powerful will attempt to crush any threat to their power.

When Christ takes control of a person's life in the midst of his or her society and culture, the power control groups quickly perceive that as a threat to their power. Most often, it has nothing to do with their fear of some vague understanding of a new religion or the Word of God, which they have never read. It is the reaction of oppressive power against those who reflect in their lives that they are free and seeking freedom and justice for others. The powerful rule by the tyranny of fear, and when Christians find the truth that frees them from fear, the oppressors see their domination begin to crumble. The pattern has repeated itself throughout history:

> The authors of oppression, those who share the privileges of might and wealth, cannot tolerate such an offense. They will

6. In the author's class notes from Charles H. Kraft's course entitled "Worldview & Worldview Change" at Fuller Theological Seminary (Oct 6, 1981).

brook no obstacle to their intent. It is not that Christians simply bear some stigma, are somehow mysteriously marked for persecution. Their persecution is for altogether concrete reasons. A despotic power feels threatened, and will feel secure only when the disturbers have been eliminated, and so it unleashes its oppression. In order to maintain themselves in power, oppressors crush their opposers.[7]

In 2 Timothy 3:12, we are clearly told "everyone who wants to live a godly life in Christ Jesus will be persecuted." When a person or a group allows Christ to change its way of life and makes that known to others, they call into question all totalitarianism that purports to control all of life.

> *Observation: The general cause of all persecution is the threat to an existing power or powerful group.*

This threat to power is common to persecution in both internal sources and external sources. In family persecution, for example, a father's status in his family or in his village may be threatened by a member of his family becoming an *evangélico*. Therefore, we must look beneath the surface of the power struggle to understand the specific causes of persecution.

Specific Causes of Persecution

While the general cause of persecution is a threat to power, it is helpful to identify the more specific causes of persecution.

Change of Religious Allegiance

The most obvious specific cause of persecution, which is most readily cited by the persecutors of Christians, is the change of allegiance from traditional deities or gods to the God revealed in Jesus Christ. The term often used here has been "conversion," but it is best described as a change of religious allegiance.

When Tzotzil people demonstrate a new faith and trust in the one living God, their whole foundation is changed. They make a deep-level change of allegiance from the whole myriad of the animistic cosmology to the one God made known in Christ. The switch from polytheism to monotheism does not, at first glance, seem so radical. A Tzotzil Christian does not need

7. Lesbaupin, *Blessed are the Persecuted*, 74.

to deny the power of the *Yajval Balamil* (Earth Lord) or the *totil me'iletic* (ancestral deities), but believes that Christ has more power than the tribal gods. However, by putting all of one's faith in Jesus Christ, a person is in effect challenging the power of all other gods and deities. It is a power encounter, nothing less. This is not perceived as a simple change by the insiders in a cultural group, whose entire existence is understood to depend on the guardian protection of the ancestral and spirit deities. Since the tribal authorities see their principal function as that of guarding tribal traditions and deities, any threat to these is seen as a threat to the existence of the entire tribe.

In most societies that do not have an actual practice of separation of religion and politics, or separation of church and state, the authorities in that society determine to whom the citizens are to give allegiance. If any of the subjects of this authority decide to change that approved or traditional allegiance, they will be quickly suppressed. In observing this tension between authorities and subjects in the Old Testament, Hans Walter Wolff says: "From a sociological point of view the history of man down to the present has in part been shaped by the polarity between rulers and their subjects; between those who give and those who take orders; between the exploiters and the oppressed."[8]

The issue of change of allegiance is a threat to religious power and authority. Those who are charged with keeping local religious allegiance safe from attack give the orders. If those who are supposed to take orders suggest any change in allegiance to gods and deities that are under the care of those giving orders, that threat must be extinguished.

Why should a change of religious allegiance by even one or two people in a tribe or village meet with immediate threats of persecution? From a Western worldview it would seem that there could be some tolerance, that one or two who deviate would not be such a great threat. However, in animistic cultures, where the gods and ancestral deities are understood to be the guardian spirits of a particular area, there can be no deviation allowed. The animistic worldview tells people that allegiance to the tribal or territorial guardian spirits assures that they will, as a group, receive favorable treatment. On the other hand, the misconduct of even one person or member of the group, who owes allegiance to that deity, will cause the whole tribe or unit to suffer the consequences. Thus, an earthquake or flood, a curse or catastrophe caused by the angry reaction of a god or spirit to the deviation of one person would jeopardize the entire population. The whole tribe would suffer if there were not controls on allegiance.

8. Wolff, "Masters and Slaves," 259.

> *Observation: The change of religious allegiance causes persecution because it is perceived as a threat, not only to traditional deities, but also to the welfare and protection of an entire society.*

The early church in Rome faced a similar situation. The Romans were convinced that prosperity and victory were theirs because of faithfulness to their gods. They also believed that calamities were caused when their gods were annoyed by some infidelity. They felt that the gods would be annoyed by anyone present who would worship another God and deny the worship due them.[9]

When new Christians pray directly to God, they are bypassing the tribal gods. They are denying that the gods have power and that these gods have control over life. For one to even suggest such a possibility is a threat to the whole cosmological system. There are only two ways to handle such threats of change of allegiance:

1. pressure the innovator to get back into line;

2. expel the innovator from the tribal area so that the territorial deity will not be affected.

In either case the result is persecution.

Threat to Practitioners' Status

In the Tzotzil cultures, the principal religious practitioner is the *h'ilol*, or shaman. The shaman functions mainly as an exorcist who gains status from his supernatural power to contact and contract with the spirit world. If that status is threatened, it will bring a defensive reaction that will result in persecution.

The majority of Tzotzil indigenous people who become *evangélicos* do so as a result of an illness from which they have not found healing through the tribal and village shamans. When these people discover that they can be healed through the power of prayer without the expensive and exhausting ceremonies required by the shamans, they find it very attractive to reject the shaman and turn to direct prayer to God for healing of diseases. These new *evangélicos* literally believe in power healing as it is described in James 5:14–16. And they soon depend on the elders or preachers of the church to be the functional substitutes for the tribal animistic shamans.

---

9. Lesbaupin, *Blessed are the Persecuted*, 5.

This, of course, presents a very real threat to the shamans, who lose both clients and professional status. Direct prayer to God implies that someone who is sick no longer needs a tribal practitioner as a medium. This challenge to the main religious practitioner in the Tzotzil tribes presents a clear worldview threat, as Fabrega and Silver observe in their ethno-medical analysis, *Illness and Shamanistic Curing in Zinacantan*:

1. Only h'iloletic [shamans] can pulse the blood; other people cannot pulse.

2. Only h'iloletic know how to speak [pray] at the shrines [the sacred mountains]; other people do not know how to pray at the shrines.

3. Only h'iloletic know how to leave candles at each mountain. They know how to leave the k'esholil [a black chicken of the same sex as the patient, which serves as a substitute for the patient's soul]. Those who are not h'iloletic do not know how to do these things.[10]

The list of the abilities of the shaman, or *h'ilol*, also includes divination, prophecy through dreams, the power to stop epidemics and disease, and the knowledge of how to pray for the person who has suffered *balamil*, or soul-loss, which is the cause of illness. The shaman also settles disputes and quarrels between family members, thus playing an important social role as well as a healing role. In a spiritual sense, shamans mediate the dispensing of forgiveness in connection with illness and healing. "Zinacanteco curing, in brief, puts a potent, albeit informal, power of mediation in the hands of the *h'ilol*."[11]

When a pastor or elder from a Protestant evangelical group threatens the status of a shaman by showing that one does not need a shaman (*h'ilol*), to have direct access to God's healing power and forgiveness, the reaction is most often persecution. Anthropologists who have studied the Zinacanteco culture acknowledge that status is one of the main controlling forces of Zinacanteco culture.

> *Observation: When the gospel is perceived as a threat to the status and power of traditional religious practitioners, persecution will be their reaction.*

---

10. Fabrega and Silver, *Illness and Shamanistic Curing*, 39.

11. Fabrega and Silver, *Illness and Shamanistic Curing*, 74.

These same dynamics take place in the cases of some Roman Catholic priests who find that their role of revered and almost deified religious practitioner in a particular tribe is being jeopardized by the growing group of *evangélicos* who no longer give them that status. In this case, the persecution comes from a priest, who would be considered an external source.

Spiritual healing power does not present a threat to the worldview of a culture that has a strong spiritual-animistic base, as long as that power is in the hands of traditional practitioners. However, the worldview is threatened if power encounter and power healing become a part of the witness of new *evangélicos* who are not supposed to have access to that knowledge or power. A society will feel that to allow such power to be in the hands of unauthorized lay people presents a threat to its worldview, and thus will react strongly to a direct threat to a practitioner's status. That reaction will usually be persecution.

Disruption of Social Norms

Social and economic conditions often exist in specific cultures and societies that not only determine receptivity or resistance to the gospel, but also give indications of the stability and cohesiveness of a particular group or society. Persecution is often initiated by a society that feels insecure because of problems and changes that cause disruption or disintegration of its social norms. Donald A. McGavran has made a similar observation: "At this point, it is interesting to observe that most opposition to the Christian religion arises not from theological but from sociological causes."[12]

Land Shortages

A sociological problem present in areas of the world where population is increasing is land shortage. Especially in areas where the economic structures are based on farming and agricultural production, the decreasing availability of good farmland puts extreme pressure on the society. As the increasing numbers of people for a limited land base threaten the local economy, the people begin to search for immediate solutions. Persecution that forces *evangélicos* off their tribal land can provide a quick solution to land shortages.

The Chamula tribe is a good example of this kind of dynamic exemplifying itself in the persecution and expulsion of *evangélicos*. As has been

12. McGavran, *Understanding Church Growth* (1990), 239.

documented by several anthropologists who have studied Chamula history, Chamula (and most of the Tzotzil-speaking tribes) can be described as living in "continued land-poverty."[13] There is not enough land for the expanding population, which is living in the midst of a national economic breakdown that is forcing many who have lost other employment in nonagricultural work to go back to the land. The land crisis has been brought about by both external confiscation of land by Latino (dominant Spanish-speaking) interests and by the internal misuse and erosion of the farmable land in the Chamula tribal area.

Because there is not enough good farmland left to meet the needs of those who make their living from what they can grow, there is ever-increasing pressure for families to obtain more land. This is further heightened by the inheritance system of land distribution. As a father passes on an equal share to each child, each parcel of land becomes so fragmented that the inherited land is not able to support the next generation.[14] This pressure has forced many indigenous men to share-crop or rent land at exorbitant prices from Latino land owners in the lowlands of Chiapas.

The pressure to obtain more land in Chamula and other Tzotzil areas has played an important role in the persecution and expulsion of many Protestant evangelicals from their tribal lands. Taken in combination with some of the factors discussed in this chapter, the land shortage problem creates an explosive pressure within the society. The expulsion of Protestant evangelicals from their family-tribal land holdings provides a much-needed safety valve to release some of the pent-up land pressures.

Since *evangélicos* are initially accused of threatening tribal equilibrium and authority in the areas of religious allegiance, religious practitioners, and political power, they are easy targets for those who see a chance to expand their land holdings. Upon discovery that members of a family have become evangelicals, they are usually given warnings in public trial, and failure to revert to traditional practices results in an immediate sentence of expulsion. Often the period of grace granted for the victims of this expulsion to gather up their personal possessions is no more than twenty-four to forty-eight hours, but the point is always clearly made that they are not allowed to sell their land. The disposition of the land is left in the hands of local authorities.

The result of the expulsion of evangelicals and the confiscation of land and buildings is the creation of a system of land redistribution based on persecution. Neighbors and relatives become effective spies who report the first indications that a person or a family might be evangelical. The rewards

13. Rus, "Managing, Mexico's indigenous" 13.

14. Cancian, *Economics*, 115.

of being granted the "abandoned" land after the expulsion make it a high-gain, low-risk endeavor for anyone who wants more land and can validate an accusation of religious deviation against a person from one's own village.

> Observation: Land shortage is one of the social factors that heightens the potential for persecution and expulsion.

Distribution of Wealth

Every society and culture seems to have some form of wealth distribution to attempt to level off the material goods accumulated by certain members of the society. In some, this is done through taxes, and in others through socialistic structures or by the religious system's requirements. If the particular system that a society has established to control that redistribution of wealth is threatened, the whole of society is threatened with imbalance.

In the Tzotzil tribes, *evangélicos* soon accumulate more wealth than their animistic neighbors when they no longer spend money on *posh* (the home-brewed liquor) and expensive animistic fiestas to appease tribal deities, when they cease to serve in the costly cycle of religious *cargo* system duties and when they no longer spend their money on shamans and ritual curing ceremonies. Since their culture understands material possessions in terms of a limited good or limited pie theory in which one person's having a bigger slice of the pie means that another person in that culture gets a smaller slice,[15] the increased wealth of the evangelical Christians presents a threat to what they see as proper distribution.

Even though Protestant evangelicals pay their *cooperaciones* (donations for tribal fiestas), unless they are willing to take part in the entire system of wealth distribution, they threaten the economic equilibrium. The traditional leaders find that the easiest and most efficient way to handle this threat is to expel *evangélicos* from their tribal homes and confiscate their property and possessions. In this way, they resolve both the problem of immediate redistribution and the threat of future imbalances. Although the stated purpose of the expulsions is usually because they are Protestant evangelicals, the root cause is basically financial.

In addressing this specific cause of persecution, J. Samuel Hofman shares a clear example of a man named Enrique from the Tojolabal tribe of Chiapas. Enrique stated it as follows:

15. Foster, *Traditional Societies*, 35.

You know, brother-in-law, how hard-hearted the people are in my colony of Tabasco. You know how they chase out anyone who shows any interest in the Word of God, or who sings hymns in their home. You know how they want us all to be alike, how we must drink together and celebrate the fiestas to the saints together. You know how they don't want anyone to have more than anyone else.

Over the past few years, I have planted banana and orange trees and sugar cane. I don't drink like the others do, so I have a bit more money than the others. When I have my work done, I go to the ranch to work to earn a bit of money to buy the things we want. My older brother has become envious of me because I have more than he does. So, about three weeks ago, he went to the leaders of our colony and said that I was studying the Bible and was reading tracts. He accused me of not being one-hearted with the colony because I was going to the ranch to work real often. He is very envious of my fruit trees and of the things I have, so he talked against me very hard.

The men of the village came to my house and said that I had to leave. They said I was reading and studying a differ- ent religion. They threw all of my things out of my house, and they tore down the roof and walls of my house. I had to leave, brother-in-law.

It is all my brother's fault. I would like to kill him. I know that he will now eat the fruit of my trees and take my land where I have worked hard to grow good corn, beans, and squash.[16]

> Observation: The persecution of believers in Christ is not only caused by the change of religious allegiance and the threat to practitioners' status, but by financial and agrarian factors.

Jon Sobrino has noted in his quest for why the early Christians were persecuted: "In general terms these persecutions were not due solely to the fact that the Christians were preaching a new doctrine, a new Lord, and a new God; they were due also to the visible social consequences of this teaching."[17]

Donald McGavran calls this visible social consequence of the gospel "redemption and lift."[18] He notes that the growth of the church can be halted

16. Hofman, "Enforcing Village Solidarity," 6.

17. Sobrino, *True Church and the Poor*, 239.

18. McGavran, *Understanding Church Growth* (1990), 209–20.

when believers in Christ experience educational, medical, vocational, and financial improvement or "lift" that is more rapid than that of other villagers or neighbors. When this is perceived as a threat to a society's wealth distribution patterns, the potential for persecution is greatly increased.

Threat to Ethnic Cohesion

Another major social factor that contributes to the persecution of Christians is the threat to ethnic cohesion. In the past thirty years, the Tzotzil tribes of Chiapas have been feeling the stress of both social and cultural disintegration, which puts extreme pressure on ethnic cohesion. This is not new to the Mayan people of Mexico and Central America. For almost five hundred years, since the arrival of the Spanish conquerors, the indigenous tribes of Chiapas have had to build an elaborate system of defenses against external threats.

Observers and admirers of the Tzotzil cultures of Chiapas have marveled at the cultural resilience and tenacity demonstrated in the face of the external threats and pressures. However, in recent years many anthropologists such as Haviland, Rus, Cancian, and Gossen have watched the interior disintegration of cultural norms and forms that is being brought on principally by the *cacique* system. Anthropologist John Haviland notes that the *caciques* no longer respect or give proper status to the traditional patterns or tribal elders. They instigate and invent new patterns and customs at their own political and economic whims, thus calling into question many of the traditional cultural values and traditions.[19] The observation has also been made by Mexican scholars and writers "that the indigenous leaders have been the first in breaking with the ideals and customs of their communities in exchange for political power."[20]

The result of the disruption of cultural patterns, values, and traditions is that basic felt needs are no longer adequately being met. The corruption and oppression committed by the mafia leaders in the tribal areas create an atmosphere of grassroots frustration and rebellion that causes tribal people to search for answers to their felt needs outside of the cultural limits.

Anthropologist Jan Rus has pointed out that much of the Protestant evangelical church growth in the Tzotzil tribes can be attributed to the fact that the *evangélicos* were waiting in the wings with culturally acceptable options for those who had become disillusioned with the breakdown of cultural

19. John Haviland, interview by Vernon Sterk, San Cristóbal de Las Casas, Chiapas, Aug 1986.

20. Pérez U., "No puede," 2–3.

norms.[21] A similar motif is noted by writers of the history of the persecution in the early church. W. H. C. Frend accredits much of the growth of the early church as well as the persecution that resulted as follows: "The Christians were strong precisely where contemporary paganism was weak. In contrast to the resignation and fatalism of so many pagan intellectuals, theirs was both a liberating and a fighting creed, good news worth dying for."[22]

Frend notes that the traditional "behavioral code was breaking down in spite of the old restraints. Family life and values were faltering just when Christianity was raising these to new heights. The Christians protested against the cruelties and immoralities of the time."[23] The Christians at that time appeared to be seeking answers to the downfall of the traditional system.

This same dynamic has taken place in many areas of Mexico and especially the Tzotzil tribes of Chiapas. The religious practitioners, the tribal authorities, and the *caciques*, those responsible for guarding against cultural disintegration, looked for scapegoats outside of the culture whom they could blame for threatening ethnic cohesion. It is at this point that Protestant missionaries were accused, and the indigenous Protestant evangelicals were persecuted for being agents of imperialism or foreign religions.

To further complicate the issue, during the 1970s and throughout most of the 1980s, Mexico was experiencing a strong wave of nationalism that picked up the issue of ethnic cohesion. During this time anything foreign was seen as a threat to Mexican nationalism. The claim made by the tribal *caciques* that foreign religious entities were dividing and threatening Mexico's indigenous cultures was given credence by most government and anthropological organizations. Thus, the *caciques* were able to carry out open persecution against Protestant evangelicals for about twenty years with nationalistic support and with almost complete impunity.

In China, just as in Chiapas, nationalism was a supportive force behind persecution. As Wing-hung Lam writes about the severe persecution of Christians in China under the communist government: "The dislike for foreignness is a part of the Chinese response to the Gospel. There has been a long history of struggle toward indigenization. Nationalism made this a big issue. Nationalism was the supportive force behind the anti-Christian hostilities."[24]

21. Jan Rus, interview by Vernon Sterk, 1989.

22. Frend, *Martyrdom and Persecution*, 257.

23. Frend, *Martyrdom and Persecution*, 257.

24. Lam, *Chinese Theology*, 52.

> *Observation: Persecution against the Christian church can result from a perceived or construed foreign threat to ethnic cohesion or national identity.*

Threat to Institutions

Persecution is often caused or initiated by some institution or organization that views the spread of Protestant evangelicals as a threat to their power or domination. In many areas of Latin America institutional attacks instigated by the Roman Catholic Church against Protestant evangelicals have presented the main causes of persecution.

RELIGIOUS INSTITUTIONS

James E. Goff wrote on the persecution of Protestant evangelicals in Colombia during the years of 1948–58. According to Goff,

> The church growth of the Protestant churches in Columbia alarmed the Roman Catholic Church. The hierarchy, unable to make the mildly anti-clerical Liberal Government retard the growth, worked to create the impression that Protestantism was a divisive and unpatriotic movement which endangered national unity and threatened the security of the Republic. In this effort, the Jesuits took the leading role. The persecution took a strictly religious form with local Roman Catholic priests urging the police on.[25]

Thus, the threat to the power and control of the Roman Catholic Church as a religious institution was the cause of the persecution. In Chiapas, although the persecution has not been primarily the Roman Catholic Church as an internal source in the indigenous areas, certain elements and leaders of the Roman Catholic Church in Chiapas have launched external source campaigns with the intention of encouraging opposition that would halt or limit the growth of the Protestant evangelicals.

Such an anti-Protestant campaign was very common in Mexico during the first half of the twentieth century, and it has reared its ugly head in recent years in scattered incidents in Chiapas and in other areas of Mexico. The March 1990 visit of Pope John Paul II to Mexico resulted in increasing acts of violence and persecution against Protestants by Mexican Catholics. As was reported in *The United Methodist Review* of September 28, 1990,

25. Goff, *Persecution of Protestant Christians*, 11.

the pope gave numerous televised speeches urging the populace to "defend the continent from all non-Catholics or 'sects.'" The Catholic news service of Mexico reported that much of the pope's trip to Mexico was "an effort to reconvert the growing number of Catholics lost to Protestant fundamentalism and sects."

Making his strongest appeal in southern Mexico, where Protestantism is strongest, the pope urged Catholic bishops and priests "to end their timidness and indifference in combating sects," the news service reported.[26]

In Chiapas, certain ultra-right bishops of the Roman Catholic Church, such as Aguirre Franco of the diocese of Tuxtla Gutiérrez, publicly encouraged the opposition to Protestant evangelicals. The purpose of such attacks was to turn public opinion against Protestant evangelicals so that persecution would slow the growth of the *evangélicos*. Strong pleas have been made to government officials to pass new laws that would eliminate the Protestant threat to the Roman Catholic Church. In the Colombian persecution, Goff saw that the goal of the institutional opposition to Protestantism was that "attrition and social opposition would gradually reduce the number of Protestants and perhaps eliminate them entirely."[27] He explains that the roots of the persecution came from the hope that the Roman Catholic institution could exterminate or expel Protestants from Colombia was based on the fact that "sixteenth century Spain, which purged itself of Protestantism, is the ideal of the Colombian Catholic Church."[28]

In Chiapas, two factors inhibited the development of this kind of institutional persecution. First, the Roman Catholic bishop who, until the year 2000, was responsible for all the indigenous areas of Chiapas was not a part of the ultra-right attack against Protestantism. Bishop Samuel Ruiz García took steps to promote ecumenical harmony, and even launched an effort that was aimed at informing the nominal Roman Catholic indigenous populations that the Presbyterians and Catholics are really brothers who believe in the same God and use the same Bible. He also supported the Presbyterian and Catholic inter-confessional translation of the first Tzotzil Bible in Chenalhó. This open attitude defused much of the institutional persecution that might have otherwise become a major factor in the highlands of Chiapas.

Second, the Roman Catholics have had many of their own people persecuted and expelled from the tribal areas by the *caciques*. As a July 17 newspaper article published in the state capital reports: "In the latest expulsion carried out in Mitontic, they [the *caciques*] got carried away and also

26. Huie Balay, "Mexican Methodists Seek Help."

27. Goff, *Persecution of Protestant Christians*, 11:7.

28. Goff, *Persecution of Protestant Christians*, 11:7.

ran off [i.e., persecuted] many Catholics because they got confused when they saw them reading the Bible."[29]

In other words, it has become common that anyone who wants to become a true Catholic and study the Bible, and anyone who does not accept the mafia-style control of the *caciques*, will be persecuted as if they were Protestant evangelicals. This has had the effect of uniting, in a common cause, both Protestant and Roman Catholic groups, at least on an informal and unofficial level. The new indigenous *evangélicos* themselves place little importance in the difference between the Catholic and Protestant institutions. Their first concern is freedom for worship, prayer, and Bible study. Therefore, the negative effects of institutional religious persecution have not posed the same kind of problems in Chiapas as they have in other areas of Mexico and Latin America.

POLITICAL INSTITUTIONS

The principal effects of the threat to institutions in Chiapas have been seen in the area of political parties. When the political party that had historically dominated and controlled the country of Mexico was threatened with the rising power of other political parties, the ruling party reacted by supporting groups that guaranteed votes for their party. Even if those groups were promoting illegal persecution and expulsion of *evangélicos*, the Revolutionary Industrial Party (PRI) became an accomplice in the crimes of violation of human rights by giving tacit permission to the persecutors in the mafia and *cacique* groups. While publicly declaring a legal end to all religious expulsions, the state government through the Indigenous Affairs Bureau made secret agreements with the *caciques* allowing them to continue to persecute and expel Protestant evangelicals. The same government lawyers then covered for those who tortured, beat, and expelled the Protestant evangelicals by producing legal documents that denied that any of the events associated with persecution ever took place. The obvious motive for the government and PRI complicity in the persecution of *evangélicos* was that they could not afford to lose the votes of the large indigenous populations that were controlled by the tribal *caciques*. As a San Cristóbal newspaper article reported about the 1990 expulsion of thirty-six families from the Zinacanteco village of Tzequemtic: "The strangest thing is that these expulsions are being allowed within the year of municipal elections and of the governor's second

29. Palacios, "Mitontic," 1.

report, which leaves us with a nagging question: Could it be that the *caci-ques* are exchanging these expulsions for votes?"[30]

Although there were many other factors involved in the PRI politi-cal party aiding and abetting the persecution and expulsions, the fact was that as a threatened institution they could not risk losing any more of the indigenous votes. Therefore, they chose to woo the favor of the persecutors in order to continue to be guaranteed the 100 percent vote that the *caciques* controlled in their tribal municipal areas. Political institutions, such as the PRI party in Mexico, played an important part in the causes of persecution.

> *Observation: When religious and political institutions feel a threat to their power, they become external sources in causing persecution.*

Challenge to Political Power

Often the most crucial factor in the cause of persecution is political power. This factor was very obvious in the early persecutions of the first-century church. As Leon H. Canfield writes: "The persecution of Christians was not begun on religious grounds, but for reasons purely social and political."[31]

The political factors were very important to my wife and me, even in our first years of village living. Although we were not immediately identified as missionaries, we found that just living with an indigenous family on one side of the village identified us with the political faction that controlled that side of town. The opposing political faction that controlled the other side of town immediately held us as their political enemy by association. An im-mediate neighbor on our side of the village was the owner of one of the two motorized corn grinders in the village. Whenever he would have mechani-cal breakdowns, I would be called to help repair his corn grinder. However, when his corn grinder suffered fewer mechanical breakdowns than the rival political party's corn grinder on the other side of town, I was accused of casting a curse on the other corn grinder. I was actually taken to trial in the village and accused of witchcraft. At the trial, it soon became obvious that the accusations were a direct result of the rival political factions. Both wanted to use me as their pawn.

Political factions often want to use persecution to fortify their posi-tion in a conflict or power struggle with another party or faction. In the Zinacanteco tribe, even though the small group of *evangélicos* had done everything possible to avoid persecution caused by changing allegiances or

---

30. Sierra Martinez, "En Zequentic," 4.

31. Canfield, *Early Persecutions*, 18.

by threatening the religious practitioners, they soon found themselves in the midst of a political power struggle in the tribe. The two rival political parties began tangling over what should be done with the Protestant evangelicals. One of the parties mounted a violent campaign of physically expelling anybody who was identified as an *evangélico* in order to show that their party was the strongest defender of traditional values. As anthropologist John Haviland observed: "All of the carefully observed principles of avoiding persecution and expulsions were nullified by the political factors."[32]

The church often finds itself being used by political groups and exposed to persecution and pressure to conform to particular ends. In "The Basil Letter," which was written during the International Congress on World Evangelization in July 1974, the Christians who came from around the world recognized this fact:

> Some churches are growing rapidly but are finding the civil authorities eager to use them to further political objectives. Other churches are tiny minorities in vast pagan populations. Frequently they are opposed by secular political powers and, on occasion, dismissed with savage contempt. Still others are being enticed to abandon their distinct Christian identity and reduce their mission to mere political activity.[33]

> *Observation: Persecution can occur when Christians are caught in the midst of a political power struggle.*

The Chamula tribe of Chiapas, Mexico, was a group of over fifty thousand people controlled by tribal *caciques*. These political and economic bosses for the whole tribe decided among themselves who was to be the next tribal president. When one of the early *evangélico* Chamulas, Mol Miguel, challenged the traditional *caciques* by mounting a campaign to replace the traditional tribal president with the choice of the grassroots people, this open affront to the *caciques'* authority was not taken lightly. The immediate response of the tribal political bosses was to place the blame for all of this disruption on Mol Miguel, who had been expelled from his tribal home several years earlier for becoming a Protestant evangelical. However, because he had moved outside tribal land, the *caciques* mounted their own political campaign of ousting all known *evangélicos* from the tribe. Thus

32. John Haviland, interview by Vernon Sterk, San Cristóbal de Las Casas, Chiapas, Aug 1986.

33. "The Basil Letter," 7.

began the severe persecution of Protestant evangelicals in 1974, affecting over two hundred believers from the Chamula tribe.

In this Chamula persecution, the political threat was cited from then on as the cause of the expulsions and conflict, and tribal political-religious leaders would proceed to expel more than five thousand *evangélicos* from their tribal homes in the next several years. Even though the Protestant evangelicals had not been actively involved in politics in any way, they were seen as a political threat.

Those who control political power are always threatened by any challenge to their authority. This factor has played a major role in all of human history. The history of persecution against the Jews has usually centered around political, rather than religious, issues. In the Roman Empire, as Lesbaupin points out: "Judaism was the target of persecution only when it presented itself as a political threat to the empire (on the occasion of the messianic insurrections of the Zealots in 66 and 135 A.D., for example)."[34]

> *Observation: Political power uses persecution to restrain any challenge to its authority.*

Certainly, the Christian presence in the Roman Empire was used by Nero as a political scapegoat in the burning of Rome. We could trace this same kind of political factor in nation after nation right up to the twenty-first century. This factor has always played an important role in the cause of persecution. Because religion and politics tend to intertwine, even in those places that claim a separation of church and state, the politics of power groups must always be taken into account as one of the root causes of persecution.

Primary Cause of Persecution in Chiapas: Caciques

The number-one specific cause of persecution in Chiapas, Mexico, has been the *caciques*. These political mafia bosses have used the Mexican government system under the PRI (Institutional Revolutionary Party) to build economic and political power. These tribal bosses, who controlled almost all industry, commerce, business, transportation, and government aid, maintained their domination over all the life of an indigenous tribe through typical mafia strong-arm tactics.

---

34. Lesbaupin, *Blessed are the Persecuted*, 5.

Over the past sixty years, these *caciques* have bolstered their political-economic control over their own tribal people by physical violence and forced expulsion of any individual or group that might challenge their power and authority. In the Chamula tribe alone, approximately half of the population can be found in settlements outside tribal land, a clear witness to the expulsions carried out for political reasons before the first Protestant evangelicals even existed.[35]

Over the past thirty years, the internal political bosses have exploited the traditional worldview mix of religion and politics to effectively justify the persecution and expulsion of both Protestants and reformed Catholics. In this way, the political bosses successfully used religion to eliminate any internal political threats.

> "The leaders (*caciques*) say they expel us because of religion, but there is really another reason," says Salvador Santis, a Protestant, whose face was still swollen and bruised a month after the incident (in which he was beaten and expelled). "If we have our own religious service, they wonder what will come next. Will we demand loans at fair interest? Will we demand land to farm on? The bosses control religion, so they can continue controlling everything else."[36]

Development of the Cacique System

The establishment of political mafias in the tribes of Chiapas began between 1930 and 1940, when the PRI (Industrial Revolutionary Party), sought to secure a firm political hold on Indian areas. One technique was to name younger, Spanish-speaking indigenous men to tribal political positions with the intention of using these appointments to maintain control over the indigenous areas. These new agents, however, soon learned that they could monopolize on their special relationship with the state, and so eventually they evolved into *caciques* or political bosses. "In a pattern historically parallel to the original '*caciques*' of noble class, these world-wise brokers both exploited their position (their knowledge of Spanish, the Latino political system and their connections with it) for personal gain."[37]

Until about 1980, federal and state government officials denied that they had created any political-boss system in the tribal areas. They found it very convenient to blame all of the mafia violence and conflict on the

---

35. Earle, "Appropriating the Enemy," 19; and Rus, "Social Change," 16.

36. Moffett, "Mexicans Convert," 20.

37. Earle, "Appropriating the Enemy," 19–20.

Protestant evangelicals, who, they claimed, were threatening to destroy tribal cohesion and cultural values. The term "religious conflict" was used to describe any disturbance or expulsion by tribal *caciques*. However, in the 1980s, both the national and international news sources began to expose the *cacique* system. The June 1, 1988, *The Wall Street Journal* states:

> For decades, Mexico's ruling Institutional Revolutionary Party, known by its Spanish initials PRI, has put many Indian groups under political and religious strongmen called "caciques." In return for seeing to it that the indigenous maintained their allegiance to the party, the caciques were allowed to exploit them so completely that some anthropologists describe the system as "internal colonialism." To control indigenous, the PRI began by choosing a handful of ambitious young indigenous. It taught them Spanish, which allowed them to dominate contacts with the outside world. The PRI encouraged its protégés to take on the sponsorship of important religious festivals, which gave them prestige at home.
>
> The leading *cacique* of these highlands, Salvador Lopez Castellanos, known to the indigenous as Tushum (pronounced Too-SHOOM), gained a monopoly on the area's commercial trucks, liquor stills, and credit, for which he charged ten percent monthly interest. Tushum amassed extensive landholdings while most villagers had about half an acre.[38]

Similar *cacique* systems were encouraged in almost all the tribal areas of the Chiapas highlands by both INI (National Indigenous Institute) and SUBSAI (Sub-secretary of Indigenous Affairs Bureau). These federal and state government agencies used a political system that had been established before the turn of the twentieth century. As anthropologist Jan Rus points out, "The system dates from 1892, and lasted until 1911."[39] Although it was placed again under direct Latino authority in 1928 when non-indigenous secretaries took the place of the *caciques* in the *municipios libres* (free municipalities), these *caciques* continued to serve the same basic role:

> Their function was to be the government's "inside men" in the Indian communities: collecting taxes, organizing work-crews, as requested by the state government, and pursuing those of their fellow indigenous who happened to escape from the *fincas* [coffee plantations]. While they were separate from the formal civil-religious hierarchies of their communities, they seem to

38. Moffett, "Mexicans Convert," 20.
39. Rus, "Managing Mexico's indigenous," 11.

have commanded the hierarchy members, and to have used them to achieve their own ends.[40]

Eventually, these bilingual Indian politicians became the bosses (*caciques*) of Chamula, securing positions of almost dictatorial control.[41]

> *Observation: The most common specific cause of persecution in the Indigenous tribes of Chiapas is directly related to internal political caciques who use the issue of change of religious allegiance as a justification for acts of violence, injustice, and expulsions.*

Pretext of Religion

The *caciques* used the pretext of religion to justify persecution. But their purpose was clearly to maintain their dictatorial control and power over the indigenous people. Protestant evangelicals became the main victims of the persecution and violence of the *cacique* mafias. By using the pretext of being traditional Roman Catholics who wanted to protect their indigenous cultures from the incursion of foreign religions, the *caciques* were able to effectively win the approval of most government officials and most of the sociologists and anthropologists who worked in the highland area. Even though these actions and persecutions were completely unjust and illegal in terms of the political constitution of Mexico, the *cacique* bosses continued to maintain political control over almost all tribal areas through payoffs and bribes to Chiapas legal authorities and political officials. Thus, most of the so-called religious expulsions perpetrated by the mafia bosses in the tribal areas were, in fact, politically and economically motivated.

> *Observation: Caciques use the pretext of religious conflict in order to maintain mafia-like control over all aspects of Indian life.*

Cacique Exploitation and Expulsions

In 1989, the public press began to publish articles recognizing the fact that the so-called religious conflict was related much more closely to the system of mafia-like exploitation in the tribal areas than to religious differences. On July 16, 1989, two years after the *caciques* of the Mitontic tribe inflicted their well-known persecution, abuse, and violence on the Protestant evangelicals,

40. Rus, "Managing Mexico's indigenous," 11.
41. Rus, "Social Change."

a newspaper from the capital of the state of Chiapas, *Diario El Dia*, printed the article "Mitontic, Pueblo Sin Ley" (Mitontic, People without Law). The article named those expelling the *evangélicos* and called them *caciques* who "form an oligarchical group which for over 20 years has controlled at its own whim the volition of its people, and have mounted an exceptional system of exploitation."[42]

Just one day later, another newspaper in the same capital city of Tuxtla Gutiérrez, *Semanal Ambar*,[43] published a very clear article called "Mitontic: Caciquismo, no choques religiosos" (Mitontic: Caciqueism, Not Religious Conflict). In this article, the reason for the expulsion of hundreds of Protestant evangelicals was clearly shown to be the *caciques* who exploited and terrorized their own people to increase their own political power and economic control. After showing how the Mitontic mafia family used its control of the sales and commerce to become very wealthy, this article points out: "Here is the key to the supposed religious problem, the soft drink business for each tribal fiesta which yields more that twelve million pesos for the mafia family. In Mitontic there is a mafia system not a holy war."[44]

Even top-ranking government officials eventually realized that the real cause of the supposed religious expulsions was that the mafia-like political groups in the indigenous tribes have been allowed to gain despotic power. In a recent newspaper interview with Mexican national congressman Jaime Sabines, entitled "Chiapas es un Estado de caciques" (Chiapas is a State of *caciques*), the issue was stated very clearly:

> With respect to the expulsions in Chiapas for supposed religious problems, he indicated that in background they are really not so, "they are more political than anything, but based on religious sustenance, which is used as an artifice"; expressing that there do exist some problems that are apparently religious, but internally there are local interests that are opposed to the Protestants because they prejudice the business of liquor sales.
>
> Jaime Sabines said that it is very probable that the expulsions are due to the fact that Chiapas is a state of mafia bosses that lack respect for the institution [of the law] and even though there have been governments that have combated the mafia system, ultimately these mafias have devoted themselves to "methods and means" of continuing to exercise their authority on the edge of the law. The problem of the mafia bosses is due to the fact that we, as a nation, have permitted them to get where

42. Samayoa Arce, "Mitontic, Pueblo Sin Ley," 4.

43. Palacios, "Mitontic," 3.

44. Palacios, "Mitontic," 3.

they are, but some day we will tire of them and we will cause them to fall.[45]

Endorsement of the Government

Recognizing that these mafia-like political groups within the tribal areas are responsible for the expulsions and persecutions on both the religious and political level, the Protestant evangelicals began calling on the Mexican government to put the brakes on the violent and unlawful acts of the tribal *caciques*. In the newspaper, *Diario Popular*, the defense lawyer for the *evangélicos*, Pablo Salazar Mediguchía, called for the application of the law against the crimes and violations committed by the mafia-like bosses.[46]

For several years, the government agencies had intentionally acquiesced to and even endorsed the *cacique* system in the indigenous tribes. All calls for justice in persecution cases were easily pushed aside by claiming that the problem was a religious conflict between Roman Catholics and Protestants. Thus, the government agencies claimed that the separation of church and state in Mexico gave immunity to *caciques* and other public officials who perpetrated persecution. The mafia-like bosses used this protection to justify further persecution and expulsions.

The Cargo System

In the Tzotzil tribes, a cultural element that performs many important functions in society is called the cargo system. It provides a good case study of how the various factors that cause persecution combine in one social system. The *cargo* system has been well described by anthropologist Frank Cancian: "The *cargos* are religious offices occupied on a rotating basis by men of the community. That is, the office-holders serve for a year and then return to their roles in everyday life, leaving the office to another man. The incumbents receive no pay for their year of service. Rather they spend substantial amounts of money sponsoring religious celebrations for the saints of the Catholic church."[47]

In many instances of persecution in the Tzotzil tribes, the Protestant evangelicals' refusal to participate in the *cargo* positions sparked the beginnings of overt persecution. The obligatory system of enlisting men in these

45. Sierra Martínez, "Chiapas," 4.
46. Sierra Martínez, "Chiapas," 1, 4.
47. Cancian, *Economics*, 1.

costly ceremonial duties performed a function of wealth distribution. The more taxing *cargo* positions were often given to the wealthier and more prosperous, thus providing an effective means of economic leveling. When Protestant evangelicals refused to participate in this required social activity, they set into motion several factors that led to persecution.

Not only is there the immediate notification of the change of religious allegiance in the refusal to serve the saints and tribal deities, but also the whole cultural system of gaining and maintaining status is threatened. The degree and manner of a person's participation in the hierarchy is the major factor in determining one's place in the community. Manning Nash points out that in the Mayan cultures the *cargo* system is an integrating social structure in which "the hierarchy is virtually the entire social structure of the Indian *municipio*."[48] Frank Cancian has said: "The *cargo* system is the key to the community-wide social structure of Zinacantán. *Cargo* service is the most important single determinant of a man's position in the community."[49] Anyone who refuses to participate in this system is not only seen as a threat to the traditional religious practices but also to the entire cultural structure of the tribe.

The *cargo*-holders are also those who carry out the traditional fiestas, and are therefore seen as the protectors of cultural values and norms. Therefore, the refusal of *evangélicos* to participate in the rituals and to hold these *cargo* positions is seen by the community as a threat to ethnic cohesion. This threat was further complicated at this time in history by the fact that the entire *cargo* system was being weakened by economic and social factors. Frank Cancian's book, *Economics and Prestige in a Mayan Community*, is a study done in 1965 predicting the demise of the religious *cargo* system in Zinacantán. The potential disintegration of this central element of cultural integration forced society to take a very defensive stance in safeguarding the *cargo* system.

Thus, the various factors that cause persecution can be seen in this case study to combine to bring the potential for violent persecution to a point of near-inevitability. In the refusal of Protestant evangelicals to participate in *cargo* positions, the traditional culture can find nearly all of the rationale that is needed to justify the persecution and expulsion of this menace to their political, social, and economic existence. At the same time, it poses a serious and difficult problem to the *evangélicos* who would seek to avoid this

48. Nash, "Political Relations in Guatemala," 68.

49. Cancian, *Economics*, 27.

cultural clash, for it presents such a complex set of persecution causes that there are no easy solutions.[50]

> *Observation: The factors that cause persecution combine in such a complex web that there are no simple solutions to resolving the conflict.*

The Underlying Cause of Persecution

While this chapter has gone into great detail about the cultural and social-economic factors that cause persecution, there is an underlying cause or source that should not be forgotten. Satan and the power of evil are behind all persecution and opposition to the gospel. In most areas of the Third World, and specifically in the indigenous areas of Chiapas, those who view persecution from a supernatural worldview recognize the spiritual environment that surrounds persecution. Satan certainly uses all of the factors mentioned in this chapter to impede the growth of God's kingdom. When the church and its missionaries attempt to evangelize in an area where Satan has so distorted and disintegrated the cultural and worldview elements, it is imperative that the need for spiritual warfare be recognized. To quote James Marocco: "It is not only the church's relationship with its cultural and physical surroundings and its own inner dynamics that brings growth, but its ability to confront its spiritual environment. This is what I call the unseen war."[51]

---

50. This is evident in the case of Santa Marta. In this dialect group of Tzotzil the persecution and expulsion of the evangelicals centered around the *cargo* position issue. In an effort to appease the traditional leaders of Santa Marta, the Protestant evangelicals decided to allow several of the men to serve in the *cargo* positions, with the understanding that they would not have to participate in the ritual drunkenness nor in the actual veneration and worship of the saints and tribal deities. After several months of experimentation with this arrangement, the traditional leaders of Santa Marta dismissed the evangelicals from the *cargo* duties and renewed the persecution. They said that the half-hearted participation of the evangelicals was more destructive than no participation. It encouraged disinterest in all of the *cargo*-holders, they claimed, and turned the entire system into a farce. Besides, they pointed out, the evangelicals often used their presence in the tribal center as a platform for speaking to more people about the gospel.

From the point of view of the Protestant evangelicals there were also serious defects in such a solution to the persecution. They found that some of the evangelicals who became involved in *cargo* participation would fall back into alcoholism and the worship of tribal deities when pressured by the system. Some could not maintain an evangelical witness in the midst of such pressures.

51. Marocco, "Territorial Spirits," 5.

Satan and Spiritual Warfare

Satan is certainly behind all persecution and efforts to keep the message of Jesus Christ from penetrating the hearts of people and the core of cultures. We could even say that opposition to the gospel is his major role and goal. The words of 2 Corinthians 4:4 refer clearly to the work of Satan: "The god of this age has blinded the minds of unbelievers, so that they cannot see the light of the gospel of the glory of Christ, who is the image of God." Scripture is clear about calling Satan "the ruler of this world" (John 12:31; 14:30; 16:11), "the tempter" (Matt 4:3), "the Evil One" (Matt 13:38), and "the one who deceived them" (Rev 20:10).

> Observation: All persecution and resistance to the gospel is the work of Satan and the result of spiritual warfare.

Satan almost always does his work through his emissaries or his evil spirits. Many indigenous people living in the Central Highlands of Chiapas, Mexico, explained that their illnesses were being caused by specific and identifiable evil spirits. The Zinacanteco people were attempting to maintain some control over these evil spirits through shamans and a sacrificial system of curing ceremonies.

All of the Tzotzil tribes could identify specific tribal deities that acted as guardian spirits (saints and ancestral gods), and they could also name specific evil spirits that are in charge of the various kinds of evil in their culture. The *Yajval Balamil* or Earth Owner (Earth Lord) controls sickness and curing through soul loss and redemption. There are many demons, like the *poslom* that takes the form of a ball of fire and attacks people at night to cause severe swelling, and the *h'ic'aletic* or blackmen, looters and rapists who commit indiscriminate attacks of evil. There is a seemingly endless list of frightening evil beings or spirits referred to as *pucujetic* or devils.[52] When the Tzotzil people became Protestant evangelicals and underwent persecution, they attributed persecution more to the evil spirits than to the people who acted against them. Since the worldview of these indigenous people includes spiritual warfare, it was not difficult for them to recognize that the work of Satan is the underlying factor behind all persecution. Prayer and all of the spiritual weapons must be employed in confronting this underlying source of persecution.

---

52. Vogt, *Zinacantan*, 304.

Summary

In this initial chapter on the analysis of persecution, I have observed that the origins of persecution are varied. Persecution originates from the confrontational nature of the gospel. This confrontation brings opposition from both internal and external sources, but the internal sources are usually those which initiate persecution.

While the one general cause of all persecution is the threat to some existing power or powerful group, the specific causes of persecution are numerous. Specific causes can be categorized under a change of religious allegiance, a threat to practitioners' status, the disruption of social norms, and the challenge to political power. In the indigenous tribal areas of Chiapas, a specific cause of persecution was the *cacique* system that developed out of political exploitation. Government endorsement helped establish the *cacique* system as a primary cause of persecution in Chiapas. The short case study of the *cargo* system in the indigenous areas of Chiapas illustrates how the various factors combined to cause an almost inevitable potential for violent persecution. However, it is important to note that Satan is the underlying cause of persecution, and spiritual warfare is the result.

Chapter 5

The Stages of Persecution

THE MORE DEEPLY WE investigate the dynamics of persecution, the more we find that the factors that cause persecution are so complex that there are no simple ways to avoid it, nor are there any easy solutions to resolving a persecution conflict when it has erupted. In light of this, it is important to understand the stages of persecution with the goal of enabling people to move through these intervals with the least amount of individual, family, and cultural disruption.

While persecution patterns may vary somewhat in differing situations and cultures, the stages are quite predictable. This does not necessarily mean that all of the stages will occur with the same intensity or length; stages may even overlap. This analysis will delineate three principal stages through which persecution can be analyzed: the first stage is threats and warnings; the second is ostracism and expulsion; and the third stage is recuperation.

Threats and Warnings Stage

The initial indication and first stage of persecution invariably comes in the form of threats and warnings. In a family or community setting, this would take place soon after any deviation from cultural or religious norms is noticed. The Tzotzils are aware of their tribal norms and of the penalty for deviation when they make clear choices that lead them into the persecution stage of threats and warnings.

Manuel Ts'uj was a middle-aged Zinacanteco shaman with a wife and six children. He became interested in the gospel through his wife's deliverance from demonic forces that were causing not only illness but also a life ravaged by fear and terrible nightmares. When his wife was freed from this oppression through our visit and prayers in his home with some local evangelicals, Manuel made his first appearance at one of the house worship services. Threats and warnings soon followed. This is a very common pattern. Most often new *evangélicos* were found out by their attendance of a worship service in the home of another villager or of a missionary who might live nearby.

Attempt to Delay Persecution

Most new *evangélicos*, especially those who have seen others persecuted before them, attempt to delay this first stage of persecution by never being seen at a worship service. However, they are soon discovered to be believers in Christ by their change in behavior. For example, they avoid calling on the shamans and they stop frequenting the *cantinas* (bars) with their former drinking buddies. In some cases, they reveal their interest by being caught in possession of a Tzotzil Bible, gospel tract, Bible CDs, or videos. Thus, even though *evangélicos* try to remain unidentified, the resulting first stage of persecution will still be threats and warnings.

The effort to delay persecution within this first stage of threats and warnings is important. If persecution can be kept from moving quickly to the second stage, that of ostracism and expulsion, the dangers of inoculation (discussed in chapter 7) can be greatly reduced. For the gospel to penetrate to the family level, which is the principal decision-making structure of Tzotzil society, it is crucial to allow time for the ripple effect to have impact. As we have already discussed in the affirm and fulfill model (chapter 2), the fuzzy areas in the worldview must be filled with biblical concepts that fulfill felt needs. This is very difficult if the innovator, who comes with the gospel message to fill that fuzzy area of the worldview, is immediately cut off or ostracized.

> *Observation: The longer violent persecution can be delayed, the better chance the gospel has to take root and penetrate to the worldview level of the culture.*

The reason for delaying persecution is to allow time for more people to respond positively to the message of Jesus Christ before the storm of persecution drives many to take shelter and to postpone any decision to see if the storm will blow over. So, it is a crucial time for the initial growth of the church in a specific area or tribe. Since this growth will take place mainly through the direct communication of early innovators within their own family, it is essential to delay any obstacle that might cut off that contact.

The idea of delaying persecution is diametrically contrary to the notion that has traditionally been suggested by missionaries and church leaders in the face of pending persecution. It has often been presumed that new Christians should be encouraged to stand up and to witness to their new faith. This approach would pose the confrontational style of evangelism which invites either an immediate positive or negative reaction to the message. However, in resistant areas, this confrontational approach (see chapter 2) can have disastrous effects on the potential growth of the church.

Shune Tontic was only fifteen years old when he became the first person in the Zinacanteco tribe to respond positively to the gospel message we had explained to him during the time he was our neighbor in the village. When he finally volunteered that he wanted to become an *evangélico*, we were excited and convinced that this was the start of the witness of the gospel to many Zinacantecos. So, we shared with him New Testament passages that showed how the apostles and early Christians had been bold witnesses, publicly standing up to share their new faith. Shune probably felt pushed by us to witness openly to some of his friends and peers. When we saw the severe and immediate persecution that came upon Shune, we realized that this public evangelism approach not only was counter-productive but that it nearly cost Shune his life and faith.

> *Observation: In the threats and warnings stage, the missionary should be in the business of planting seeds and setting roots, not already looking for the harvest.*

The missionary must use all of the options for delaying persecution and emphasize non-confrontational worldview transformation. It is also important to impede persecution in this first stage so that adequate preparation for persecution can be given to those who will face opposition. If the fury of the storm can be held off long enough to do adequate preparation and teaching, then both the individual believer and the new body of *evangélicos* can gain enough strength and maturity to stand up to the severe winds of persecution that will surely come.

> *Observation: Delaying violent persecution in the threats and warnings stage allows preparation time for believers in Christ to gain strength and maturity.*

Advantage of Affirmation Versus Attack

Central to delaying persecution in this stage is the word "affirmation." As has already been discussed in chapter 2, the model to be applied is affirm and fulfill. The goal is to affirm whenever possible such qualities and values as ethnic cohesion, political unity, cultural norms, and even certain religious allegiances, such as the saints or some concept of the ancestral deities. The idea is to present the Christian faith as a positive and fulfilling influence to counter the negative attack represented by the threats and warnings. It is precisely for this reason that the Christian must not attack or become defensive in this stage of persecution.

One of the first Zinacanteco *evangélicos* was violently dragged to public trial and threatened with beating and imprisonment because he was suspected of no longer bowing to the patron tribal images. He countered by arguing that "the saints are no more than wood and plaster. When there was a fire in the tribal church building housing them, they weren't able to save themselves, so how do you suppose they could help us?" This offensive attack on the venerated tribal saints came at a critical time in the history of the Zinacanteco tribe. Just a few years previous an actual fire in the shrine at the tribal ceremonial center had destroyed the most sacred deities. This affront not only brought the wrath of the village leaders upon this young man but caused persecution to move immediately into the ostracism and expulsion stage.

An even more common error at this stage is that of Protestant evangelicals fiercely claiming their rights under Mexican law. Some *evangélicos* will threaten to get a Spanish lawyer and challenge the persecutors to legal battle. All of these tactics may have some validity at other stages of persecution, but in the threats and warnings stage they are extremely counterproductive. They will be seen as an attack and will increase possibilities for premature expulsion.

The Bible teaches us in Hebrews 12:14 that we should "make an effort to live at peace with all men." In Romans 12:14–21 we are counseled to "bless those who persecute you; bless and do not curse." And in verses 16–18 it continues with: "Live in harmony with one another . . . Do not repay evil for evil. Be careful to do what is right in the eyes of everybody. If it is possible, as far as it depends on you, live at peace with everyone." Protestant evangelicals should use all the wisdom given by God and all of the options available to seek to live at peace during the threats and warnings stage. One way to do that is to always respond in positive and affirming terms.

> *Observation: In the threats and warnings stage, the affirm and fulfill model can help avoid premature ostracism and expulsions.*

A young man named Mariano was brought to stand trial for being an *evangélico*. He did not deny the accusation, but rather replied that he believed in what is written in the Bible, the Word of God. He then produced his New Testament and told them that it was the same Bible that was being used by the catechists all over the tribal area. After checking to see if what he said was true, the village leaders warned him that he should not be a part of the Protestant evangelicals, and they released him. He then went to tell all of his family members that they would not be persecuted for reading the Word of God.

Thus, it is essential to delay persecution in the threats and warnings stage while there are still options available to the *evangélico* or missionary. It is a time to weigh the options that are presented by those who threaten persecution, in an attempt to choose options that might be acceptable both to the traditional worldview and to the biblical guidelines.

The Options

The threats and warnings stage presents the new *evangélico* with two basic options. They are usually phrased in a statement that goes like this: "If you . . ., you will . . ." Shune Tontic, the first Zinacanteco Protestant evangelical, was told: "If you believe (act on) the Word of God, you will be killed and your body will be fed to the vultures!" A Chamula *evangélico* was told: "If you don't give up this interest in the Word of God, you will be expelled from the tribe."

The *evangélico* is warned that he or she has clear options: either give up the innovation, or be persecuted. This means, of course, that there is a choice. Option number one is to heed the warnings; option number two is to face the threat of persecution.

Since a choice is still being presented at this stage, a new Christian must learn to pay close attention to the options being presented. In some cases, the option being presented can be acted upon. In the Chamula tribe of Tzotzil, the Protestant evangelicals were told that they would be persecuted if they refused to pay the annual *cooperaciones* (fiesta fees) for the traditional veneration of the patron saints. The Chamula *evangélicos* decided that if this was the principal demand in the either/or option, they could justify the delaying of persecution by calling this fee a kind of local tax that everyone in the tribe must pay to live in the municipality. The *evangélicos* determined that biblical guidelines would allow them to "pay to Caesar what belonged to Caesar." By making such a decision, the Chamulas were able to gain valuable time in which there was tremendous church growth in the villages, even though new threats and warnings as well as the second stage of ostracism and expulsion would eventually occur.

Negotiation for Acceptable Options

In most cases of threats and warnings the persecutors will not offer any acceptable options. It is at that point that the *evangélicos* must initiate negotiations for acceptable options.

My wife and I found it necessary to negotiate for acceptable options in order to be allowed to continue living in the village of Nabenchauc. When told that we must participate in paying for the construction of a new Catholic church building in the village, we decided that this was an option that we could accept in exchange for the right to stay in that village. A few years later when we were told that the village leaders did not want us to hold worship services in our village home, we agreed to the option of going with the small group of new believers to worship outside of tribal boundaries. We always attempted to negotiate with the village and tribal leaders to find options that would lessen the threat of our innovations. For almost ten years, we were able to live in that resistant village setting and do village evangelism by negotiating for such options.

This approach has been used widely by indigenous *evangélicos* in Chiapas when they are confronted with the threats and warnings of persecution. They have found that often the issue of ethnic cohesion can work in the believer's favor in this stage of negotiating for acceptable options. The *evangélico* may be able to delay the escalation of persecution by presenting counter options that display a desire to maintain his or her position as a real part of the culture. This can open the possibility of placing a list of new options in the hands of the tribal or traditional leaders by asking: "What can we do so that you will not threaten to cut us off from our tribe and our people?" Then, depending on the perceived causes of persecution, the *evangélicos* will propose some new options. The new option might be: "If you will give us a chance to show that we are true Zinacantecos (or other ethnic group), then we will volunteer to serve our people in community positions like the school committee or some civic-municipal assignment." This approach emphasizes the importance of maintaining tribal unity and affirms it with an offer to give community service or another ethnic option as a substitute to the *cargo* position.

> *Observation: Since persecutors are reacting to a perceived threat to their cultural norms, we must counsel believers in Christ to attempt to determine the perceived causes of the threats and warnings and begin to bargain for acceptable options.*

The specific option held out by the Protestant evangelicals must counter in some way the perceived cause of the persecution. This may require a combination of various options such as: "If you will allow us to read the Bible and meet with other *evangélicos* for worship, then we will attend all of the tribal fiestas, and we will show respect to our ancestors by attending *Q'uin Santo*" (the elaborate festival for veneration of the ancestral deities that is observed for the immediate ancestors). The local group of believers must decide together how far they are willing to bend in their negotiations. Unless the *evangélicos* can come to a consensus about specific options that they might offer, these might be the cause of dissension and eventual division.

> *Observation: In the threats and warnings stage, options must be discussed and agreed upon by the body of believers in Christ in order to avoid divisions in the church.*

Acceptable versus Unacceptable Options

Obviously, there are options that will be presented to Protestant evangelicals by persecutors that will be completely unacceptable. In the threats and warnings stage, the Christians must be prepared to weigh carefully the acceptable and unacceptable options.

In the Mitontic tribe, the Presbyterians were rounded up at gunpoint and imprisoned for three days without access to food or water. "At 4:00 am, four days after the ordeal began, López Vazques (the tribal president) released the prisoners with a final warning: Either forget your faith or get out. If you sing hymns, we'll kill you. We will destroy your temple."[1] One of the options in this case was considered to be unacceptable for the Mitontic *evangélicos*. It demanded that they renounce their faith.

The *evangélicos* as a group will find that many options are unacceptable. The most common of these is the suspension of any gathering for worship, prayer, and singing. Traditional leaders will often give this as one of the options in the negotiations, but *evangélicos* realize that agreement to

1. Open Doors USA, "Standing Strong," 23.

such a demand would be fatal to the church. On the other hand, *evangélicos* have often discovered that if they offer to refrain from building and meeting in a *templo*, or church building, and propose the option of meeting in small house churches or private homes, the tribal leaders will weigh that as a positive option.

Options such as refraining from all evangelism and preaching are usually not acceptable to the body of Protestant evangelicals, as it would undermine their biblical reason for existence. However, many *evangélicos* are willing to suggest options that would assuage the anger of traditional leaders over a specific type of witness that has proven offensive to the tribal people. In the Tzotzil cultures, door-to-door evangelism and public witness are especially objectionable. To offer to refrain from these specific forms of evangelism without committing oneself to desist from all evangelism, is often a key to the temporary appeasement of potential persecutors.

This, of course, does not mean that we are to advise new believers in Christ to compromise everything to keep peace or to delay persecution. It would certainly be ill-advised to invite syncretism or encourage reversion through such counsel. The persecuted Protestant evangelicals in Chiapas have made it clear that certain issues are not negotiable. When the only option given at this stage is that which demands complete worship and homage to the traditional gods and deities, then the *evangélicos* must openly state to the traditional leaders that they cannot agree or negotiate at that point. However, the importance of always looking for and affirming positive options cannot be forgotten. When persecuted Protestant evangelicals come under attack at this stage, the temptation is to become defensive and go on the counterattack. It is this counterattack that we must avoid.

Outward Denial

One controversial option employed by Protestant evangelicals in the stage of threats and warnings is that of outward denial, while inwardly continuing to attempt to live as believers in Christ. It is an attempt to remain hidden even after they have been discovered.

In some cases, the use of this option has resulted in a delaying of persecution and the rapid growth of the church. In 1985 the *caciques* of the Zinacanteco village of Tzequemtic expelled the main Protestant evangelical leaders and their families. The five other families of *evangélicos* decided to deny their faith; several of them even appeared to fall away for a time in an attempt to avoid expulsion. The expelled *evangélicos* assumed that those who had publicly denied their faith would revert, and the seed of the gospel would be lost in that village. However, a few years later reports began to emerge that those who had denied their faith to avoid expulsion had continued to be *evangélicos*. They also used the time that they had purchased through the use of the denial option to quietly witness to family and neighbors. In 1990 the remnant group in the village had grown to over seventy families of *evangélicos*. They then felt strong enough to start holding house church services in the home of one of the leaders. As the growth continued, they split into two house churches.

In September 1990, following the violent expulsion of thirty-five families from the village of Tzequemtic, several families decided to deny that they were *evangélicos*, ask for forgiveness from the tribal leaders, pay the $50,000 peso fine, and make it appear that they were again reverting. However, just a few weeks after the expulsion of the *evangélico* leaders from their village, a few families of those who had made public denials came to our home to inform us that they were not actually denying Christ, but choosing the option that allowed them to avoid expulsion from their homes and village.

> The idea of taking the church underground is, of course, not at all a new idea. In the persecution of the church in the Second and Third Centuries the church often had to go underground to survive. In many 20th Century cases of persecution of the church in communist or Marxist States, Christians have often found it necessary for them to resort to the "underground life for the Church and commit it to Providence."[2]

However, the outward denial option is a form of going underground that carries real dangers with it. As Pierre Pascal notes about the underground church in Soviet Russia: "Persecution which forces Christianity underground presents the danger of syncretism and distortions of the faith."[3] There is also the danger of complete reversion in attempting to remain as an underground *evangélico*.

Mateo Ocots was a skilled Zinacanteco tribal musician. He played the Indigenous harp for all of the animistic ceremonies. When he became an *evangélico* along with several of his brothers and their families, the threats and warnings became very serious. Mateo decided to deny that he was an *evangélico*, but told us that he would continue to be a believer. To test the veracity of this denial, the tribal leaders placed a condition on Mateo's attempt to avoid severe persecution and the threat of expulsion: they compelled him to continue to play the harp in all of the tribal ceremonies. This also implied some participation in adoration of the tribal deities and in the drinking of

---

2. Pascal, *Religion of the Russian People*, 100.

3. Pascal, *Religion of the Russian People*, 119.

the rounds of liquor at the tribal events. It seemed that Mateo's intention to continue to be a secret *evangélico* was sincere, but within less than a year he had completely reverted and totally lost interest in the gospel. Mateo has never returned, even though his brothers and mother and their families were later expelled for being Protestant evangelicals. Mateo has never again shown any interest in being an *evangélico*.

> *Observation: Outward denial may be an acceptable option for some groups of hidden believers in Christ, but it does present clear dangers.*

Thus, there are real dangers in the outward denial option, especially for individual believers or families. It can so easily lead to actual denial. Because the persecutors will continue to be suspicious of the person who makes a denial, they will keep that person under surveillance for a long period of time. During this time the secret believer will have to go through a long series of denials and actions that prove his or her innocence. It is extremely difficult to maintain a new faith without any fellowship, and the required involvement in traditional practices will cause many to fall back.

However, the outward denial route can have positive results if there is a sizable group of *evangélicos* who have agreed to this secret approach and who can continue to help and support each other. It is almost impossible for one individual to be able to survive the pressure of living under the subterfuge of outward denial. But it may be a way for groups of *evangélicos* to delay expulsion and stay in the village to maintain a hidden witness.

Many Protestant evangelicals in the indigenous cultures of Chiapas continued to use the outward denial option as a way of bargaining for time to remain in their villages until expulsion was the only option. Some used this time to sell property and possessions before they were found out and eventually expelled. In this way, they suffered less of a financial loss upon expulsion. A few used the time to attempt to win their family members to Christ before ostracism or expulsion cut them off. At any rate, outward denial was very seldom more than a temporary gain and proved to be a very hazardous venture that often led, not only to possible syncretism, but also to eventual reversion and denial of faith.[4]

4. Although I do not discuss the moral validity of the outward denial option, I personally feel that it can be wrong because it is dishonest. When a believer in Christ bases his or her stand on an outright lie, God does not honor that witness. Of course, the Scripture is very clear on the matter of false witness, and the New Testament also teaches, "If we disown him [the Lord], he will also disown us" (Matt 10.33; 2 Tim 2:12b). In Luke 12:9 Jesus says, "But he who denies me before men will be denied before the angels of God."

Fines and Penalties

Another option that must be weighed by believers in Christ in the threats and warnings stage is the paying of fines and penalties. Fines and penalties is a form of punishment that is intended to discourage others from becoming *evangélicos*. Some form of monetary fine demanded of those accused of religious deviation is often connected with the physical punishment of imprisonment. In the Tzotzil tribal areas, as a normal condition of release from prison, the accused will be asked to pay for all transportation costs, for estimated costs of lost time from work for all who come to the communal meetings, and for so-called administrative expenses charged by the tribal authorities for their attention and work. The total amount of such fines is extremely large since, in cases of religious deviation, large groups of men are transported in expensive hired trucks to the tribal center.

Additionally, a Protestant evangelical who was brought to trial or was imprisoned on religious charges would be asked to show agreement with the sentence by paying fines in the form of liquor. Prior to an *evangélico's* release, he or she would be required to participate in a cultural ceremony of appeasement through the purchase of rounds of *posh*, a tribal sugar-cane liquor. The final test was to force the *evangélicos* to drink a large amount of the liquor, since the persecutors know that the evangelicals oppose drunkenness.

Since the Protestant evangelicals knew that these forms of threats and warnings were intended to discourage them and dissuade others from their interest in the gospel, they usually felt that they should be willing to pay a price for the right of staying in their tribal villages. Several anthropologists who have studied the Tzotzil cultures have noted that fines and imprisonment are used as community sanctions. "Social pressure, public criticism, gentle harassment, fines and the threat of imprisonment, applied singly or in combination, are the means by which the village as a corporation enforces conformity with decisions made at the community level under the guidance of the leadership."[5] The goal of the indigenous *evangélicos*, in this stage of threats and warnings, was to avoid being expelled. Thus, they tried to appease village and tribal leaders by doing all they could to delay the passage to stage number two, which is ostracism and expulsion. The options had to be weighed. Everything possible was done to present a positive image through personal example and non-confrontation. The believer in Christ who chose to use all of the options available for staying in the tribal area had to exemplify a strong faith and great courage. Some were even confident

5. Miller, "Cultural Change," 61.

enough to call the bluff of those who openly threatened to kill them by answering: "We were born on this tribal land, and we will die on this tribal land. If it is for us to die today or tomorrow, that is for God to decide."

Imprisonment

In many cases, the persecutors allowed no options other than imprisonment. It was typical to be thrown into prison before being given an opportunity to speak in a public trial. At times, *evangélicos* were jailed after other options failed to satisfy the traditional leaders. In the early stage of persecution, imprisonment was the most common form of discouraging others from following in the footsteps of the *evangélicos*. This punishment was intended as a threat, but should be viewed as a way of delaying expulsion.

Both from the view of the New Testament and from the opinions of many persecuted believers in Christ, to be jailed for the sake of the gospel is to be accepted with a sense of joy. The apostle Paul certainly did not seem to think of imprisonment as a terribly negative thing. He describes it with a sense of joy and of serving to advance the cause of the gospel (Phil 1:12–14).

The older Tzotzil evangelicals in Chiapas told the newer *evangélicos* to look at imprisonment as an opportunity. "If you have exhausted all of your options and the persecutors threaten you with jail," they counseled, "accept jail as an opportunity." This may sound strange, but the *evangélicos* have found that because imprisonment was seen as a form of punishment, it could be a way of delaying expulsion from their homes and tribal land. As Mol Chep, a former alcoholic who became a believer in Christ said: "I spent many cold nights in jail for being a drunk; I certainly can suffer a few nights in jail in my witness for the Lord."

> *Observation: Fines and imprisonment can serve as options for delaying the ostracism and expulsion stage if they are seen as an evangélico acceptance of punishment.*

Constant Pressure

The difficult part of living in the threats and warnings stage is that there is constant pressure. As those who have suffered the pressure of persecution under communist regimes state: "It is not so much the imprisonment that weighs so heavily on the shoulders of men, but rather the crushing feeling of not being able to escape from the constant pressure."[6]

In 1966 and 1967, the early *evangélicos* survived daily death threats by working their fields near their homes in the daytime, and slipping off at night to sleep in caves among the rocks and trees in the mountains above their tribal homes. With their wives and children, these courageous Protestant evangelicals endured intense pressure and hardship for many long months.

Zinacanteco *evangélicos* who attempted to live with the constant threats and warnings resolved to never accept expulsion from their tribal homes and villages. Yet, when the pressure became extreme, almost all of them chose to leave and joined those who were already in an *evangélico* relocation community. As one Tzequemtic *evangélico* said: "Don't try to help us stay in our village; we're weary of the lack of freedom and constant threats. We're ready to trade our homes and lands for freedom and more peaceful life in a relocation community."

While the counsel to use all of the acceptable options to avoid being pushed into the ostracism and expulsion stage is essential for the growth of the church, it takes a very special kind of believer to be able to live under the constant pressure of persecution. It is easy, from the relatively safe position of living in a city outside of tribal control, to tell others that they should not accept premature expulsion. In the final analysis, it is only those who are putting their own lives and the lives of their families on the line almost every day who can decide when the danger or the pressure has become too great.

Ostracism and Expulsion Stage

When fines, imprisonment, and constant pressure fail to halt the growth of the Protestant evangelical movement, the next stage is an attempt to cut off the innovators from their people in an area or tribe. This consists principally of ostracism and expulsion. This stage usually does not begin until there is a group of *evangélicos* and the gospel shows signs of spreading in spite of the threats and warnings.

In this second stage of persecution, the time for any kind of negotiation is over. The persecutors have come to a desperate point of frustration, and they are no longer willing to consider any new options or concessions to the Protestant evangelicals. At this point they are saying: "No options! Just get out!" Their goal is no longer to slow the growth of *evangélicos* with

6. Grossu, "Methods of Degradation and Brainwashing," 60.

threats and warnings; now it is an attempt to either isolate or expel all who might be witnessing believers in Christ so that the persecutors can completely end the threat to existing power and structures.

Method of Ostracism

The initial step in this second stage of persecution is often that of ostracism. This is the attempt to exclude or isolate people from the rest of society so that there is little contact or communication between the two. The most common form takes place in circles of family or friends who cut off a person or group and no longer permit opportunities to talk, discuss, or have any relations with the persecuted *evangélicos*. Within family groups, ostracism is carried out either through the silent treatment or through the attempt to leave the believers in Christ out of normal social activities.

This kind of ostracism is common in Islamic persecution. "Nearly every Christian convert from Islam, whether in Riyadh or Los Angeles, is at least shunned by his or her family and other Muslims in the community. This poor treatment is often manifested through the loss of jobs, inheritances, homes, and even children after a parent's conversion. Would I, as a father of three children, leave Islam to follow Christ if I thought the government might take my children and bar me from seeing them?"[7]

Grandmother Loilin, grandmother and widow, had become an *evangélico* through the influence of her nephew Shune, a truck driver in the Zinacanteco tribe. She knew that she would be challenged when her relatives and neighbors found out, but she wasn't prepared for her family's ostracism. The most difficult part for her was that her own grandchildren, who always visited her daily, were warned to stay away from her home so they wouldn't be influenced by her strange new beliefs. At the water hole, former friends would simply turn and walk away. She felt hurt and lonely. In a culture in which these social relations form the only source of communication and companionship, Grandmother Loilin felt completely isolated.

The ostracism is, of course, an intentional tactic with two objectives. First, communication is cut off so that there can be no more proselytism or persuasion by the *evangélicos*. Second, these *evangélicos* are ostracized so that they will feel pressured to return to the cultural norms to avoid repercussions from tribal deities. It is a form of forced isolation to show the disfavor of society, with the hope that this pressure will cause new *evangélicos* to revert.

7. Richards, "Price of Leaving Islam."

This kind of ostracism takes place right in the family and village set-tings. It is probably the most difficult and most discouraging kind of per-secution pressure that new *evangélicos* in newly formed groups face. It is very effective because it threatens to cut off all of the essential family and ethnic ties before there is any significant support group in the larger body of *evangélicos*. Marvin K. Mayers points out that when conflict results from a person or group attempting to control or modify another, this control calls on the use of weapons such as "social ostracism." He says, "Social ostracism is another weapon in a neighborhood where the people are somewhat close and do many things together."[8] Social ostracism is a powerful persecution weapon that uses the culture's values of ethnic and family solidarity to per-suade a member of the society to conform to the accepted worldview and behavioral patterns.

There is a high incidence of reversion at this stage of persecution, un-less there has been significant preparation to provide support and fellowship for new believers in Christ. Fortunately, this form of ostracism doesn't last for a long period of time, since it is also hard work for families and society to sustain for more than short periods.

Severe ostracism makes it imperative for new Protestant evangelicals to organize as a group and meet together for support and fellowship. When ostracism cuts people off from their normal social roots and relationships, it is essential that these believers find substitutes in Christian community and fellowship.

> *Observation: Ostracism must be met by fellowship and support of the local Christian group in order to avoid reversion.*

Kinds of Expulsion

While ostracism is the effort to cut off communication with certain people while still living with them, expulsion is a way of putting these people out of sight and ridding society of their actual presence. Expulsion takes two forms: (1) coerced withdrawal and (2) forced removal.

Coerced Withdrawal

Coerced withdrawal is a form of expulsion that gives the appearance of a voluntary exit by those who have been unwilling to conform to the demands

8. Mayers, *Christianity Confronts Culture*, 184.

of a particular society. This makes it look like those who are persecuted choose to leave on their own volition, and that they were not expelled.

The six families of *evangélicos* living in the village of Tojtic were told in a public hearing that if they didn't return to their traditional religion, they would be expelled. Since the believers assumed that if they did not leave voluntarily there would be the inevitable step of forced expulsion and possible violence, they immediately began to pack their personal possessions onto hired three-ton farm trucks. The *evangélicos* were able to take out all of their personal possessions and even some of the roofing and building materials from their houses. There was no incidence of physical violence, and except for the verbal abuse and mockery of the onlookers, the departure looked like a group of families simply moving to another village.

The advantage of withdrawal in the face of coercion, and the reason that many *evangélicos* submitted to this pressure, was that it reduced greatly the risks of physical violence and loss of material possessions. They pointed to other *evangélicos* whose homes had been burned, or some who have been forcibly loaded like cattle into trucks and shipped off with only the clothes on their backs.

The first Zinacanteco believers were loaded onto trucks
with only the clothes on their backs.

Sometimes they were beaten, and a few have paid with their lives. Thus, many believed that when *evangélicos* are asked to leave, they should consent to do so.

Another justification for accepting coerced withdrawal without putting up any kind of fight is that it is non-confrontational. When *evangélicos* voluntarily withdraw, the tensions are reduced since the persecutors feel that they have won the battle. They confiscate the land and possessions that are left behind and feel that the threat to their power has been removed. In some cases, this makes it easier on those who remain as hidden believers since it takes some of the pressure off for a short time.

However, there are definite negative aspects to the acceptance of expulsion by coercion. First, it sends a message to the tribal mafia leaders that *evangélicos* are cowards who are easy marks for oppressive mafia tactics. The persecutors learn that they can run believers off their land and confiscate their property by using scare tactics. Second, when *evangélicos* leave without so much as attempting to resolve the situation so that they can stay near their families and relatives, it communicates the message that Protestant evangelicals are those who possess no real strong connections with their land or ethnic background. This not only demeans *evangélicos* before others, but also invites the criticism that Protestant evangelicals intentionally destroy cultures and ethnic unity. External political and anthropological critics take real advantage of writing negative reports on how *evangélicos* are dividing and destroying culture and communities, and corrupt internal mafia factions in the tribal areas are encouraged to use the excuse of religious expulsions to usurp more land and financial power.

After many years of witnessing the results of coerced withdrawal, many Tzotzil church leaders were counseling those who came with reports of threatened expulsion: "Do not leave voluntarily. Trust the Lord to care for you and protect you and your family, but do not leave until they forcibly remove you from your tribal land." This policy and counsel have proven to be very effective in most of the cases in which it is tried. At the very least, it delayed expulsion for valuable periods of time.

After several families had left the Chamula village of Chicubtantic due to coercive pressure, the growing group of *evangélicos* decided to follow the advice of their pastor to stay until forced out of their village. For almost a year, in spite of the intense pressure to scare the believers out, they lived by faith and courage. Finally, out of desperation, the village leaders called on the help of tribal center authorities to help them carry out a forced removal of the *evangélicos*. The positive point here is that the number of believers in Christ in that village more than doubled during the time that was gained in not yielding to the temptation of coerced withdrawal.

While this same approach has been employed successfully in many cases, it is definitely not a principle that can be recommended to everyone suffering persecution. First of all, it is only applicable for those who have had the time to mature in their faith in the reality and power of God. It takes strong faith to submit to the threats and pressures of the persecutors on a daily basis. Ostracism, mockery, humiliation, terror, and threats of forced expulsion are used against *evangélicos* in a torturous fashion. Only those who have built a strong community at this stage of persecution are able to withstand this kind of pressure. Thus, while the temptation for the missionary or church leader is to counsel the believers to always remain in their homes when under coercion, it is not feasible for many.

My wife and I faced this kind of choice in our early years in the village of Nabenchauc. After being threatened in various ways over a period of several months, the bullet hole in the rear of a car that we had borrowed to hasten our escape from that village in case of real trouble convinced us that it was no longer safe for us to stay in the village with our family. We chose to use the path of coerced withdrawal. I must admit that, having lived under the pressure of persecution, I could not demand that anyone must stay in his or her village until there is a forced removal. It is only those who are living in the specific situation of persecution that can decide when it is no longer wise to persist in confronting the dangers.

Any premature departure from the village under persecution pressure leaves believers in Christ with two serious dilemmas. First, leaving prematurely gives indication that they do not trust God to protect them during times of persecution. Second, it also makes it virtually impossible to negotiate any future return, since the perception is that the departure was voluntary and that there was no expulsion. This means that *caciques* and animistic leaders who mobilize the persecution are able to exonerate themselves from any wrongdoing before legal authorities.

> Observation: In the expulsion stage, believers in Christ generally should not leave their tribal homes until it is absolutely imperative.

It may be a matter of placing people and possessions at risk, but it is extremely important to hold out and stay in the village and in one's home until there is a legal document or an actual act of violent forced removal. Until there are severe physical beatings, the actual burning or destroying of houses or churches, or a legal declaration of expulsion, the believers in Christ who have been properly prepared to face persecution should be counseled to remain in their villages and trust the Lord for care and protection. Otherwise, both the insiders in the tribe and outsiders in legal and government agencies deny expulsion. Thus, when *evangélicos* leave without a clear indication that they are being forcibly or legally expelled, it is almost impossible to ever return. All of the internal and external political and legal authorities pointed out that the departure from their tribal land was voluntary, and that all rights and privileges had thus been forfeited. Believers in Christ must be counseled to openly resist and denounce this kind of manipulation by corrupt political leaders. Those who are tempted to withdraw from their tribal homes should be encouraged to stand fast until there is some clear act of forced removal. However, when the pressure and ostracism becomes very intense, the difference between coerced withdrawal and forced removal becomes very hard to define.

Forced Removal

Forced removal of believers in Christ from their homes and land by persecutors is the real meaning of expulsion. To be forced off of one's land by the dominant political and physical control of the persecutors, to be removed from one's home by sheer physical force, is a picture quite common in violent persecution.

Expulsion has been one of the more notable features in the persecution of Protestant evangelicals in Chiapas. It has played a major role in almost every Tzotzil tribal area. In some tribes, such as Chamula, it was so pervasive at times that there were almost no *evangélicos* living within the tribal boundaries. They had all been expelled, and almost all of them by forced removal.

The first problem created by expulsions of believers was the loss of their houses and land. New land and housing had to be provided for those expelled, since the persecutors almost always confiscated the land and houses of the expelled Protestant evangelicals. In this way, the tribal political leaders or mafias added to their own wealth and power, while the *evangélicos* were left to the mercy of other Christians for emergency aid and help in finding places to live. Expulsion thus created an urgent need, especially when large numbers of families were expelled at one time. This urgent need must be met with prompt and decisive action, either by a missionary or by the local or national church organization. If expelled believers in Christ are not reorganized into both a worshiping community and a residential community, serious damage will occur in the unity and growth of the church (see chapters 6 and 7).

The second problem caused by expulsions of believers in Christ was the loss of all witness in a tribal area. For this reason, the missionary and the church must continue to look at ways of responding to expulsion so that the loss of the *evangélico* witness in the tribal areas can be minimized.

Responses to Expulsion

The first questions asked by those who are expelled are: "Do we accept expulsion as the final word? Would a better response be to return to our homes and land in spite of the threat that we will be killed if we return?" I will answer these questions and discuss three responses that can minimize the negative effects of expulsion on the *evangélicos* and their families.

> *Observation: The proper response to expulsion is essential in lessening the negative effect on the growth of the church.*

Immediate Return

The first possible response is to say: "They put us out today, but we will get on a truck and be back in our village in a few days." This resistant response is highly confrontational and carries with it many risks and dangers for the families who choose to try it. Yet, it is also a viable possibility for strong and more mature *evangélicos*, especially if such a response was planned and prepared in advance. It also yields the greatest potential for the continued growth of the church. On the other hand, because of its confrontational quality, this response usually results in a more violent expulsion. There are only a few instances when *evangélicos* in Chiapas were willing to risk this kind of confrontation in the stage of expulsion. One instance of the immediate return response to expulsion that has proven that this response can be feasible and effective is the Aldama case.

On November 10, 1989, 154 Chamula Protestant evangelicals were forcibly expelled from the community of Aldama. As was reported in the national newspaper, *Excelsior*: "Following the exile, the indigenous people who profess different beliefs arrived in this city [San Cristóbal] to take refuge in the facilities of the National Indigenous Institute, where the Indigenous Affairs Bureau of the state government is trying to gather food and medicines for 81 children and 73 adults."[9]

In the same article, it was pointed out that the governor of the State of Chiapas, Patrocinio Gonzalez, had made a public statement that there would be no more expulsions allowed in the state. The same report also indicated that the community of Aldama was composed of Chamula Mayans but that it is located in the jurisdiction of the Chenalhó municipality. The tribal president of Chenalhó was interviewed about the Aldama case and he stated: "Definitely, the authorities of Aldama headed by the municipal agent

9. Gonzalez, "Autoridades," A-2.

[town mayor], Alfonso Sántis Hernández acted illegally, and it is necessary for the proper authorities to investigate the problem in depth."[10]

In an unusual occurrence, the municipal authorities actually arrested and imprisoned the head *cacique* of Aldama, Domingo Pérez Gómez, only two days after the expulsion. On November 15, the headlines of the San Cristóbal newspaper, *Tiempo*, carried the following surprise: "Todos los expulsados de Aldama regresan hoy" ("All of those expelled from Aldama are to return today").[11]

Although the expelled Protestant evangelicals had to accept some very rigid restrictions and conditions surrounding their return, the immediate return was accomplished and did not result in another expulsion. However, we must recognize five unique circumstances that made an immediate return possible in this case: First, the government gave the expelled *evangélicos* asylum, so felt an urgency to help them return; second, the Chiapas governor had widely publicized his program to end expulsions; third, the expulsions took place in Chenalhó where there are more *evangélicos* and few *caciques*; fourth, The Chenalhó tribal president arrested the main persecutor; fifth, the *evangélicos* were willing to make compromises so that they could return to their homes.[12]

> *Observation: Whenever circumstances allow it, the first and most desirable response to expulsion should be an immediate return.*

Calculated Return

The second and more common response to expulsion was to say: "We were expelled today, but if we wait a few months for the tensions to subside, we can slowly and quietly go back." This response assumed that a small element of the tribal leadership was able to stir up strong public opposition to the *evangélicos* and that a cooling off period would allow this pressure to dissipate. Often political factions who wanted to make a public show of power incited expulsion during certain ethnic festival events. Once they had made their point, it was possible to quietly and unobtrusively make reentry.

10. Gonzalez, "Autoridades," A-2.

11. Henríquez Tobar, "Todos," 1.

12. The governor's new program for halting religious persecution and expulsions had been initiated only a few months before the Aldama expulsions. He had made a public radio statement that promised an end to all expulsion and the punishment of authorities who did expel people on religious grounds. The government had to make an example of this case to prove that the new program was to be taken seriously.

In 1985 the 116 *evangélicos* from the area of Santa Marta were expelled from their village homes following several years of threats and warnings that included beatings and imprisonment. For more than three years they lived in exile in the neighboring tribe of Chenalhó. In 1988, after numerous attempts to return to their tribal homes with government guarantees, most of the expelled families tried a calculated return. They agreed with the persecutors to serve the tribal *cargo* positions in exchange for the right to live in their village. Even though they continued to struggle with threats and warnings about holding worship services and planning a church building, the calculated return was successful. Not only did the Santa Marta *evangélicos* manage a continued presence in the tribal area; they witnessed nearly 100 percent church growth in the next two years.

It has proven true in Chiapas that the slow, quiet return to tribal villages was the most advisable response to expulsion. This approach allowed for a cooling off period, as well as a gradual testing of the waters to determine if the timing was right for families to return. The positive features of this response to expulsion was that it communicated that the *evangélicos* were not running away in fear, and it restored a witness in as short a time as possible. The communication potential for the gospel was enhanced by the fact that the people of the village admired the faith and courage exemplified by this action.

Following the coerced withdrawal of our family from the village of Nabenchauc after a time of intense pressure, my wife and I decided to try this kind of quiet return to the village after a cooling off period of about three months. Not only were we able to avoid another expulsion, but found that the source of the coercion that had caused us to withdraw had himself been expelled. If we had not risked going back, we would never have realized that only a small faction was behind the persecution. After our return, we found that most of the people of the town were in favor of our presence because during our three-month absence they had missed the medical work that we had been doing. A month later we were able to obtain official approval from the village leaders for our residence there. As it turned out, our position in that village was more secure after our withdrawal than it had been before. If we had not chosen to return, we may have never realized such a breakthrough.

> *Observation: Whenever circumstances allow it, the first and most desirable response to expulsion should be a calculated return.*

However, there were limits to this persecution response. First, this calculated return often required some formal negotiation with tribal leaders in the presence of some external government authority. These tribal leaders often specified rigid conditions for return. Second, the government agencies began an exhausting and endless series of meetings that were supposed to renegotiate the conditions for return. The tribal authorities either failed to respond or were unwilling to negotiate. After several months, the Protestant evangelicals found that their finances, their patience, and their hope became depleted. Third, when this return was negotiated, the tribal *caciques* began to make impossible lists of illegal conditions that took away many basic human rights. Fourth, government agencies that acted as the mediators in negotiated return cases tended to give approval to the conditions demanded by persecutors, even if they were illegal and unconstitutional. Fifth, if the tribal authorities did not live up to the agreements that had been negotiated, and if the growth of the church continued and there were renewed expulsions in spite of the agreements, the government took no immediate action against the persecutors who broke the agreements.

All of these limits to the calculated return could be seen in the expulsion of six hundred Protestant evangelicals from San Miguel Mitontic.[13] The government-sponsored conditions presented by the traditional *caciques* included fifteen points, many of which were both unconstitutional and unacceptable to the *evangélicos*. The document proposed by a state government commission reads as follows:

> The return of the *evangélicos* to their native communities will be accepted if and when the following conditions are formulated:
>
> 1. The construction of any *evangélico* church building is prohibited in the municipality
>
> 2. They must fulfill the costly religious *cargos* that are assigned to them.[14]

Other conditions listed in the document were: no personal witnessing; no practice of Protestantism; no visits or contact with Protestant evangelical pastors or leaders from any other municipality; no house-church services; no reading *evangélico* literature; no practice of Protestantism in any private home. The Mexican constitution guaranteed all of these points as basic human rights, but the government agencies claimed that they could not be applied in the indigenous tribal areas of Mexico.

---

13. Sanchez, "Mas de 600," 1.
14. State Government of Chiapas, 1989, 1.

Only five days after the government-sponsored agreement allowed the Protestant evangelicals from Mitontic to return to their villages, the tribal *caciques* arrested and took mob action in beating and almost killing two of the first evangelicals who had attempted to return. The persecutors claimed that they had heard a tape recorder playing gospel music in Tzotzil coming from the house of one of the *evangélicos*, even though that prohibition was not included in the final conditions agreed upon with the government negotiators. On that basis, the tribal authorities ordered the nullification of the return agreement, asserting that the Protestant evangelicals had broken the agreement. The expulsions were immediately renewed, and the government agencies maintained that they could do nothing to enforce agreements if the majority and the mafia groups in a tribe would not comply.

> *Observation: Once the persecutors responsible for expulsions realize that no legal action will be taken against them for illegal conduct, the calculated return response becomes virtually impossible.*

The case of Mitontic is a clear example of how the government's negotiated return policy worked to slowly destroy the financial and moral resolve of the Protestant evangelicals. For more than three years, the expelled Mitontic *evangélicos* invested their time and money in countless negotiation attempts. Every time they tried to return to their villages, they were again forcibly expelled, each time with more violence and torture.

Since the Indigenous Affairs Bureau continued to tell the Mitontic *evangélicos* that a settlement with legal guarantees was just around the corner, the Tzotzil Presbytery decided that it was not wise to immediately purchase land outside of tribal restriction on which the Mitontic *evangélicos* might relocate. Even though financial aid and some temporary housing were provided for the expelled people, they suffered slow discouragement and eventual complete disillusionment. They became frustrated with the government plan for their return, and the Mitontic *evangélicos* began to search for other return options. They tried joining an opposition political party. They considered the radical approach suggested by lawyer Jonas Flores, but decided not to take up an armed struggle. Finally, the Pentecostals offered to find them more help than they were receiving from the Presbyterians, and that served to further fragment and divide the group. Over a period of about three years, the Mitontic *evangélicos* became dispersed in various areas around the state of Chiapas as they struggled to find work and survive physically. By the time the National Presbyterian Church of Mexico responded by offering to help purchase relocation land for them, the *evangélicos* were so fragmented and dispersed that there was little interest in trying to get everyone back together to form a relocation community.

Two conclusions can be drawn from the above case study: First, the government approach seemed to be an attempt to please the tribal political mafias while appeasing the Protestant evangelicals with promises of solutions for their return. The result, which almost seemed to be an intentional goal of the government plan, as that the *evangélicos* would get tired and worn down physically and financially until they finally would give up and accept voluntary expulsion and become disillusioned and dispersed. Second, if the church or the missionary insisted on the calculated return to tribal villages as the only option for expelled Protestant evangelicals, they risked disintegration of the unity of the indigenous *evangélicos*. At a certain point, decisions had to be made that the calculated return was not going to be possible, and the *evangélicos* needed to look at the third response to expulsion, which was accepting expulsion and maintaining contact.

Continued Contact

The third response to expulsion says: "We have been expelled from our homes and cannot go back permanently, but we will go to visit our family and friends and maintain contact with our people in every way possible." This acceptance of expulsion as an irresolvable reality is the most popular response of Protestant evangelicals, and then the emphasis must be on the importance of maintaining family, ethnic, and evangelistic relationships and contact.

When all of the Zinacanteco Protestant evangelicals were expelled from their tribal villages in April 1982, they immediately determined that they would only foolishly risk their lives if they tried to return immediately. Their pressing need of finding land and rebuilding their homes and their lives was their uppermost concern. Even after several months had passed, their assessment of a quiet and calculated return to the tribe was that it would be irresponsible. After receiving help from the Reformed Church in America to buy land and establish a relocation community, these Protestant evangelicals began to make cautious visits to their families in the tribal areas. As the church grew through family lines and as other *evangélicos* were also expelled, they developed an organized plan of secret visits to those who expressed an interest in the gospel or who requested prayer for someone who was seriously ill. They maintained contact with their tribe through family ties and commercial dealings in the city market.

The advantage of this third response to expulsion was that the Protestant evangelicals found escape from the pressure of persecution. They felt that the peace and security of being able to worship and live as *evangélicos* without the fear of repression and persecution made the isolation and disruption more than worth it. They insisted that they were consequently freer to witness to their faith because they no longer had anything to fear. On the other hand, the separation and disruption of being permanently expelled from ethnic roots and family structures caused severe readjustment problems that resulted in a struggling community and a weakened church.

There are other negative implications of permanent expulsion. First, many who are willing to choose to become *evangélicos* are not willing to face the probability of expulsion if it implies a definite separation and disruption in family and ethnic relationships. Thus, the growth of the church is significantly hindered, at least for a time, by this response to expulsion. Second, the secret visits are often discovered. The tribal leaders see these intentional contacts as an insidious form of proselytism that violates the intention of the expulsions. The tribal leaders' response is to heighten the pressure against any new Protestant evangelicals. This increased tension and confrontation between the traditional leaders and the *evangélicos* tend to take the form of violent political clash in which the cycle of expulsions becomes more intensified and more difficult to halt.

> *Observation: Accepting expulsion and maintaining contact should only be a choice after the first two possible responses have failed.*

Maintaining contact is certainly preferable to another possible response to expulsion, which is acceptance of expulsion with no attempt to continue communication with family or ethnic roots. Although there are scattered examples of this response, it runs counter to the principles of church growth and thus cannot be encouraged.

Recuperation Stage

The third major stage of persecution is the recuperation stage. After believers in Christ have gone through the wearisome rigors of persecution, no matter how well they have survived the threats and warnings, and ostracism and expulsion, they will need a time of recuperation. There is no schedule that can tell how much time this will take, but it does consistently follow stages one and two.

Recuperation involves people on the two opposite poles of persecution. Persecution tends to threaten the equilibrium of the persecutors and of the persecuted, of those who continue to live in tribal or traditional communities and those who must relocate and form new communities. Therefore, both levels of the dynamics of recuperation from persecution must be observed.

Recuperation in the Traditional Community

While it is often assumed that the tribal or traditional community suffers no ill effects from its role in persecution, cultural norms and ethnic cohesion have been questioned and threatened during the stages of persecution. In the battle that was waged in the form of threats and warnings, and especially in the stage of ostracism and expulsion, many wounds are inflicted upon families and structures of the culture and society that must be healed.

Troublesome Questions for Persecutors

The persecution of Protestant evangelicals raises many troublesome questions in the minds of the people in the traditional society. Even though they seem to simply drift with the winds of rationale proffered by those who direct the persecution, many members of a tribe or ethnic group are presented with a whole series of new options and possibilities that expand and challenge their worldview. They are forced to struggle with certain issues and questions for the first time in their lives.

Some of the troublesome issues and questions during and after violent persecution are:

- These are our own people who are being beaten and thrown out for being *evangélicos*. Are they really so bad that we must treat them this way?

- That man used to be a drunk. Since he became an *evangélico* he is no longer bound by that curse. Would that work for me?

- Since that couple became *evangélicos*, her husband no longer beats her. Is this a better way?

- The *evangélicos* no longer pay the high costs of sacrificing to the ancestral gods and calling on the shamans, and yet prayers to God heal them without spending any money. Is it possible to get free help from God?

- Evil spirits no longer affect the *evangélicos*. Is their God more powerful?

- Our tribal leaders are corrupt and we suffer much abuse because of them. The *evangélicos* are free from that political system. Is that an option I should consider?

- We expelled several families of *evangélicos* five years ago. They left with nothing. Yet today they are more wealthy and better off than we are. Did our gods really punish them as we were told would happen?

- Our leaders told us that the *evangélicos* practice all kinds of perverse and despicable activities, and we believed them at first. But we have visited *evangélicos* and they don't do those things. Could it be that our leaders told us deliberate lies?

- We were told that if the *evangélicos* were expelled, we would no longer suffer illness due to curses, but more people than ever before are dying of curses in our villages. Did the *evangélicos* really cause the curses?[15]

Such troublesome questions as these are in the minds of many who remain in the traditional communities, and by the ripple effect they increasingly bring about worldview transformation that causes others to be interested in the gospel message. If the traditional leaders do not make serious attempts to offer valid explanations and give believable reorientation to those who discuss these questions in their family and clan circles, the society may never recover its former equilibrium.

Explanation and Reorientation

Traditional leaders must react immediately to such troublesome questions by attempting to reorient their people so cultural norms are reestablished. At the same time, they must use renewed ostracism to deny any contact with what they consider the destructive influence of Protestant evangelicals. In other words, the persecutors must continue to make those they persecute look very bad, and they have to create answers to the new questions being asked.

At this stage, the importance of maintaining an *evangélico* presence in the traditional community cannot be overemphasized. If *evangélicos* have stayed in the tribe on the basis of an outward denial, they may be able to take part (through family lines) in giving balanced answers to the questions being raised. Those who have been able to avoid expulsion or were able to make a calculated return will play an even more important role. The actual physical presence of *evangélicos* in the traditional community provides a

15. Interviews with various *evangélicos*.

living witness in the midst of an atmosphere that is attempting to destroy the credibility of all Protestant evangelicals. When a believer in Christ can respond in love to those who persecute him or her and show respect for the culture (see chapter 8), the positive effect on the traditional community will be immeasurable and the growth of the church reaches its greatest potential.

This presence, of course, does not assure the lessening of persecution. As a matter of fact, ostracism and expulsion may be renewed with increased intensity, but the believer's response is to keep coming back with a persistent love that eventually brings healing of relationships and recuperation of equilibrium. The affirm and fulfill model is again the key to valid cultural transformation, and in this case to cultural recuperation. But it is also essential to avoid the isolation of *evangélicos* from their tribe or people so that the ripple effect can take place in the traditional community or tribal group.

Recuperation in the Evangelical Communities

If persecution of Protestant evangelicals has resulted in the physical dislocation of families and individuals from their tribal homes and traditional communities, recuperation is very complex. Not only must the immediate needs for survival be met, but also there is an urgent need to reestablish community in order to avoid both spiritual and cultural disintegration.

When hundreds of expelled Chamula Protestant evangelicals were thrust into the city of San Cristóbal de Las Casas, not only did they need to find places to eat, sleep, and work, they also needed to recover some sense of normalcy in their families. Since no preparations had been made for this stage of recuperation, almost all of the families were on their own to find a means of survival. The church must be involved in meeting the emergency needs of food and shelter for the basic survival of the refugees, but one of the most important needs that the church can fulfill is the need for community. This need for community should be met on two levels: the worshiping community and the residential community.

Worshiping Community

Even before expelled *evangélicos* are able to begin thinking and planning for where they might find a permanent residence, they should form or join a worshiping community. This first step in recuperation or recovery from expulsion is essential, especially for people groups whose worldview has a spiritual emphasis.

Observation: The establishing of a spiritual worship community is at the core of maintaining worldview balance for believers in Christ who are suffering the disintegrative effects of persecution.

The expelled believers may have already had an established worshiping community in the village or villages from which they were expelled, but they will need help in the recuperation stage to put the broken pieces back together. Because the recently expelled believers in Christ are suffering a form of shock at this stage, they will often need some leadership help from outside of their own group of persecuted people. They will normally need guidance and encouragement to initiate worship and Bible study, to define leadership roles in the worship group, and to determine a place for worship. Such help will have a dual role.

First, this assistance will affirm the spiritual faith and foundations for which the believers in Christ have been expelled. Since violent persecution threatens and challenges their new faith, expelled believers can recuperate more rapidly if they are immediately given teaching on the biblical perspective of persecution. When *evangélicos* are knocked off balance by the terror and disruption of vehement persecution, they need to take some time to hear a practical summary of the faith of the believers in Christ so that they can regain stability. In the emergency situation in which the expelled *evangélicos* find themselves, their immediate concerns are going to be to recover some physical equilibrium in terms of basic food, clothing, and shelter. They must be reminded and encouraged to take time for worship and biblical teaching to recover their spiritual equilibrium.

Second, this assistance will also play a key role in organizing a caring support group to meet the felt needs of the refugees. The displaced believers in Christ need help to join together with other indigenous *evangélicos* to form a kind of base Christian community for believers in Christ. The severe pressures of persecution and expulsion tend to push *evangélicos* to concentrate on their own personal and family survival needs. It is a time that easily spawns jealousies, strife, and disunity. That tendency needs to be countered by structuring the community so that it is loving and caring.

The caring and sharing community was one of the marks of the early church under persecution (Acts 2:44). The love and concern of Christian community is the central component in maintaining the unity and the growth of the church in the recuperation stage of persecution. However, it does not happen without careful preparation and planning. The missionary and/or local church leaders play an important role at this stage.

> *Observation: Persecuted believers in Christ move through the recu-*
> *peration stage of persecution more rapidly and naturally if they form*
> *a homogeneous community with their own ethnic group.*

Donald A. McGavran raised the issue of the homogeneous unit principle and its importance for the growth of the church.[16] People "like to get
together with those who worship in their own language."[17] "The establishment, in each linguistic and ethnic group, of congregations whose members
worship God with delight in their own mother tongue should be the aim."[18]
This principle of church growth can help people recover from persecution.

When *evangélicos* of a particular ethnic and linguistic group are expelled from their tribal homelands, they cannot be submitted to the shock
of adapting to other ethnic and cultural groups in forming a community of
believers in Christ. Even among the culturally similar tribal groups of the
Tzotzil-speaking Mayans of Chiapas, ignoring this observation has proven
to be very damaging. The prime example in the Tzotzil persecution has been
the Mitontic tribe.

The Mitontic people constitute a sub-dialect group of the Chenalhó
dialect of Tzotzil. Most ethnologists list them as a separate ethnic group
because of distinctive dress, customs, and leadership structures. However,
when more than six hundred Mitontic Presbyterians were ejected from the
tribe and forced to live in San Cristóbal de Las Casas, it seemed an easy
solution to relate these expelled believers with a congregation of Presbyterians who had been evicted from the Chamula tribe some years earlier.
Since the Chamula Presbyterians already had a church building and a well-
established worship community, it seemed valid for the Mitontic refugees
to find a church home there. However, after a couple of years of attempting to relate to the Chamula community, the Mitontic group had become
fragmented and dispersed. Many of the Mitontic Presbyterians became
disillusioned and joined other congregations and denominational groups.
The Mitontic group of Presbyterians quickly went down the path of disintegration because of a failure to recognize the need for the ethnic unity and
homogeneity of the worship community.

This observation was clearly recognized by the leadership of the
Tzotzil Presbytery. The president of the Tzotzil Presbytery, Pastor Tumin
Chicbiltenal, notes that the attempt to mix different ethnic groups of per-
secuted *evangélicos* had caused nothing but problems and divisions in the

16. McGavran, *Understanding Church Growth* (1990), 165–66.

17. McGavran, *Understanding Church Growth* (1970), 289.

18. McGavran, *Understanding Church Growth* (1970), 290.

relocation village of Betania.[19] The strongest churches grow out of groups of expelled Protestant evangelicals that join together because of close linguistic and ethnic ties. The church at Vida Nueva is a good example of this, and shows that recuperation from persecution is much easier if it can be done with the support and care of one's own ethnic group or homogeneous unit.

Even if this homogeneous unit is established, there is potential conflict in defining who will take leadership in the new *evangélico* worship communities. This is especially difficult when mass expulsions force leaders from numerous worship groups from various villages to form one worship community. When the leaders, preachers, or elders from numerous worship groups get expelled from their villages, they will most often try to join with others from their own ethnic group to form one new worship community. The problem is that this places respected leaders from various congregations in the unfortunate position of having to choose who will become the main leaders of the new worship community. The leadership struggle that ensues often leaves some of the former preachers or elders out of the picture. Those excluded from the leadership often feel slighted and move to politically pull enough of the believers to their side to be able to create a division. They then form a separate congregation in which they can be the main leaders. Some initial leadership conflicts can be resolved with little struggle if a neutral indigenous church leader from the same ethnic group can take a temporary role in giving counsel and organizational advice to the new worship group. If the church is new, the missionary may have to take this role.

> *Observation: Expelled believers in Christ and their leaders will be able to recuperate more successfully if they find some unbiased indigenous help to reorganize the worshiping community.*

A slightly different dynamic takes place when a group of expelled *evangélicos* decides to join an already established and organized worship community. Even if the established community is of the same ethnic and linguistic background, the problem of recuperation is complicated by the potential leadership conflicts. Since the already existing worship group has its chosen leaders, the newly expelled *evangélicos* must be encouraged to submit to that leadership and patiently gain integration of its own leaders into the older worship community.

In the recuperation stage, the help and guidance of a church leader, consistory, or presbytery can be valuable. This assistance can give some

19. Tumin Chicbiltenal, interview by Vernon Sterk, San Cristóbal de Las Casas, Chiapas, 1990.

outside perspective and wisdom learned from previous persecution and recuperation. Such impartial participation can allow the recuperation from persecution to take place in an atmosphere of love, by avoiding the leadership conflicts that create long-lasting animosities and destroy the caring worship community. In spite of impartial participation, divisions may occur. It is helpful at this point to maintain a unity in the relationship of these groups by relating them to a mutual consistory or presbytery.

Relocation Communities

In the formation of residential communities or relocation communities for expelled or persecuted Protestant evangelicals, the recuperation process is even more complex than it is in the worship community. The recuperation stage is a crucial period that goes beyond the urgencies of land, housing, and food. Recuperation requires the rebuilding and reformation of lives within a new community. Much more is involved than the emergency needs of relocating refugee *evangélicos* who have been exiled from their homeland. At stake in a relocation community is not only the formation and choosing of new leadership, but also the social issues of property ownership and the distribution of wealth. It is also in the residential community where *evangélicos* struggle to replace the physical and material losses that they suffered when expelled.

In the establishing of original relocation villages for expelled Protestant evangelicals, all of the social and political relationships should be recuperated. Much of the responsibility for land purchases, including loans and credit to rebuild houses, will be a part of the role of the missionary. Community structures for settling administrative and ownership problems must be reestablished with a minimum of cultural disintegration. All of the cultural and social forms for handling disputes and divisions should be recreated. However, since much of this becomes the role of the missionary, it will be discussed in the next chapter.

Summary

The stages of persecution consist of threats and warnings, ostracism and expulsion, and recuperation. In the stage of threats and warnings, options must be sought in order to delay further persecution and avoid expulsions. When hostilities lead to the ostracism and expulsion stage, all efforts should be made to remain or return to tribal homes and villages. It is essential that the expelled Christians maintain contact with their tribal people in order to advance the growth of the church. Finally, when expulsions become inevitable, believers in Christ need to form worshiping communities.

Persecuted *evangélicos* will depend heavily on the missionary while they move through the stages of persecution. Chapter 6 will analyze the role of the missionary in dealing with persecution.

Chapter 6

The Missionary's Role in Dealing with Persecution

THE ACTIVE PARTICIPATION OF the missionary in all phases of persecution in a hostile environment is implied in all we have studied thus far. Therefore, we must consider a few of the main contributions that the missionary can make in helping others deal with persecution so they can rise from the ruins it has caused. This chapter will not be inclusive in discussing the role of the missionary; it will only attempt to approach a few of the principal areas of that involvement in solidarity with the persecuted.

Personal Exposure to a Hostile Environment

The first requirement for a missionary who will be involved in counseling persecuted believers in Christ is personal experience in the hostile environment. Too often we stand on the sidelines and attempt to counsel and help those undergoing persecution and oppression without having lived through it ourselves. This does not mean that every missionary must have been involved in a traumatic or dangerous experience. However, it is valuable for the missionary to have personally experienced the pain and suffering of persecution. This is true for all of the stages of persecution, even though the missionary, as an outsider to the culture, will experience these stages at different levels than the indigenous believers.

> *Observation: A missionary who has personally experienced the pressures of persecution is better equipped to counsel persecuted indigenous Christians.*

It is important that the missionary understand the dynamics of persecution through personal experience. The indigenous people who undergo the various stages of persecution will respect the counsel of one who can speak from actual experience rather than just theory about persecution. People who are suffering the pain and pressure of persecution find both comfort and counsel from one who has gone through a similar experience. In Hebrews 2:18 and 4:15–16 we are given indications that Jesus is truly able to help us in our time of need "because he himself suffered and thus understands our weaknesses and struggles." In the same way, the missionary can be of help in the stages of persecution.

There are two ways that a missionary can experience persecution: village living in a non-Christian setting and intentional involvement in times of persecution. Both of these involve face-to-face confrontation and encounter.

Village Living in a Non-Christian Setting

The first way that the missionary finds exposure to persecution is by living and witnessing for Christ in a village or local setting. It is essential for a missionary who is preparing for work with Christians in hostile situations to initially locate in a non-Christian village. Not only does this village living afford excellent language learning and cultural insight; it also exposes the missionary to the reality of persecution. There is no substitute for this experience.

a village at the first indications that the leaders no longer want Protestant missionaries to live with them. However, such premature and hasty departures from hostile situations pose a model for future Protestant evangelicals, teaching them to flee persecution at the first stage of threats and warnings.

At the same time, if missionaries are pressured by persecution to the point that they feel that they must escape the hostilities and dangers, the important lesson that must be illustrated by the missionary and his or her family is that of maintaining contact and continuing to make concerted efforts to regain acceptance in the village. The mistake that is often made is to take the easy way of moving permanently to an *evangélico* village or an area where there is no opposition or threat of persecution. This communicates a model for any future Protestant evangelicals that they, too, can simply take the path of least resistance and risk. Usually, the missionary will find it difficult to counsel persecuted *evangélicos* to trust the Lord for protection and to risk staying in the village, if that has not been the pattern set personally by the missionary.

It is also important for the missionary to personally work for a calculated return or at least maintain contact so that the negative results of persecution are minimized. Maintaining contact through personal visits and relationships, even though some personal risk may be involved, is essential if we are to avoid the inoculation and immunization effects of persecution and expulsion.

Intentional Involvement in Times of Persecution

The second type of missionary involvement is living outside the actual area of hostility, and then responding by personal involvement in specific times by going into the tribal village in spite of the pressures or dangers. Much of the growth of the church has taken place because expelled Protestant evangelicals have been willing to risk returning to their tribal areas, either secretly or openly, to respond to needs and invitations to share the gospel. Missionaries can best counsel *evangélicos* to take that risk when they have also experienced what is involved in such a risk and are continuing to take that risk themselves.

Spontaneous Response

One of the most frightening experiences that I personally had as a missionary occurred a few years after we had moved out of the village of Nabenchauc where we had lived for almost ten years. We had left that village to work with all five of the major Tzotzil dialects and therefore were no longer living in Nabenchauc when the violent persecution broke out. After a yearlong period of threats and warnings, we knew that the persecution had reached a volatile phase since expulsion threats had already been issued to the Protestant evangelicals. It was a Sunday morning when one of the Zinacanteco *evangélico* leaders from the tribe arrived breathlessly at our door to report that several of the believers from Nabenchauc had been forced onto a truck and were on their way to be executed by order of the tribal president.

My spontaneous response was to jump into a vehicle and try to meet the leaders from Nabenchauc whom I had known and worked with for years. With a Zinacanteco *evangélico*, I headed out to wait at the road where the assassins would reportedly be passing. When I saw the truck carrying the condemned believers, I recognized it as belonging to Manuel PatOsil from Nabenchauc with whom my family had lived for two years.

The Sterks shared a village home for their first two years.

Considering him my friend, I flagged down the truck. However, before I was able to negotiate anything, five other large trucks loaded with about 250 enraged and drunken Zinacanteco men surrounded us. One man named Antun C'atish, who had been the captain of the village basketball team that I had organized and coached a few years earlier, shouted a command: "Let's kill René (my name in the tribe) and put an end to all of the *evangélicos*."

Before I knew what was happening, I was struck in the face, sending my glasses flying. Because I am half-blind without my glasses, I automatically moved to retrieve them so that I could see. As I picked them up in one hand, someone shouted: "He has a gun!" Evidently the way I was holding my glasses gave the appearance of a pistol, and through a miracle of the Lord, the mob suddenly split, opening a clear path for my escape on foot. When the crowd saw me running full speed, they shot at me and threw rocks that zipped past my head. I didn't stop running until I reached the outskirts of the city about two miles away.

The *evangélicos*, including the man who had reported to our house, were immediately taken back to the tribal center, but beaten severely on the way. Since the tribal president feared that I would report him to the city police, he ordered the believers released, and they all appeared at our door late that night, badly beaten but thankful to be alive.

I relate this story to illustrate the first kind of intentional involvement, the spontaneous response. To this day, the believers recount that they surely would have been killed if the missionary had not been willing to risk being involved. Although I must admit that I had not made a conscious decision to risk my life, it was important that I had made a previous commitment to respond to the persecuted believer's call for help. It formed a foundation upon which I could build a ministry of counseling and encouraging others who would face persecution.

Conscious Decision

The more difficult decision for the missionary involved in persecution comes when one must consciously decide how much to risk on certain occasions. Such occasions may be to show solidarity with *evangélicos* who live in hostile areas, to respond to opportunities for evangelism, or to accept an invitation to pray for the seriously ill. In every case, the missionary must determine if the involvement and encounter are worth the risk. In such a case, one must make a conscious decision that is very similar to the decision that indigenous believers in Christ must make to maintain contact and witness in the tribal area.

I remember clearly an invitation to return to a village in the Zinacanteco area soon after the tribal president had issued a decree that I was not allowed to enter any part of the tribe. It was at the height of the expulsion of the *evangélicos*, and there was clear risk involved. The invitation, however, was from a former tribal president who was asking that I go to witch "divining" (searching with a forked branch) for water in the village of Ch'aynatic where there was a serious water shortage. Since I had done this kind of work for several years while living in the tribal area, I was known for offering such assistance to communities. When one of the young men who had shown interest in the gospel urged me to go and assured me that there was no conspiracy to kill me, I agreed to go. Although I was convinced that this visit could provide a unique opportunity for evangelism to several families who were interested in the gospel, I was also concerned that it could be a trap. After much prayer, I followed through with the visit after asking one expelled Chamula *evangélico* to accompany me. The result was a positive one. We not only found a good spot for a well, but we also were able to open a serious discussion about the good news of Jesus Christ before we left the village.

It is this kind of evangelistic opportunity with its accompanying risks that the missionary must encourage believers to accept in order to maintain contact. If the *evangélicos* see that the missionary is willing to trust God to protect and guide in high-risk evangelism, they also will be willing to do so. Persistent love that is willing to go back to the tribe in spite of the risk of persecution is one of the essential elements in the growth of the church.

On other occasions, the missionary is called to risk a persecution encounter in order to respond to calls for help from the seriously ill. The Chamula *evangélicos* were willing to risk the dangers of being caught and killed, making courageous midnight visits into areas from which they had been expelled. They would walk for hours to the village home of a potential believer to pray for and to lay hands on a seriously ill person.

Mol Antun was the *agente* (town mayor) in the village of Nachij, one of the major witchcraft centers of the Zinacanteco tribe. Doctors in Mexico City diagnosed his cancer as terminal, and he came to our home in San Cristóbal de Las Casas on various occasions for prayer. However, God did not heal Antun, and his cancer soon brought him near death. When several of the Zinacanteco *evangélicos* who had earlier been expelled from that village came to ask us to drive out to Antun's home at about midnight for a prayer service with the extended families, I wanted to think of a good excuse for not being able to go on this high-risk adventure. However, since the expelled believers were willing to go, both my wife and I decided to make the trip.

The extended families of Mol Antun and his wife were both gathered around the open fire that night, and God's Spirit was present in the prayer and sharing of the gospel during the two-hour visit. Antun died a few weeks later, but both extended families became believers in Christ as a result of the witness at Antun's home. When the anti-*evangélico* leaders of that village heard that we had been there during the night, they issued a savage warning concerning any future visit we might make. However, none of us were sorry we had risked making the trip.

The missionary must not only be willing to make the conscious decision to be involved in the risks of persecution; he or she must also be willing to allow the judgment of other church leaders to be the guide whenever possible. This does not always mean that the believers will choose to expose either themselves or the missionary to unwise or unnecessary risk in facing potential persecution.

On another occasion, when a family from the village of Nabenchauc came to request that I go out at midnight to pick up a dying woman, the Zinacanteco *evangélicos* would not let me go. I insisted that the people who had come were sincere and were not planning any kind of devious trap for me. However, the believers who had been expelled from that village had an uneasy feeling about the missionary going alone into a potentially dangerous situation when they could do the same task with another vehicle. They pointed out that I was the one in that particular village that had been named as the target, so I should not go. Although there turned out to be no obvious danger on that particular night, I learned an important lesson from the Zinacanteco *evangélicos*: Even though the missionary must demonstrate a willingness to risk, the decision should be in the hands of the believers, for they know their own people and villages best.

> *Observation: Indigenous Christians are better qualified than the missionary to decide what personal risks should be taken in times of persecution.*

This does not mean that the missionary must be the perfect example of facing persecution encounters, which the indigenous believers must follow. However, the missionary does, in the early days of persecution, implant an attitude toward encountering persecution that will very often set the tone for the indigenous church. The apostle Paul used his own experience in persecution to both guide and encourage those who were suffering for the cause of Christ. In Romans 5:3 and 2 Corinthians 12:10, Paul affirms the positive aspects and even the joy of encountering persecution and suffering.

> *Observation: The personal example of the missionary in facing persecution will often set the pattern for how indigenous Christians will react in a similar situation.*

In hostile and difficult evangelistic situations, the courage and attitude displayed by the missionary may be the key to the growth of the church. We must remember that it is not the presence of persecution that causes the growth of the church. Rather, it is the response of believers in Christ, the courageous witness of indigenous Christians who are willing to risk their lives to show their faith by returning to tribal villages, by maintaining cultural contact, and by witnessing to the power of God. This is what results in the growth of the church in spite of persecution. And the first role that the missionary plays is to set an example of courageous witness in times of persecution.

Preparation for Confrontation and Conflict

The second major role that the missionary can play is that of preparing the church for persecution. The missionary must be honestly and actively preparing new believers in Christ to expect confrontation and conflict and to understand that all who want to follow Christ must be willing to count the cost. This is probably the most common area of neglect. Too often we have wanted to downplay the coming persecution so that it would not act as a deterrent to interest in the gospel.

General Preparation

The good news is often presented in such a way that those who accept the message get the idea that there will be no cost. New indigenous believers in Christ share how they have been freed from evil spirits, alcoholism, disease, and fear, and tell others that their lives will be much easier and more comfortable when they become *evangélicos*. While it is truly an exciting message of freedom and victory that penetrates the hearts and lives of families when they become believers in Christ, if the pain of bearing the cross of Christ is omitted, it is not a true picture, nor does it allow for the necessary preparation for persecution. In Luke 14, Jesus emphasizes the importance of counting the costs of discipleship and then gives two examples: "Suppose one of you wants to build a tower. Will he not first sit down and estimate the cost to see if he has enough money to complete it?" (Luke 14:28). "Or suppose a king is about to go to war against another king. Will he not first sit down and consider whether he is able?" (Luke 14:31).

Peter and Anita Deyneka, in their 1977 book on persecution in Russia, *A Song in Siberia*, point out that there was great emphasis placed on the preparation of new Christians for ensuing persecution:

Christians frankly discuss the cost of following Christ in Russia
with the new believer: "Are you prepared for persecution? Will
you be able to stand true to Christ if only you alone are left? If
you are questioned by the police and asked to inform on your
brothers and sisters, will you be able to withstand pressure?"
Finally, members vote whether to accept the candidate for bap-
tism. The decision must be unanimous.[1]

Often, we have failed to emphasize to new believers in Christ that they
must count the cost, that they may have to be willing to give up everything
to hold on to their new faith in Jesus Christ. Thus, we fail to communicate
the importance of preparing for upcoming persecution. We make Christianity out to be nothing more than cheap grace, and we do not emphasize to
new believers in Christ the need to prepare for battle so they can face the
onslaught of persecution.

Even in areas of the world where persecution has been widespread,
Christians are seldom prepared. In Africa, for example, where persecution
has been a longstanding problem for Christians, there is a great lack of preparation for coming persecution. Referring to Africa's lack of preparation,
Ugandan Daniel Kyanda, a witness to the terror of Idi Amin, believes that
despite persecution's prevalence, Africa's Christians are largely unprepared
to face it. "Many people think naively that somehow persecution will not
strike them," says Kyanda, Nairobi representative for Christian Solidarity
International. "For one thing, it isn't even taught. Many people turn to Jesus
at evangelistic campaigns, but hardly anyone tells them that, like their mas-
ter, they will be persecuted."[2]

Thus, the role of the missionary in preparation for persecution is to
use methods of evangelism that are balanced and honest and that also include the cost of taking up the cross of Christ (Matt 10:38). The missionary
must also remind the indigenous church of the need for preparation for
persecution. Both believers and church leaders often try to ignore the fact
that persecution is coming. They seem to favor the idea of attracting many
to the church before people find out that there might be some suffering and
cost involved. However, the missionary must give perspective by sharing
that many will fall away, and most will lack proper commitment if a partial picture of Christianity is developed in evangelism and in teaching. As
Brother Andrew said, addressing over five thousand Filipino pastors and lay
leaders in "Alert '86," a seminar dealing with preparation for persecution,
"If you do not train yourselves in times of liberty, you will not be equipped

1. Deyneka and Deyneka, *Song in Siberia*, 71.
2. Moore, "Ugandan church leader," 4.

when the battle erupts."[3] The main objective of the seminar was to teach the participants how to equip themselves and their church members to respond appropriately if and when traditional methods of evangelism, discipleship, fellowship, and worship are forbidden.[4] If the church is to survive when persecution comes, it must be made acutely aware of the need to prepare.

Specific Areas of Preparation

If we know that a battle is coming, we must make specific defensive preparations. Although there are other areas that could be emphasized in the missionary's role of preparing the church for persecution, three are outstanding.

Scripture Translation and Memorization

Of all of the tasks that the missionary performs with the indigenous Christians, the translation of the Bible into the language of the people has been proven by history to be the most important. Preserving the Scriptures in the indigenous languages is the key to the survival of the church in any place that is or will be facing harsh persecution.

The most amazing story of a flourishing Christian church that suffered complete extinction under persecution is that of the Christian churches of North Africa. I have found no other example which so clearly relates the account of a thriving Christian church, which completely disappeared when persistent persecution assaulted it.

J. J. Cooksey makes a very revealing analysis: "Why did the Church vanish in North Africa? A Church that was started by Simon of Cyrene and produced such leaders as Tertullian, Cyprian, and Augustine. The Church flourished under persecution in the third century. In the fifth century it was a Church of vigor, authority and learning, far beyond those of Alexandria or Rome."[5]

Cooksey goes on to note that even after the Donatist schism and the invasion of the Vandals in AD 429, the church "still numbered five hundred dioceses, more than a fourth of the whole number in Christendom; while in eminence, it was inferior to none."[6] He continues, "And yet this great Church internally declined and fell, and at length was utterly destroyed

3. Open Doors USA, "Standing Strong," 14.
4. Open Doors USA, "Standing Strong," 14.
5. Cooksey, *Land of the Vanished Church*, 20.
6. Cooksey, *Land of the Vanished Church*, 21.

by the Moslem invasion of the seventh century; and of it, not a vestige remains."[7]

Cooksey makes his number one judgment on why the North African church disappeared: "Because the Bible was never translated into their languages."[8] He notes that only Latin was used. Leonard R. Holme, in his 1989 study of *The Extinction of the Christian Churches in North Africa*, makes the same observation: "Latin was not the natural language of Africa, and it probably never became universal. It gained ground through the learned classes; no doubt the Church helped to spread it widely. But the Vulgate was Latin, and *the Bible was never translated into the languages of North Africa*" (emphasis mine).[9] Therefore, it seems clear that the number one area of preparation for surviving persecution is the translation of the Bible and biblical materials into the local indigenous languages.

Translated Sunday School materials contribute to the survival of the church.

7. Cooksey, *Land of the Vanished Church*, 22.

8. Cooksey, *Land of the Vanished Church*, 22–23.

9. Holme, *Extinction of the Christian Churches*, 19–20.

Stephen Neill cites a clear case-in-point in the history of the introduction of the gospel into Madagascar. He points out how, after a very severe persecution under Queen Ranavalona from the year of 1835 until 1861, the Christians reappeared.

> When a reckoning was made, it was found that the Christians were four times as many as they had been at the beginning of the persecution. How did it come about that so young a Church was able to maintain itself, without outside help, through a quarter of a century of persecution? The major factor was undoubtedly the possession of the New Testament in Malagasy. On this the Christians secretly fed their souls; this they passed on to others, in hand-written copies if the printed books were no longer available. There could hardly be more striking confirmation of the view held by almost all Protestant missionaries that the first duty of the missionary, after he has once learned the language, is to provide the Word of God, 'without note or comment,' in their own language.[10]

Bible translation is essential preparation for persecution because it is basic to the penetration of the gospel at the worldview level. Gordon Laman, in his examination of the persecution of Christians in Japan in the early 1600s, points out that the penetration of the gospel through the Jesuits was ineffective because "unfortunately, they never translated even a major portion of the Bible into Japanese."[11]

As I struggled to understand where the missionary might best spend time in preparing Christians for persecution, it was encouraging to realize that Bible translation is at the top of the list. For ten years my wife and I worked closely with Tzotzil Presbyterians and Catholics to produce the first interconfessional Tzotzil Bible.

10. Neill, *History of Christian Missions*, 319.
11. Laman, "Our Nagasaki Legacy," 108.

Catholic and Protestant Tzotzil translation team with author seated at rear of table

At times I felt uneasy about dedicating most of my time to this translation work while I spent less time assisting those suffering persecution and expulsion. However, as I became aware of the importance of the translation of biblical materials in preparation for persecution, I was encouraged that my involvement in translation was a priority in helping the church survive persecution. When the Tzotzil interconfessional Bible was dedicated, more than three thousand copies were sold that day.

Vern and Carla, with their children, Shane and Michele, at the Tzotzil Bible dedication

Another essential part of this preparation through translation is the need for an emphasis on Scripture memorization. In a consultation on "The Church in the Midst of Suffering" that was held in Hong Kong in February 1988, one of the strategies suggested "to prepare local churches in Asia to face possible adverse times in the years ahead" was "studying and memorizing the Word of God diligently and regularly."[12] The missionary can play a lead role in teaching the importance of the memorization of Scripture in the indigenous languages. When persecution denies access to the written Word of God, the most valuable preparation is the memorization of major passages from the Bible. This has been the testimony of Christians who have suffered repressive persecution under communism, Islam, and others. Daniel Kyanda identifies this as one of his tactics in preparation for persecution: "We need to have internalized the Word of God sufficiently to be able to meditate on it and use it when Bibles have either been banned from publication or distribution."[13]

> *Observation: Bible translation and Scripture memorization are specific areas in which the missionary can assist in preparation for persecution.*

Indigenization

An essential aspect in preparing the church to survive and grow in the face of persecution is indigenization. It is imperative that the church develops its own leadership as well as indigenous forms of evangelization. Therefore, a significant contribution that the missionary can make in the area of preparation is that of working toward a truly indigenous church. The church can survive and even grow under persecution, but only if it has become an indigenous church.

12. "A Letter to the Churches in Asia," 4.

13. Moore, "Ugandan church leader," 4.

Missionaries trained the first Tzotzil pastors.

In Holme's analysis of the church in North Africa he says: "It will seem that the Church perished because it was the Church, not of the native population, but of the alien conquerors. If it took deep root it was not amongst the indigenous peoples of N.W. Africa, but amongst the foreign immigrants and Roman officials."[14]

When severe persecution first came under the Vandals, there existed not enough grass-roots Christianity for their faith to remain strong.[15] Cooksey confirms this analysis of the reason the church in North Africa fell to persecution, both in Carthage and Alexandria. He says, "It had ceased to be a truly indigenous Church centered in the heart of the people, native to its own culture, and propagated by the expansive spiritual life shared by all its members. It had fallen into the hands of the Latin and Greek theologians, hot on the quest for the perfect theological definition, expressed in their respective classical tongues, not understood by the mass of the people."[16]

When severe and violent persecution threatened the Church, all of the expatriate leaders were killed or expelled. Because there was no strong indigenous base, the Turks and Islam had very little trouble in wiping out the very few native Christians that were left. That was the end of Christianity in North Africa.[17] In his conclusions on why the church disappeared in the

14. Holme, *Extinction of the Christian Churches*, 3.

15. Holme, *Extinction of the Christian Churches*, 53.

16. Cooksey, *Land of the Vanished Church*, 27.

17. Holme, *Extinction of the Christian Churches*, 240.

face of persecution, Leonard Holme is very clear: "There can be no doubt that the African Churches were destroyed not because of their failings, not because they were corrupt, but because they failed to reach the hearts of the true natives of the Province."[18] He continues, "But as it was, the Church in Africa as an organization was sure to disappear, not because its members fell away, but because they were dispersed, and when the foreign population was gone, there were hardly any Christians left to carry on in Africa the life of the alien Church of its former rulers."[19]

George Elison drew much the same conclusion in his study of the virtual destruction of Christianity in Japan in the 1600s. He says: "Buddhism had set deep roots in Japan and adapted to Japanese conditions. Christianity could do neither, and was an alien religion. That was the crucial difference. Buddhism could not be erased and was used; Christianity could not be used and was erased."[20]

> *Observation: Indigenization is a fundamental responsibility of the missionary in preparing the church for persecution.*

The missionary's concern for preparation must include indigenous principles, indigenous forms, and indigenous theology. The role of the missionary, even before persecution becomes a major menace, is also to insure indigenization in the areas of finances and leadership. The establishing of a truly indigenous church that has not been built on foreign dependencies is critical if the church is to survive the vicious attacks of persecution that will be coming.

The persecution of the church in China during and after the communist takeover did irreparable damage. Leonard M. Outerbridge claims that the institutional church in China was actually lost in the persecution that was a part of the communist takeover. It is interesting that Outerbridge makes such a statement in the context of a study that traces the effects of dependency versus indigeneity through the history of China and the Christian church there. His conclusions: "The Chinese Church became lost because it was so largely dependent upon the Western Church which first lost its way. Certainly, the church in China will never again be controlled by missionaries of the West."[21]

18. Holme, *Extinction of the Christian Churches*, 254.
19. Holme, *Extinction of the Christian Churches*, 255.
20. Elison, *Deus Destroyed*, 253.
21. Outerbridge, *Lost Churches of China*, 189.

Foreign control and dependency are the main roadblocks in the path to indigenization, and it is usually the foreign missionary and faulty principles of mission that cause dependencies to continue. Missionary control not only contributes to the weakness of the indigenous church itself, but it also invites persecution for the wrong reasons. In many cases, Christians suffer persecution due to anti-Christian feelings stirred up by nationalism which is a powerful issue in many countries of the world today. Unless the church is visibly indigenized, it will be identified as a pernicious foreign religion.

The dislike of foreignness is often a part of the persecution reaction to the gospel.[22] Lam writes how nationalism made this a big issue for persecuting Chinese Christians. Lam indicates that out of this nationalism arises the charge of imperialism against the church. It accuses the church of oppression and capitalism. It accuses the church of allegiance to foreign influences and aggression. It persecutes the church because there is enough truth in the accusations for it to become an anti-Christian movement.

This issue of nationalism has been used in the tribal areas of Chiapas to call for the persecution of *evangélicos*, making the claim that tribal customs and traditions would be preserved. The finger was pointed at the indigenous Protestants for having become the agents of foreign imperialists. The Protestant evangelicals were accused of having intentionally disrupted, divided, and discarded indigenous forms and customs. Thus, persecution and clear human rights abuses against *evangélicos* were justified and excused in the eyes of government and justice department officials since they felt they had to defend national interests against imperialism.

Missionaries should constantly be preparing believers in Christ to defeat this persecution threat by in-depth indigenization, by affirm and fulfill evangelism, by emphasizing the importance of tribal dress and patterns, by encouraging the use of indigenous hymns and worship patterns, and by insisting on indigenous leadership and financial responsibility.

Broad Spectrum of Leadership

Another of the principal tasks of the missionary is the training and preparation of indigenous leaders. This is, of course, basic to the indigenization of the church. However, in the face of imminent persecution, missionaries should not only be involved in the preparation of a few leaders, but they should be aware of the necessity of preparing a broad spectrum of leadership in the church.

22. Lam, *Chinese Theology*.

From his insight gained as a missionary with the China Inland Mission, Arthur F. Glasser indicates that the first attack against the church is felt by the leaders, and if there are only a few highly placed or highly trained pastors or bishops, the church can be left without leadership.[23] Even if the church is highly indigenized, when the gospel itself brings eventual persecution and confrontation, the first members of that community to be attacked will be the leaders. Thus, while it is important for the missionary to emphasize indigenous leadership, it is even more important to spread out that leadership so that violent persecution cannot successfully wipe out the church by simply attacking its leadership.

The missionary can play an essential role in encouraging and preparing lay leadership. Glasser observes that to highly train a few pastors and leaders is not the ideal. If we know that persecution is coming, the preparation should be broad-spectrum, including as much lay leadership as possible. The house church setting will demand the participation of many lay teachers and preachers. It is neither possible nor preferable to invite outside trained leaders for teaching and leading house churches in persecuted areas. The believers must be encouraged to choose several lay leaders who can begin to receive training and preparation.

In the Zinacanteco village of Tzequemtic, as the gospel spread rapidly and as many as seventy families were gathering in the house church that was organized, four men were chosen by the group of Presbyterians to officially be the preachers and leaders of the group. Two leaders were added when another house church was formed. These indigenous lay leaders assumed the responsibility for all aspects of the house churches, including preaching, teaching, administration, and finances. The training for their lay leadership roles followed, and since their own people chose them, they took their responsibilities and need for training very seriously. The training also included preparation for the persecution that they knew would soon come down on their group.

When violent persecution and imprisonment struck the Tzequemtic group, the persecutors could not simply attack a pastor who had come from outside the village. They attempted to round up and arrest all six lay leaders in the Tzequemtic area, but because their houses were widely scattered, the band of persecutors only captured two of the lay leaders. This allowed the other leaders to escape and find help. In persecution and expulsion, the broad-spectrum of leadership provides a much-needed unity and mutual

23. Arthur Glasser, interview by Vernon Sterk, Fuller Theological Seminary, Pasadena, CA, Jan 30, 1989.

support, as the believers in Christ do not permit only a few leaders to take the whole brunt of the pressure and punishment.

The church in Mitontic offers an opposing example. Even though the congregation was over twenty years old, they never named their own local leadership, but relied on an outside pastor and elders from a neighboring tribal area. Therefore, when persecution separated them from the outside leaders, their group disintegrated and was not able to join in a unified response to persecution.

The missionary can play a key role in helping the indigenous church prepare for persecution by encouraging each house church or congregation to choose several lay leaders. This broad-spectrum leadership will not only multiply the number of indigenous leaders who can receive training, it will also make it virtually impossible for persecution to halt the Christian movement by eliminating a few respected pastors and leaders.

> *Observation: In preparation for persecution, the missionary must encourage a broad spectrum of leadership in order to insure the survival of the church.*

Solidarity of Christian Community

In all stages of persecution, one of the most important roles that the missionary can fill is that of encouraging solidarity and unity. While this encouragement can take place in the one-to-one relationship of missionary to persecuted believers in Christ, that is very limited, especially if the believers have not yet been expelled from the traditional community. The best way the missionary can encourage solidarity in all stages of persecution is by advocating for the formation of Christian community.

One of the most difficult trials of those who suffer ostracism and expulsion is that they feel cut off from traditional family and community support systems. The Christian community should be the functional substitute for the traditional community, and it should supply fellowship and encouragement. This community element is, of course, a well-known feature of the Christian faith. However, the role of the missionary in times of persecution is to intentionally emphasize this community. It is imperative that the missionary encourages, establishes, and insures Christian community during all stages of persecution.

Christian Community within Traditional Community

During the stage of threats and warnings, the missionary can encourage Christian community in the villages. Since there are only a few scattered believers in Christ at this stage, it often means that they must be taught the importance of meeting with other believers, even if that means going to visit each other on Sunday or some other day of the week for worship, Bible study, and prayer, which includes singing if the persecution pressure has not become so great that their meetings have become secret. The first meetings are naturally begun in house church settings. Believers are encouraged to rotate the worship services by taking turns at the homes of those who are willing to host the small group, which may gather from various nearby villages.

While living in a Zinacanteco village during the stage of threats and warnings, my wife and I held worship services in our small, one-room Zinacanteco house.

The first Zinacanteco believers gathered at the Sterks' one-room home.

As the *evangélicos* became aware of the importance of the fellowship and encouragement gained in this new community, they responded eagerly to the idea of rotating the meetings to different houses each week. This helped prevent the premature arousal of suspicion or anger on the part of village neighbors who might object if they observed that someone's home was becoming a weekly place of meeting. Thus, the missionary can promote the house church model to initiate an early community of believers in Christ.

House Church Model

The house church model is the preferred form of Christian community when gatherings are being held in a hostile environment. The informal family setting not only provides a relaxed and nonthreatening atmosphere for first-time visitors, but it also avoids the immediate ostracism that comes if a group sets aside a special building that can be identified as a church building or *templo*. This model has been widely and successfully applied in countries such as Russia and China where for many years the church could only maintain its spiritual life in this restricted form. In the face of severe repression of Christian worship in Russia, Deyneka reports:

> Many groups chose to opt for house and home meetings without government sanction. These took different forms. Some went from home to home, changing constantly. Others settled on one home since "the unity gave us a stronger witness." In one instance the church would take the local custom of celebrating house warmings to hold services in different homes. When police complained that they were conducting a gospel meeting, they replied, "No, a housewarming!"[24]

The development of the house church movement in China after 1950 became a matter of survival of the church. Jonathan Chao explains that the church did not die out because

> the church in China became a lay movement and had to work underground in house churches. The slow house church movement developed as an underground movement. God raised up a number of young house church leaders who itinerated or traveled from place to place regrouping the individual, scattered, scared Christians and rebuilding house churches anew.[25]

The missionary can play the critical role of establishing a house church model that will meet a felt need of the growing number of new believers

24. Deyneka and Deyneka, *Song in Siberia*, 44–45.
25. Chao and Covell, "Questions," 9.

in Christ. As the number of believers increases through family lines, the number of house churches will increase. As the size of a specific house limits the number that can meet together, new groups will have to be formed in other houses. When visitors from other villages realize that they can form a worship group in one of their own homes and that it not necessary to travel to other villages to find fellowship, the house church model will continue to be the method that the missionary teaches and encourages in each village.

Vern enjoys a meal following a house church gathering.

As Donald McGavran writes in *Understanding Church Growth*:

> *Emphasize house churches.* The congregations should meet in the most natural surroundings, to which non-Christians can come with the greatest ease and where the converts themselves can carry on the services. Where non-Christian leaders are antagonistic, the meeting place should neither attract attention nor throw out a challenge to them. Obtaining a place to assemble should not lay a financial burden on the little congregation. The house church meets all of these requirements ideally.[26]

26. McGavran, *Understanding Church Growth* (1970), 285–86.

> *Observation: The house church provides an ideal model for Christian worship in the midst of hostile environments.*

An early Tzotzil house church

The Church Building Decision

When the number of *evangélicos* either outgrows the house church possibilities or becomes too numerous for the lay leaders to handle in small groups, the natural desire of the believing community will be to construct a church building. At that point, the missionary will find that he or she has a role of counseling lay leaders concerning the advisability of such a step. The risk of inviting violent and destructive persecution will be the main topic of such a discussion. The decision has to be made if the importance of building a recognizable place of worship warrants the peril of possible violent persecution and expulsion.

The first Protestant evangelicals in the Zinacanteco tribe were faced with this decision in 1982. At that time, they were gathering in house churches with new *evangélicos* from various villages in the tribe. The number of believers coming for weekly worship was growing rapidly, and the lay leaders felt that it was time to attempt to build a meeting place. They felt that they could construct something that would appear to be a large house, and in that way avoid any immediate negative response from the traditional community. However, before they were able to complete the raising of the adobe walls, a mob came at night and tore down the walls.

At that time, I, as a missionary, counseled the Zinacanteco *evangélicos* to continue to meet in the house church format, as it was obvious that a church building was not acceptable to the local and tribal leaders. However, the lay leaders felt that they could not continue to accept those restrictions from the tribal leaders. When the *evangélicos* raised the walls a second time, it was seen as a deliberate threat to the tribal authorities, and only a few weeks later the forced expulsion of all of the known Zinacanteco Protestant evangelicals began with violent expulsions in several different villages.

The role of the missionary at such decision times is to clarify to the believers in Christ what options are available and what their results might be. The leaders must make the decision on the basis of those options, and they must follow what they feel God is leading them to do in each case.

In 1990, a similar decision about constructing a formal church building had to be made. There were so many new Tzequemtic *evangélicos* that they either had to build a meeting place or divide into two separate house churches. After discussing the option of making a formal and legal document requesting the state government to give them legal guarantees in the right to build a *templo* (church building), the believers decided that it would be better to split the house church into two groups and name new leaders in each new house church group. They were sure that even making a legal request for a church building would initiate persecution and expulsions. By avoiding that immediate confrontation with tribal leaders, the Tzequemtic *evangélicos* were able to delay violent persecution for almost six months.

The role of the missionary is to help the witnessing community of believers in Christ avoid premature persecution within the traditional village. The missionary's role is unique in that he or she is the only one who can share the broader perspective of persecution. At the same time, the missionary can continue to emphasize the solidarity of the community of believers and the importance of regular worship and Bible study.

Christian Community outside of Traditional Community

Whether or not persecution has moved to the stage of ostracism and expulsion, there will be a need for a worshiping community of believers in Christ outside the boundaries of the tribal or traditional community. If the threats and warnings have become intense and believers have been denied the right of meeting in house churches, then the missionary must play the role of establishing places and opportunities for worship and fellowship outside the area of control of the tribal authorities.

Provisional Communities

Believers should avoid unnecessary persecution by attempting to meet every possible demand of the traditional leaders. However, one of the principal things that believers in Christ cannot abandon is the meeting together for worship and fellowship, even if tribal leaders have prohibited such gatherings. This will imply forming provisional worship communities to assure that worship and fellowship will not be discontinued. Donald A. McGavran insists that "worship must be central! While it must be indigenous, it must also be continuous. If regular worship is eliminated, a people movement will be halted. Without fellowship, singing, and regular Bible study, nurture and growth will be lost."[27]

In his book *The Bridges of God*, McGavran points out the dilemma of trying to prevent new Christians from being ostracized from their families and tribes, and yet making sure that the Christians are not so dominated by the non-Christians that they are denied all worship and witness.[28] In my interview with McGavran, he concluded that new believers in Christ must be able to gather for worship and nurture, or they cannot survive. Worship cannot be sacrificed. He noted that this involves "instituting regular worship and securing a place of worship. For congregations to continue for long with no place to meet is to court disaster."[29] Thus, provision must be made for a place of worship outside the village or tribe when house churches are no longer permitted. To avoid premature persecution, worship must be held outside tribal boundaries or outside the view of those who would deny Christian community.

In the case of tribal areas that border the city of San Cristóbal, it was possible for many Zinacanteco and Chamula *evangélicos* to maintain a community of believers by traveling the relatively short distance into the city. Since many of their people go to buy and sell in the city markets, it was no major step to attend the worship service that was arranged by the missionary at the Tzotzil Bible Center. Since it was held in a building behind the customary Spanish-styled walls, it provided seclusion in the city so that

27. Donald A. McGavran, interview by Vernon Sterk, Fuller Theological Seminary, Pasadena, CA, May 8, 1975.

28. McGavran, *Bridges of God*, 11.

29. McGavran, *Understanding Church Growth* (1970), 326.

evangélicos could enjoy fellowship, spiritual growth, and encouragement without fear of being found out by other tribespeople. This offered a partial solution for Christian community under persecution, but it had the severe disadvantage of serving only those who lived close to the city and those who could finance the weekly bus or truck trip.

Those who could not worship in the city were encouraged to find a place just outside of tribal boundaries where they might meet. In some cases, meetings were held outdoors, in other cases they borrowed houses. In still another case, the *evangélicos* actually got together to buy a piece of land just across the tribal border and built a small house church where they could meet. The problem with these worshiping communities gathering just outside the tribal boundaries was that they were very obvious and open. Soon word of these meetings traveled back to tribal leaders, who made raids across their borders and quickly closed down these suspicious gatherings. As it turned out, this kind of attempt by believers not only failed to provide more safety from persecution, but it also stirred up even greater suspicion of deception on the part of traditional leaders.

For many *evangélicos* who, because of locality, could use neither of the first two options, the only choice remaining was to meet in secret in their villages. This often took the form of extended family gatherings. They had to refrain from singing or using musical instruments in their services in order to keep secrecy. Along with the fact that music-loving Tzotzil *evangélicos* consider worship incomplete without audible music, the secret services also suffered from the lack of trained and capable leadership. Too often the small groups could find no one who felt able to lead Bible study or prayer. Many were very new believers who were not ready to accept leadership roles. To add to the difficulties, family members or neighbors would soon inform on the secret meetings.

> *Observation: The church cannot exist without worship and fellowship opportunities. The missionary can provide options by helping the believers in Christ determine which possibilities are feasible in the particular situation.*

The gathering of *evangélicos* for some form of worship and community is essential. Suspension of worship for long periods is never an option. It is necessary to risk persecution in hostile environments in order to maintain nurture and fellowship. It will be a part of the missionary's responsibility to make indigenous believers in Christ aware of the importance of maintaining a community of believers and worship.

Relocation Communities

While relocation communities represent another form of Christian community outside the boundaries of traditional community, they must be dealt with under a separate category since they present a very different situation with unique problems. It is especially important to discuss the relocation communities related to the role of the missionary, because often the major burden of responsibility for the establishment and organization of these communities is placed on the missionary. This is especially true when the persecuted church is young and undeveloped or when national church leadership is either unprepared or unwilling to become involved. The role of the missionary then is to establish communities for expelled believers in Christ. When believers are placed on emergency refugee status by sudden and violent expulsions, the missionary must be involved in meeting urgent needs.

IMMEDIATE PHYSICAL NEEDS

Since the believers in Christ have often been exposed to harsh physical treatment, the most urgent need may be for medical attention. Professional medical care may be needed for such injuries as knife or machete wounds and broken bones. Others will have been exposed to conditions that led to illness or dehydration. Until the local or national church is in a position to meet these emergency needs, the believers who have suffered from violent persecution and expulsion will invariably go to the missionary. He or she is often the only one they know who has access to emergency resources. This is especially true when the missionary is living in the city or market center.

The urgent need for shelter and food also tends to fall on the missionary when believers are expelled from tribal homes. Even after the local church is organized to help with some of these emergency needs, the missionary will continue to be asked to help. This is especially true when mass expulsions bring twenty or more families into town. Finding emergency food, temporary housing, gatherings, distribution of provisions, and accounting of the emergency funds are just a few of the services that are expected of the missionary.

IMMEDIATE SPIRITUAL NEEDS

Just as urgent as the obvious physical needs of the expelled believers are the less apparent spiritual needs. The missionary must be aware of the importance of organizing and even leading times of worship and prayer. At the actual time of expulsion, often following physical and spiritual abuse, the persecuted believers in Christ need to be united in prayers of thanksgiving and praise for God's help, and prayer for God's guidance in the crucial decisions ahead. If the missionary does not encourage and organize daily prayer and worship, the physical needs cry so loud for attention that even the indigenous church leaders fail to make this a priority.

RELOCATION LAND AND HOUSING NEEDS

When forced expulsion has been accompanied by violence and death threats, the believers do not see immediate return to their homes as even a remote possibility. Within a few days of living with their families in emergency shelters, those who have been expelled will come to the missionary to ask for assistance in finding places where they can arrange for permanent relocation housing or for land for relocation. Even if this effort is later coordinated with national church leaders, the missionary will find that a major investment of time and effort is required at this point.

Vida Nueva (New Life), the first Zinacanteco relocation community

Ethnic cohesion will make it desirable to keep the community of believers in Christ united. This unity will be destroyed if the believers are forced to disperse in all directions to find places to relocate. The ideal, especially for groups of the same ethnic background, is to purchase land where relocation communities can be established. If there are no existing communities, or if property has not already been purchased, there are many tasks that become the responsibility of the missionary in cooperation with indigenous leaders. These tasks would include the purchase of land, the fair distribution of plots, the administration and financial arrangements, and the repayment of loans and credits for land and housing materials.

The missionary cannot easily assign indigenous leaders these responsibilities until relocation communities are well developed, or until local church leaders and pastors are prepared to assume these tasks. It takes a number of years of missionary participation before pastors are ordained or members of relocation communities have been taught how to take over these responsibilities.

Petul was ordained as the first Zinacanteco pastor.

The coordination in establishing some of the first *evangélico* relocation villages, at a time when there was no organized Tzotzil Presbytery, was placed almost completely in the hands of missionaries. In communities such as Betania and Vida Nueva, there was a wide range of spiritual, material, and interpersonal needs that required almost my full-time attention. It is a role that the missionary should fulfill until the church leaders are organized.

The missionary should encourage solidarity and unity of the community of believers throughout the expulsion and relocation phase of persecution.

The first expelled Zinacantecos united to form a relocation community.

> *Observation: A major role of the missionary is to encourage and help maintain Christian community and worship both before and after the expulsion stage.*

Summary

The involvement of the missionary in persecution includes personal exposure, preparation of materials and leaders, and meeting needs in the Christian community. Other specific needs will arise according to the type and intensity of the persecution. For instance, the missionary may be called on to give counsel, biblical teaching, historical perspective, and anthropological insight during any of the stages of persecution. Communication and coordination tasks are often time-consuming responsibilities that will be thrust upon the missionary when the church is young. Because the missionary is so intimately involved in all phases of persecution, it is crucial to gain an in-depth understanding of the how persecution affects the indigenous people, the church, and the missionary. The following chapter will therefore deal with the results of persecution.

Chapter 7

The Results of Persecution

WHILE IT IS IMPORTANT to analyze the origins and the stages of persecution, another essential issue is the results of persecution. Many Christians assume that persecution yields mostly good and positive results. They feel that it commonly results in church growth and strengthening of the church, and that it is literally true that "the blood of the martyrs is the seed of the church."[1]

This chapter takes a more balanced look at the results of persecution by surveying both the positive and the negative consequences. While there can be certain positive aspects that result from persecution as it relates to the growth of the church, there are also serious negative considerations that must be taken into account before we conclude that persecution is a helpful factor in the growth of the church or in other aspects of the development of society.

The Negative Results of Persecution

The most obvious and immediate result of persecution is human pain, suffering, and death.

---

1. Tertullian, *Apol.* 50.

The first three Christians from Ic'alumtic were brutally slashed to death.

The physical and emotional agony and misery that result from the conflict that develops in persecution may be, in itself, enough reason to want to avoid all persecution. Descriptions and accounts of those who have suffered violent repression and persecution make our hearts ache and cause us to wonder what good or positive results could come out of that. At the same time, there are other factors and results which cause us to perceive that persecution has a negative effect on the growth of the church of Jesus Christ. As Herbert B. Workman notes:

> We may not under-rate the "secondary causes" of Christianity's growth. But neither may we neglect the external circumstances which promised only, it might seem, to surely destroy it. Persecution may be a sign of strength. It is hardly a cause of strength when it is cruel and persistent. Persecution may kill a religion and destroy it utterly, if that religion's strength lies only in its numbers, by a simple process of exhaustion. The opinion that no belief, no moral conviction, can be eradicated from a country by persecution is a grave popular fallacy.[2]

Persecution has negative and destructive elements, and we must be careful not to allow popular fallacies to deceive us. "It is also obvious that there are places where persecution has not brought revival. One thinks of

2. Workman, *Persecution*, 350.

the whole of North Africa and the Middle East, which provided so many of our early church leaders like Tertullian and Augustine. Now there are only the sandy ruins of churches, and Islam."[3] An entire church in a tribe or geographical region can be destroyed by persecution. Even though it is unusual that persecution, no matter how cruel and persistent, actually wipes out the entire church in a tribe or area, it certainly can bring with it many detrimental consequences.

Inoculation and Immunity

One of the first negative results of persecution that can already be seen in the threats and warnings stage is inoculation. Using a medical analogy, a small dosage of the good news of the gospel message is introduced into a society and the worldview of a people. The dosage they receive is not nearly enough to make them catch the "disease": the gospel has not had time to penetrate into the worldview of that society. Persecution then strikes before people ever understand the meaning of the message or before they see any of its life-changing results. What they do experience are the negative side effects of confrontation, disruption, ostracism, and expulsion. Because they experience the pain without knowing the power, the reaction is not only rejection, but also something similar to an inoculation. They see the gospel as a threat or a disease to their society, often causing an entire generation of people to be immune to any further presentation of the gospel.

Miguel Buluch was still a young man when the gospel message was presented to him by missionary Ken Weathers who lived in Nabenchauc for a few years. Miguel expressed interest in becoming a believer in Christ but was immediately threatened with the imminent possibility of ostracism. He quickly denied his interest in the gospel and cut off his contacts with any Protestant evangelicals. Premature persecution had proven painful enough to result in the inoculation effect on this man and his entire family. When another missionary attempted to rekindle this spark of interest in the gospel years later, his response seemed like a defense that cried out: "That hurt, and I don't ever want to have another shot of it again."

Immunity caused by persecution that is perceived as a painful little shot of the gospel not only takes place in individuals and families; it also has devastating results in specific villages and entire tribal groups. In such cases, the immunity results from premature persecution that leads entire villages to reject the gospel and to cut off any Christian witness.

---

3. Open Doors USA, "Standing Strong," 14.

The village of Potovtic, located in the San Andrés tribe of the Tzotzil-speaking people of Chiapas, is an example of immunization at the village level. A Protestant missionary lived and witnessed in the village for a few years, and a few men from the town began to show interest in the gospel. However, before the message had a chance to penetrate to the worldview level, the Roman Catholic priest with jurisdiction in the village convinced the town leaders that they should ask the missionary to leave. Thus, before the people of the village of Potovtic ever experienced the power and life-changing effects of Christianity, they were loaded with negative propaganda about Protestant evangelicals and missionaries. This missionary's attempt to relocate in a neighboring village failed, so before anyone became a strong confessing believer in Christ, he and his family moved a significant distance away and found it difficult to maintain contact with the village or make visits to the men who had shown interest in the gospel.

A few years later, when San Andrés *evangélicos* from another village attempted to renew evangelism in the village of Potovtic, they were told that Protestant evangelicals were no longer welcomed in the village. Inoculation had taken effect, even though the persecution had been fairly mild. It might be said that immunity resulted from an untimely exit by the missionary and the failure to maintain contact. Thus, not only was the witness lost, but also the small dose had the negative effect of inoculation.

Inoculation against Christianity can also take place on the level of nations and entire countries. An example of such national inoculation can be found in the history of Christianity in Japan. Gordon Laman wrote of the devastating effect of persecution in Japan, which became so ruthless that by 1650 most Christians had either apostatized, been exiled, had left the country, or had been killed. As many as three hundred thousand Christians perished in Japan by 1650.[4] Laman observes that the persecution was so effective that it "had been eminently successful in eradicating Christianity from Japan."[5] However, he goes on to point out that the more profound and lasting effect of persecution on Japan was inoculation. "By means of all that happened during the period of persecution, Japan has been effectively inoculated so as to not contract the disease called Christianity. And if the original period of persecution served as the initial inoculation, then perhaps we could draw out the metaphor further and say that subsequent Japanese history has provided repeated booster shots."[6]

Almost three hundred years of persecution had effectively immunized Japan against any future entrance of Christianity. "Persecution, surveillance,

4. Laman, "Our Nagasaki Legacy," 115.
5. Laman, "Our Nagasaki Legacy," 117.
6. Laman, "Our Nagasaki Legacy," 118.

and propaganda had implanted an anti-Christian and anti-foreign feeling deeply into the minds and hearts of the Japanese populace. A kind of folk memory of aversion and fear of both the Christian faith and its adherents had been created."[7]

Inoculation and immunization are among the most damaging negative results of premature persecution, and thus we must take great care that we do not allow them to happen. It is precisely for this reason that we must emphasize the importance of avoiding any unnecessary persecution, of seeking to delay overt persecution, of keeping new believers in Christ in their villages, of maintaining cultural contact, of discouraging evangelism by extraction, of encouraging indigenization, and of emphasizing translation of the Bible. Inoculation tends to take place when persecution extinguishes the witness to the gospel before the affirm and fulfill model can make any penetration into a culture's worldview.

> *Observation: Inoculation against Christianity often takes place when persecution does not allow the life-changing message and power of the gospel to penetrate into the worldview and structure of a society.*

Persecution can result in inoculation against the gospel, depending how we respond to and how we deal with persecution. If we allow immunities to take root, we will find that the result of persecution is the halting of the growth of the church for generations in specifically affected areas. If there is insufficient provision for and an ineffective response to persecution, the inoculation effect can do serious damage to any future evangelization. People will fear and reject any future contact and communication with Protestant evangelicals or the Bible, creating a people or group that is literally closed. In such instances, persecution results not in the growth of the church, but in making it even more resistant to the communication of the gospel in the future.

> *Observation: Inoculation and immunization are negative results of persecution which create opposition and resistance to the gospel and halt the growth of the church.*

Disruption and Dislocation

Another negative result of persecution is the unmistakable disruption and dislocation that it causes in the lives of individuals and in the structures of

7. Laman, "Our Nagasaki Legacy," 119.

families and society. When persecution turns family members into enemies and when society chooses to use the weapons of ostracism and expulsion against its own members, the results are disruption and dislocation.

Family disruption is often a powerful factor in causing a negative effect on the growth of the church. Many who would otherwise choose to accept the gospel find that the threat of ostracism from family pushes them to either reject Christianity completely or at least hold it off as an option that might be attractive if the conditions change and persecution no longer poses this threat over them.

Maruch Pintol, a Zinacanteco woman from the village of Nachij, was suffering from such severe mental and psychological problems that she could no longer care for her family. In desperation, her husband allowed her to join her sister who had been expelled for being a Protestant evangelical and was living in a relocation community outside the Zinacanteco tribe. He promised that he would become an *evangélico* and join his wife if she was healed. The first time the believers prayed, God cast out the spirit that had been oppressing Maruch, and she was completely healed. However, her husband Chep was skeptical and did not want to leave his tribal land to join his wife. He waited six months before making a trial attempt at living in the Christian relocation village of Nuevo Zinacantán. After two years he decided to take his wife and family back to the tribal village where they could be with their married daughter and other extended family members. Even though they had witnessed the power of God to heal miraculously, Maruch's family could not survive as *evangélicos* if they had to be dislocated from family and Zinacanteco tribal society.

In Mark 10:29–30, Jesus promises to make multiplied restoration of the losses caused by disruption in family and society. And while this does take place in the new Christian community, there are many who will reject the offer of Christianity if it means that they have to give up their tribal land and traditional social ties. Thus, the disruption and dislocation threat involved in persecution is a clear detriment in the growth of the church.

> *Observation: The social disruption caused by persecution is a major negative factor in the growth of the church.*

In the Zinacanteco village of Tzequemtic, of the sixty families that had been attending worship with the Protestant evangelical group there, only thirty-five families were willing to face the social and family disruption when severe persecution and expulsion took place in September 1990. Even though a remnant of those who decide to reject the gospel due to the pressure of disruption will eventually openly rejoin the *evangélico* community, a significant number will become casualties of social disruption.

Caciques and leaders of the tribal mafias know that family and social disruption and dislocation is one of their most effective tools in halting the growth of the *evangélico* movement. Thus, they actively promote ostracism, family disruption, and expulsions for personal gain and for the purpose of discouraging any political or religious opposition that would threaten their power and status.

> *Observation: While disruption caused by persecution may be unavoidable, every attempt must be made to help believers in Christ reestablish family and cultural relationships in the shortest time possible.*

We cannot ignore the fact that disruption and dislocation are serious negative results of persecution. To disregard or do little to combat their effects leaves believers in Christ open to further attacks and persecution. If no conscious and clear efforts are made to counteract cultural and family disruption and disintegration, an additional negative by-product is that the opponents of Christianity will make it appear that missionaries and *evangélicos* actually incite or invite persecution conflict for the sake of the growth of the church.

Accusations of intentional cultural disruption and destruction are commonly leveled at Protestant evangelicals by the anthropological and governmental organizations. They point to instances in history in which the intrusion of missionaries has contributed to the disintegration of a particular culture. They proceed to attribute to all missionaries and indigenous evangelists an intentional design to destroy indigenous cultures and replace them with Western cultural forms and patterns.

Government agencies and political leaders who want to divert attention from their role in the disruption and destruction of cultures also place the blame on missionaries and other Protestants for careless disregard of folk religions and colorful traditions. They claim that Protestant evangelicals actually encourage converts to emigrate from their ancestral communities, thus causing rapid cultural and social disintegration.

In a newspaper of the state capital of Chiapas, *Número Uno*, the director of the justice department of the State of Chiapas made public declarations that accused the Protestant "sects" of "encouraging the total loss of the customs and traditions of the Indian cultures."[8] While admitting that

---

8. *Número Uno*, "Editorial."

certain Protestant mission agencies have been guilty of an extreme lack of cultural sensitivity, most Protestant missionaries and indigenous Protestant evangelicals in Chiapas have worked diligently to show their respect for and concern to preserve indigenous culture. In my personal discussions with several of the well-known anthropologists who specialize in Mayan studies, several have recognized that the Protestant evangelical movement may well prove to be a force "that actually preserves Indian cultures through the extensive translation and publication of the Bible, literature, and Mayan histories in the indigenous languages of Chiapas."[9] Even though persecution does cause serious disruption, those who share the gospel in other cultures can be successful in minimizing some of the negative effects of persecution.

Persecution itself threatens cultural equilibrium. The recognition that persecution produces negative results should move the cross-cultural missionary to do everything to minimize the negative effects of persecution. The concern here is not only with the growth of the church but also with insuring that it will take place with a minimum of cultural and social dislocation and disruption. Thus, I must again emphasize my previous observations about the importance of avoiding cultural and worldview clash, of avoiding extraction of believers in Christ, of avoiding the expulsion of *evangélicos* from their ancestral villages and tribes in persecution stages, of maintaining and establishing a community of believers that is able to perpetuate its unique cultural identity, and of encouraging indigeneity at all levels.

To combat the negative effects of disruption and dislocation on the growth of the church, an intentional and public stand for justice and human rights is an essential role of the persecuted church. Also, a proper preparation for and reaction to persecution can determine the ultimate effect of disruption and dislocation on the growth of the church.

Division and a Weakened Church

An even more disturbing negative result of persecution is that it tends to spawn a weakened and division-prone church. As has just been discussed, persecution results in dislocation and disruption of cultures and lives. People who have had their family and cultural identity disrupted will in turn produce a new community of believers in Christ that is weak and impoverished. The result consistently shows itself in the formation of unstable and divisive community and church structures that may require many years to recover.

9. Personal discussion with Gary H. Gossen in San Cristóbal de Las Casas, summer, 1986.

When persecution results in expulsion and the necessity of forming relocation communities outside tribal land areas, the potential of division and internal conflict in the relocation church is especially high. In relocation villages like Betania, the merging of village and church leaders from more than thirty Chamula villages invited inescapable clashes of personal, political, and cultural interests. The status and leadership positions had to be reestablished after the persecution and dislocation. This led to debilitating and demoralizing divisions in both the community and the church that not only have a negative effect on the witness and growth of the *evangélico* community, but also cause a further weakening of the community itself.

W. H. C. Frend makes a similar observation about the effect of the Great Persecution in the early church. He says that persecution "was to complicate vastly the disciplinary and doctrinal problems which were already dividing the church. New fervent groups could no longer get along with first generation Christians. Older ones raised persecution as an issue of holiness, 'You have not gone through it.'"[10] Frend adds an even more striking note: "The ultimate legacy of the persecutions was the lasting division of Christianity into its eastern and western parts."[11]

Persecution does cause, or at least vastly complicate, problems that lead to divisions in the church. Internal problems and conflicts are the direct results of the disruption caused by persecution. Factions and divisions quickly form and make the task of cultural and social recuperation and reintegration even more complex. Outside observers are quick to notice and criticize the Protestant evangelicals for not being able to establish an ideal utopia out of the ruins of persecution. The existence of internal divisions and conflict among the groups of Protestant evangelicals is used as a powerful weapon in condemning the whole Protestant movement and in slowing the growth of the church.

> *Observation: Persecution often results in division and internal conflict in the church that weakens the witness and growth of the church.*

Division and a weakened church are such critical negative results of persecution that all efforts at minimizing expulsions should be made from the very first signs of persecution. Solutions need to be found to limit the incidence of expulsions that require the formation of large numbers of relocation villages and their congregations. It is important to recognize that persecution has a strong negative impact on the church itself, and that many

10. Frend, *Martyrdom and Persecution*, 463.

11. Frend, *Martyrdom and Persecution*, 569.

years and much effort are demanded to bring the weakened church through the recuperation stage.

Some might argue that severe persecution does force Christians to unite and join together. However, I have observed that the unity that is forced on people during persecution is not true unity but rather a temporary alliance that is formed as an emergency procedure and then falls apart when the pressure of persecution declines.

Persecution, in the long run, actually does much more to divide and break up the church than to unite it (Acts 8:1–3). In the case of the Zinacanteco *evangélicos*, their unity came out of a need for self-defense and self-preservation. When they were able to relocate in a village of believers and escape the threats and dangers of tribal persecution, the apparent unity quickly dissolved. As a matter of fact, the previous support groups of family and village identities formed their own factions within the church and caused not only disunity but outright fighting and quarreling. The same dynamic was seen in the massive Chamula expulsions and the resulting relocation communities.

> *Observation: Unity that is constructed on the foundations of persecution often collapses soon after those temporary foundations have crumbled.*

This fragile kind of Christian unity is neither what the Bible describes in Colossians 3:12–17, nor is it a strong positive factor in causing the growth of the church. The hurt and disillusionment that comes out of the fragile unity forced on persecuted Christians turns out to be more of a negative factor in the growth of the church than a positive result.

Unity that is based only on the urgencies of persecution does not provide lasting solidarity. In Acts 2, unity was born out of the desire for fellowship and prayer, not out of an emergency defense against persecution. Even the oneness and sharing exemplified in Acts 4:32–35 seems to have been a choice made by the first believers even before any severe persecution became a reason for unity. Lasting unity must be established on the basis of Christian love and fellowship, and this should be constructed before persecution strikes.

If the unity of the larger church has not been established before severe persecution attacks a section of the church, there is seldom any spontaneous demonstration of solidarity in times of crisis. This lack of Christian unity in specific times of persecution turns into a negative force in the growth of the church. During the massive expulsions of Chamula Protestant *evangélicos* in 1967, the local Spanish-speaking Presbyterian churches failed to give any aid or hospitality to the suffering Presbyterians. The Tzotzil presbyterial structures were not yet organized at that time, and state and national responses ranged from paltry to nothing. Even succeeding persecution in surrounding tribal areas did not result in any noticeable unity. The Presbyterian church of Las Margaritas, which had experienced persecution in its neighboring Tojolabal area, was the one exception; the emergency rations sent by this church in a subsequent expulsion of Tzotzil *evangélicos* was a clear demonstration of unity. Otherwise, there was very little evidence that persecution caused the unity of the larger church. The negative result was that the persecuted Indigenous *evangélicos* concluded that the Spanish-speaking Christians refused to help them because of racial prejudices. These negative feelings continued to affect the relations between indigenous and *Mestizo* Christians for many years.

> *Observation: For persecution to result in the unity of the church, that solidarity must be established before actual persecution strikes.*

Reversion of Weak Christians

Probably the most common and most widely recognized negative result of persecution is the reversion of Christians because of the pain and pressure of persecution. The unmistakable goal of persecutors is to cause potential and new believers in Christ to turn away from Christianity under the intimidation of threats, ostracism, and expulsions.

> In 2011, Amelo, a pastor working near the Colombia-Venezuela border dominated by the guerrilla Armed Revolutionary Forces of Colombia (FARC), left his house and never returned. In the aftermath of Amelo's murder, the family's faith was fragile: They stopped going to church; his wife abandoned her faith completely for a time; his family fled to Bogotá in panic amid hostile threats; once settled there, they were depleted and scared, trusting no one; they were shattered emotionally and spiritually by their grief.[12]

Throughout history every method of torture and abuse has been used to prompt people to revert to traditional practices and beliefs.

In the Tzotzil persecution, many fell away at the first sign of threats and warnings. Some increased their involvement in witchcraft or alcoholism

---

12. "From Pain to Promise," 1.

just to make a clear statement to traditional society that they were not Protestant evangelicals. There were others who remained faithful until the time of ostracism, jailing, and potential expulsion. Finally, there were those who reverted back to traditional patterns after they were tortured or beaten or forced to leave their homes. Many potential believers in Christ were trampled underfoot by the heavy heel of persecution. Many of them were permanently lost to the kingdom of God, and that was certainly a serious negative result of persecution.

Shune Tontic, a young Zinacanteco man who became the first Protestant evangelical in that tribe, was severely ostracized and threatened when it became known that he had become an *evangélico*.

The tribal leaders intimidated and terrorized this young *evangélico* until he agreed to openly deny his new faith. To prove that he had truly reverted back to the Zinacanteco animistic religion, he married the daughter of a shaman and immersed himself in alcohol and shamanism. Shune became a picture of what Jesus described in Luke 11:24–26:

> When an evil spirit comes out of a man, it goes through arid places seeking rest and does not find it. Then it says, "I will return to the house that I left." When it arrives, it finds the house swept clean and put in order. Then it goes and takes seven other spirits more wicked than itself, and they go in and live there. And the final condition of that man is worse than the first.

Shune Tontic, the first Zinacanteco evangelical

In Shune's case, he was not permanently lost to the kingdom of God. He plunged to the depths of degradation and alcoholism, and it was more than five years before he again responded to Christ's call. However, there are other cases of reversion of new and weak believers in Christ in which violent persecution drives a permanent wedge between them and Christianity.

Another man named Shune, from the village of Shulvo', had expressed his interest in the gospel when persecution struck him almost immediately. He had just decided to put aside his fear of persecution and again attend a worship service when he was captured, imprisoned, and beaten severely along with the other Zinacanteco Protestant evangelicals. Since that experience, in spite of many attempts by some of his family who remained *evangélicos*, Shune has never again shown any interest in the gospel.

This negative effect of persecution is similar to that of inoculation, but in the reversion of weak Christians we are dealing with those who basically had made family and individual decisions to follow Christ, only to be scared off when persecution strikes.

Telesh Potovtic, a corn grinder owner, and his entire family made their decision to become *evangélicos* by offering to risk holding one of the house-church services in their home. However, when violent expulsions threatened to rob them of all of their land and houses in the village, they reverted completely and have never again responded to further contacts concerning Christianity.

While the stories of individuals and family groups that reverted are numerous, there are no actual statistics. Where violent and persistent persecution prevailed in the Tzotzil tribes in Chiapas, approximately a quarter of the new Protestant evangelicals reverted under the pressure of persecution. About half of that number reconsidered their denial and joined the *evangélicos* after a number of years, while the rest reverted permanently. Although the severity of the persecution and the response of the church to the persecution would cause these percentages to vary, the fact is that persecution does result in a significant loss in the growth of the church. Simply stated, a considerable number of individuals and families deny their new faith in Christ because of the pain and pressure of persecution.

> *Observation: The reversion of new or weak Christians results in a significant repression of the growth of the church.*

While some would argue that this negative factor is offset somewhat by the purification of the church through this process of elimination of weak Christians, this does not reduce our responsibility to those who are lost in this process. The parable of the lost sheep clearly indicates that God is deeply interested in recalling those who have wandered off: "In the same way your Father in heaven is not willing that any of these little ones should be lost" (Matt 18:14). This also applies to those who have reverted because of persecution.

The purification process can leave the church with mainly early innovators who are not necessarily the best leaders. The sifting process of persecution often eliminates those who are late innovators, those who eventually prove to be the most reliable and solid leaders. Everett M. Rogers's insightful study on the *Diffusion of Innovations* points out that the best leaders are not those who are early innovators. This is especially true in social systems where the norms do not favor rapid change. Rogers says, "Innovators are poor opinion leaders in systems with traditional norms: they are too elite and too change oriented."[13] When persecuted groups form new worship communities, they often are left with a choice of leaders who are too innovative for the church. These innovative leaders later cause disruption and division in the church when they are eventually replaced by the less innovative believers in Christ who respond to the gospel after persecution risks have lessened. The charismatic early innovator is often attracted by other new options and leaves the church, taking other members with him or her.

Halting of the Growth of the Church

The negative results of persecution affect both the traditional and the Christian communities, but the principal concern for missiology is the halting effect that persecution has on the growth of the church.

Jesus made us aware of the negative effect on potential Christians "when trouble or persecution comes because of the Word" (Matt 13:21). The fact is that a large number of those who would otherwise eagerly become Christians will hesitate to commit themselves to something that might cost them more than they are willing to invest. Many potential Christians allow themselves to be terrorized or scared off by the threats and violence they see being unleashed against confessing believers in Christ. While they might admire the courage of those who stand up in the face of persecution, significant numbers of those who are interested in the gospel as a viable option for themselves and their families will merely decide to wait until a more favorable time or to choose to repudiate the gospel altogether. Trevor Beeson makes a comment on the negative effects persecution in Russia, "There are fewer churchgoers than there were fifty years ago, for oppression and propaganda do have their results."[14] It is impossible to gather accurate statistics on what percentages are lost to the growth of the church due to

13. Rogers, *Diffusion of Innovations*, 285.
14. Beeson, *Discretion and Valour*, 150.

these factors. However, in growth studies I have done in the Tzotzil tribes, I have seen that in every case of violent persecution or expulsions the growth of the church was stifled for a significant period of time.

Halting of Growth Due to Dispersion

The dispersion of persecuted Christians has often been seen as a positive factor in the growth of the church. But this can easily become negative if monolingual and mono-ethnic tribal people are expelled out of their tribal areas and relocated in areas where they are cut off completely from their culture and ethnic group. If persecutors are successful in forcing believers in Christ to move so far away that there is no further contact with their own kinship and ethnic group, scattering can have the effect of halting all further evangelization for a number of years. Unless the expelled believers in Christ respond by maintaining contact and renewing evangelism outreach back into their tribal areas, the dispersion will hinder the spread of the gospel in their own tribal region, but hopefully could advance the spread of the gospel in areas to which they flee.

Halting Momentum of a People Movement

The halting effect on the growth of the church is most notable when persecution causes the people movement in a specific tribe or area to lose its momentum. When the twelve families of worshiping Presbyterians were threatened with expulsion from the village of Amatenango, the Presbyterian worker in that area lamented: "There were at least another 20 families who had just recently said that they wanted to become Christians. But now they have all backed off because of their fear [of violent persecution]. Many more would have become Christians if they were not threatened by this outbreak of opposition."[15]

Old communities becoming Christians together, often called a people movement, can be halted by the fear of persecution. This fear has a negative affect on potential receptors, as well as on those who have been witnessing.

---

15. Roberto Sántiz Gómez, interview by Vernon Sterk, San Cristóbal de Las Casas, Chiapas, Nov 27, 1990.

THE RESULTS OF PERSECUTION

Halting of Personal Witness

This loss of momentum also negatively affects the witness of evangelists, pastors, and workers who have suffered persecution. The effect of persecution is often the suspension of evangelistic outreach on the part of those who have suffered violence while involved in such work. Antun Gómez Ruiz is a Protestant evangelical who was expelled from the Zinacanteco tribe in 1984. By 1989 he had fully recovered from the original expulsion and became one of the enthusiastic evangelists who made almost weekly trips back into Zinacanteco villages. His efforts were being rewarded with exciting church growth, especially around the area of a town called Granadia. However, in September 1990, Antun and three Presbyterians who had accompanied him to show the *Jesus* evangelistic movie were grabbed by a mob of persecutors. Following three days of imprisonment, beatings, and the humiliation of having patches of his hair chopped off with a machete, Antun was not at all ready to resume any evangelistic trips into the Zinacanteco tribe. Many others were unwilling to readily submit themselves to certain and violent persecution. In the meantime, not only was the evangelistic and church growth momentum stopped, but valuable time was lost before recuperation would allow these evangelists to regain their enthusiasm for nurturing the hidden church and for new tribal outreach.

Halting Growth because of Discouragement

Persecution can slow the growth of the church through discouragement. Repeated disappointment in finding relief or justice in the face of persecution can lead to disillusionment. When there seems to be no end to suffering and pain caused by persecution, it is easy for Christians to give up the battle. As Lesbaupin says:

> Precisely at an age of catastrophe and harsh confrontation, a time of persecution becomes a time of danger, the danger of discouragement: "You are patient and endure hardship for my cause. Moreover, you do not become discouraged" (Rev. 2:3). Defeat does not consist in being tortured or killed, but in giving up, wearing out, yielding points, going over to the other side.[16]

The Mitontic persecution continued for a number of years (1987–90) with no real hope of a solution. The *evangélicos* attempted to make calculated returns to their tribal homes on three different occasions, only to be

---

16. Lesbaupin, *Blessed are the Persecuted*, 77.

expelled with increasing violence at each attempt. The corrupt government lawyers sold themselves out to the *caciques*, and the *evangélicos* found their unity and resolve disintegrating. Most of them were crowded into borrowed rooms, many began to disperse and look for relocation possibilities, and some became discouraged and wanted to give up.

The tendency of much of Christianity has been to ignore the negative aspects of persecution and to idealize the positive aspects of persecution in relation to the growth of the church. The danger of such a lack of balance in the understanding of persecution is that we fail to be ready to help believers in Christ face the negative aspects of persecution. We fail to teach converts about or prepare them for the negative and difficult struggles that are coming. When we fail to prepare for persecution, the risk is not only the retardation of the growth of the church but also the danger of the possible extinction of whole groups of believers in Christ.

A study of the negative results of persecution and the consequent halting of the growth of the church may destroy some of the myths of the past that have taught us that persecution is strictly a positive force in the growth. Instead of assuming that "the blood of the martyrs is the seed of the church,"[17] we might conclude that persecution results in the killing of much of the seed. The parable of the sower teaches us that the seed is really the Word of God.

> Those along the path are the ones who hear, and then the devil comes and takes away the word from their hearts, so that they may not believe and be saved. Those on the rocky ground are the ones who receive the word with joy when they hear it, but they have no root. They believe for a while, but in the time of testing they fall away. (Luke 8:12–13)

Observation: Persecution, in itself, is not the seed of the church, but it often negatively results in destroying the seed of the Word of God that has been planted in human hearts.

There are other negative results of persecution that could be discussed at this point, but I prefer to simply mention them quickly: first, the reality of human pain, suffering, and death caused by persecution; second, the complacency of the church in responding to the needs of persecuted people when persecution is persistent and extended over many years; third, the desire for personal gain that may arise out of the possibility to secure material aid for persecuted refugees. Even when not persecuted, some people

17. Tertullian, *Apol.* 50.

will provoke or fabricate persecution so that they can get in on the offer of help for land, houses, and other material aid. Also, those who administer the financial aid to persecuted Christians may take advantage of these funds for personal gain.

The Positive Results of Persecution

While it is essential for us to attempt to recognize and minimize the negative results of persecution, it is equally important to understand and capitalize on the positive results. There are some constructive and favorable consequences that emerge from the process and stages of persecution.

Purification of the Church

Probably the most commonly known positive result of persecution is the strengthening of faith and commitment to Christ. During persecution, a purification of the church takes place in that only those with genuine and lasting faith endure the time of testing. This could be called the sifting and refining process because it implies that the trials of persecution result in some believers who are refined in their faith and who become mature witnesses for Christ. When those who are too weak in their faith to continue to be believers in Christ are separated out, the church is purified of elements and individuals who would only weaken the witness of the church. This is the common rationale that is used to indicate this sifting process as a positive factor for the church.

Ruth Tucker describes the reality of persecution in the early church as being "a sobering thought that excluded nominal Christians from their numbers. The fire of persecution purified the church, and the courage displayed by the innocent victims was a spectacle unbelievers could not fail to notice."[18]

This fire of purification of the church reveals its most positive effects in individual lives. Some Christians become more mature in their faith, and some future leaders are prepared and designated for God's work through the refiner's fire of persecution. The New Testament is clear about this positive contribution. First Peter 1:7 tells us that persecution and trials "have come so that your faith, of greater worth than gold, which perishes even though refined by fire, may be proved genuine."

18. Tucker, *Jerusalem to Irian Jaya*, 27.

So, persecution does provide a test of faith that reveals which believers in Christ are genuine, will remain faithful, and are actually willing to give their lives for the cause of Christ. In a sense it is a time of separating the "sheep from the goats" (Matt 25:32–33). This means that persecution forces people to make a clear choice, and for those who are ready to make this decision such pressure can solidify their choice.

Petul Votz, the uncle of the first Protestant evangelical in the Zinacanteco tribe, allowed us to live in one of his houses in Nabenchauc. He had struggled with his commitment because of his fear of persecution. He owned two houses and had inherited a large amount of tribal land from his father. So, whenever he went to an *evangélico* worship service he would sneak in and out of the tribe so that no one would see him. If he went to visit believers in another village house church, he would ask us to pick him up a few kilometers from the village so that he would not be seen getting into a missionary's car. When violent persecution against the growing *evangélico* house church movement began, Petul and his whole family were jailed, put on trial in the tribal center, and publicly sentenced to death. When God miraculously saved Petul and his family from almost certain killing, he put his fear and his concern for land and possessions behind him. When Petul and his family were expelled from their tribal village, he helped establish the new relocation community of Vida Nueva and later another relocation community of Nuevo Zinacantán. Petul deeply committed his life to Christ when he saw that God had powerfully saved him in a time of extreme testing.

Petul's family rebuilt their lives in Vida Nueva.

There is evidence that a period of testing does develop some good characteristics in individual Christian lives. James said: "Consider it pure joy, my brothers, whenever you face trials of many kinds, because you know that the testing of your faith develops perseverance" (Jas 1:2–3). Persecution often reveals which believers in Christ are unafraid and are able to stand up in the midst of extreme pressure. Perseverance emerges out of testing. It is a kind of training that produces endurance and stamina that will be needed to survive continued testing and persecution. Romans 5:3–4 reminds us that suffering produces perseverance, character, and hope. First Peter 5:10 concludes that this time of suffering will be followed by Christ restoring the Christian to one who is "strong, firm and steadfast."

Peter is careful to note that the "restoring" of the Christian to be "strong, firm and steadfast" comes after or following the time of suffering. In other words, there are some good characteristics that are produced in some believers in Christ that are developed over a period of time. Antun Gómez Ruiz, a Zinacanteco Christian, shared with me that this had been his experience:

> When I first experienced persecution and expulsion for being an *evangélico*, I was very weak and afraid. I just wanted to escape the persecution. Later, when I was just forgetting some of my fear, I was subjected to more persecution and had to again abandon the house I had built. It took me several years to get over that persecution. Five years later, I was given the courage to go to the lowland Zinacanteco area and do evangelism in the growing movement there. When I was beaten, jailed and had my hair shaved off, I decided I didn't want to be subjected to persecution again. But now that several months have passed since the last persecution, I can actually say that I realize God has been strengthening me through each experience. I no longer fear being put in jail, and I know that God cares for us in each persecution so that nothing serious happens to us.[19]

This Christian leader had to be "restored" by the power of God after each persecution cast fear in his heart. That restoration took a number of years following each incident. When asked whether the times of persecution had made him a stronger witness, Antun answered: "It is not the persecution that makes one stronger or increases one's faith. Persecution and suffering actually renew the fear in one's heart. Persecution tears down and destroys confidence. But when we survive the violent persecution, then we

19. Antun Gómez Ruiz, interview by Vernon Sterk, San Cristóbal de Las Casas, Chiapas, Nov 30, 1990.

can look back and see God's help and care. We can see that God restores us."[20]

It is the power of God revealed during persecution that brings restoration, strength, and renewed faith; it is not persecution itself that brings maturation and growth.

Reliance on God Alone

When God chooses to reveal his power and protection in times of persecution, believers in Christ often learn a positive and lasting lesson: reliance on God alone.

Manuel Chiotic was a pastor in the large Chamula Presbyterian Church. He shared the story of how he learned that he could trust God for protection for himself and his family during the killings and persecution in the tribal area:

> The gospel had been spreading rapidly in the tribal village, and the traditional leaders decided that it must be stopped. They gathered a group of assassins to kill the leaders of this new *evangélico* group in order to discourage any further growth.
>
> At midnight the small band of killers crept toward the area where the houses of the *evangélicos* were located. As they went up the last rise, one of the men shouted: "A mountain lion!" In terror the killers scattered without firing a shot.
>
> The next night, the determined killers met near the houses where they had planned to do their evil deed. But this time they were surprised to see a truck parked at the house of one of the believers. Since none of the *evangélicos* owned a truck, it was assumed that they had some foreign visitors, maybe even a government official. It would be too risky to attack if some witnesses were present.
>
> The third night was overcast with low clouds and a steady mist that made the clay path treacherous. As the resolute band of killers made their way along the slippery trail, a shot rang out. The leader of the group had stumbled and shot himself in the leg. "Let's get out of here," the men all agreed. "There must be some spirit or god protecting these people! They can't be killed!"[21]

20. Antun Gómez Ruiz, interview by Vernon Sterk, San Cristóbal de Las Casas, Chiapas, Nov 30, 1990.

21. Manuel Chiotic, interview by Vernon Sterk, San Cristóbal de Las Casas, Chiapas, Mar 1978.

When this incident was first related to Manuel Gómez Jiménez by one of the would-be killers who had become an *evangélico*, Manuel knew that it had been the protection of God, for no one had seen a mountain lion in years, and no truck had ever been parked by his home at night.

Manuel did not become a leader because he was persecuted; he found faith and maturity through learning that he could depend on God's protection. It did not come through just one incident of experiencing God's power revealed in the setting of persecution; it was a lesson he learned over a period of time from continued experience of dependency on God alone, in miraculous healings and protection in the face of persecution.

Believers in Christ are strengthened in their faith when they experience God's power revealed in times of persecution. While this dependency on God alone can be learned in other experiences, persecution provides a stage upon which God can act out his mighty deeds. When believers in Christ witness God's powerful acts in the midst of persecution, they are impressed with their need to rely on God. Learning to depend on God alone is an outgrowth of persecution that can have clear positive effects on the growth of the church. In 2 Corinthians the apostle Paul speaks of suffering and persecution in these words:

> We do not want you to be uninformed, brothers, about the hardships we suffered in the province of Asia. We were under great pressure, far beyond our ability to endure, so that we despaired even of life. Indeed, in our hearts we felt the sentence of death. *But this happened that we might not rely on ourselves but on God*, who raises the dead. He has delivered us from such a deadly peril, and he will deliver us. On him we have set our hope that he will continue to deliver us, as you help us by your prayers. Then many will give thanks on our behalf for the gracious favor granted us in answer to the prayers of many. (2 Cor 1:8–11, emphasis mine)

Exposure to the Gospel

Another positive result of persecution is that the attention of many people is attracted to the message and the claims of Christianity. Persecution provides a time of increased exposure to the gospel.

The Dandelion Effect

After several years of severe and violent persecution in the Chamula tribe in which hundreds of Protestant evangelicals were forcibly expelled from their homes and land, the traditional tribal leaders in Chamula became frustrated because they were not able to snuff out the growing *evangélico* movement. Following a long discussion of the various strategies that had been used to put an end to the believers in their tribe, the tribal president reportedly said:

> It is useless to try to stop the spread of *evangélicos* by throwing them out of the tribe, because they leave their seeds behind. They are like dandelions. We try to blow them away, and soon we find that we have just scattered their seeds all around. We get rid of one group and soon another has grown, and we again try to blow them away by expelling them, only to find that more seeds have been scattered. We cannot stop the *evangélicos* by trying to blow them away.[22]

This dandelion effect is similar to what is described in the book of Acts: "On that day a great persecution broke out against the church at Jerusalem, and all except the apostles were scattered throughout Judea and Samaria. Those who had been scattered preached the word wherever they went" (Acts 8:1, 4). Especially in ethnic groups in which family ties and ethnic cohesion are strong, the persecutors unknowingly enhance the dandelion effect by public trials and violent displays against believers in Christ.

> *Observation: Persecution can provide a time of increased public exposure to the options being offered by the gospel.*

Public Witness to New Options

One of the principal effects persecution has in society is as a witness to new options. Persecution not only opens people's eyes to other possibilities; it is sometimes able to slip these new options through cracks in closed worldview concepts. In effect, there is a positive quality in persecution that is essential to communication. That quality lies in its ability to attract public attention and slip past barriers.

Especially in areas where social and cultural disintegration is causing people to look for solutions to their felt needs, persecution can be a factor in awakening those people to new options. In areas where specific social

---

22. Interviews of Chamula converts conducted by Vernon Sterk, 1980

factors have developed a feeling of dissatisfaction with the accepted cultural ways of handling problems, persecution makes people stop to take a look at what options others from their culture are choosing. These observers will then try to keep an eye open to the relative success or failure of such innovators to decide if this new option or innovation could also meet their needs. In his book on *Diffusion of Innovations*, Everett M. Rogers says it this way: "One of the ways in which the innovation-development process begins is by recognition of a problem or need, which stimulates research and development activities designed to create an innovation to solve the problem or need."[23]

Persecution not only exposes innovations to meet specific felt needs, but it also provides a public forum in which research and development activities are stimulated. Persecution has the unique quality of publicly presenting to an entire people group the new options or innovations that are being presented by Christianity. In many instances, public trials raise the very questions that are already on the minds of many people. Believers in Christ are then given a unique opportunity to witness to a new option with everyone listening. It must be noted, however, that this can only have a positive effect if the affirm and fulfill model has been encouraged. On the other hand, when a confrontational model has been employed in the communication of the gospel message, there is a greater tendency for hearers to twist and turn any public witness into ammunition with which persecutors can justify an escalation of the battle against the new innovation.

At any rate, public attention is often drawn to a new option that may address real felt needs. When a group of Protestant evangelicals was jailed in the Chamula tribal center and threatened with expulsion if they refused to pay a special fine to the tribal mafia leaders and buy rum liquor for the persecutors, the *evangélicos* got the attention of many who were struggling with exorbitant fees and unfair demands from tribal leaders. Some of the onlookers were alcoholics who wished they had the courage to say no to the pressures of social drinking. Others may have been wishing they had the courage to stand up to the repressive tribal *cacique* authorities. These persecution incidents open public opportunities for witness. When *evangélicos* were asked why they would not drink the liquor, they simply answered that Christ had freed them from their former addiction to alcohol. They mentioned that they had tried the medical and physical treatments that others offered, but it was the power of Christ that freed them. Even though the believers' answers were treated with ridicule and contempt, many were actually listening carefully to what was being said.

23. Rogers, *Diffusion of Innovations*, 135.

Often the very people acting out the persecution, incarceration, and expulsion of others from their tribal group are the ones who are most readily affected by this witness of *evangélicos*. Although they will use extreme abuse and violence to put those on trial to a real test, they also have a front row seat to the persecution and injustice that is carried out. It so often happens that in the privacy of their own homes they will not only question their actions against their own people but will actually begin to give serious consideration to some of the new options or innovative solutions to which *evangélicos* have witnessed.

In the village of Nachij, the tribal judge had confiscated the New Testament and tape recorder and gospel cassette messages from the Protestant evangelicals. At the trial, the *evangélicos* had defended their use of these materials because they were based on the same scripture being used by the Catholic priest and catechists. It was not until a year later that the believers discovered that the tribal judge had become interested in the gospel after he secretly read the New Testament and listened to the message on the cassette tapes in his own home.

Another subgroup that pays close attention to the issues and answers publicized by persecution is that of extended family groups. In societies that hold family relationships and kinship in high regard, to have one of the family members become an *evangélico* and suffer persecution attracts intense extended family attention and in-depth discussion. Although village and tribal pressures and ostracism usually keep extended families from initial defense of a family member, the positive effect takes place as the family members become aware of new options. The family will not lose track of what is happening to this innovative family member and will quietly determine if the options that he or she has chosen are valid for them at a later stage.

Healing Option

In the Tzotzil tribes, one of the most powerful options that was shared during times of persecution was the believer in Christ's witness to God's power to heal. When those who were summoned by the tribal authorities told that one of their family members had been healed of a serious disease through the power of God, the witness of these believers promoted quick penetration into the Tzotzil worldview. An indigenous couple whose child had just died in spite of the traditional curing ceremonies of the tribal shamans listened intently to this option, especially since it fit into their worldview concept that healing comes through spiritual power. They often secretly began personal and family research to find out if it was true that *evangélicos* had found healing power through Christ. Then they began to weigh this option with their family and kinship groups.

In the Tzotzil tribes, this witness to the healing power of God has been the overwhelming factor in the growth of the church of Jesus Christ. In informal surveys that my wife and I have done, we have concluded that approximately 90 percent of the Tzotzil Protestant evangelicals originally responded to the gospel through their search for medical help and healing, which they found in the *evangélico* option.

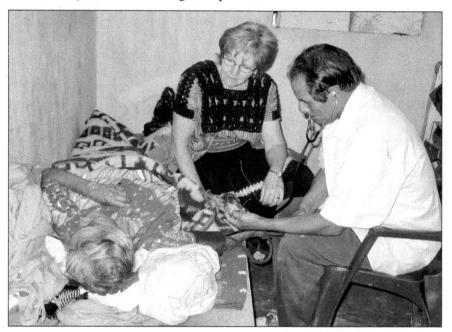

Carla Sterk worked with Tzotzil paramedics in a medical healing ministry.

Persecution plays a positive role in exposing new options for finding solutions to the felt needs of a tribe or culture. Therefore, the gospel spreads rapidly with such a combination of factors. As Charles Kraft explains, "When desired changes can be attached to felt needs, therefore, the advocacy of these changes is facilitated considerably. Usually the advocates can devote their attention primarily to winning others to their point of view (reinterpretation) concerning the issue(s) and to stimulating them into action in changing the present situation."[24]

24. Kraft, *Christianity in Culture*, 354.

In other words, a persecuted believer in Christ finds that he or she does not have to spend a lot of time trying to convince fellow tribal people of the need for a valid source of healing. An open example and witness to the power of God to heal facilitates considerably the openness to new options and thus advances the growth of the church.

Liberation Option

Another important option that is given public display in times of persecution is the longing for liberation. In situations in which people are seeking freedom from oppression or fear, be it economic, social, military, physical, or spiritual, a witness to the option for liberation is very attractive. In many parts of the world where people are dominated and oppressed, the search for liberation brings people to see the persecution of their own people in a different light.

In indigenous areas of Latin America with its history of oppression and abuse at the hands of foreign powers, any new hope for liberation from the centuries of tyranny and domination is viewed as a possible option. When that tyranny is being imposed within one's own tribal area by *caciques* and internal mafia groups, the liberation option being offered by Christianity opens new church growth dimensions. Finally, when social and cultural disintegration has increased fuzzy areas in people's worldviews, the openness to new options allows the Christian witness that is exposed in persecution situations to penetrate otherwise closed areas.

In Chiapas, as well as in many parts of Latin America, the search for liberation has found expression in the Base Christian Community movement, better known as the *Comunidades Eclesiales de Base* or CEBs. The cultural and historical oppression of the indigenous people of Chiapas has made both Protestant and Roman Catholic expressions of these small Christian Base Communities a very real option for liberation hope. Curt Cadorette states that in both the Protestant and Catholic forms, these small Christian communities or grassroots congregations "are ecclesial expressions of hope in the possibility of creating new, liberating societies where full personhood can be achieved."[25]

When oppressed people see a way to join with a community of committed believers in Christ of their own ethnic group to overcome many of the oppressive forces in their lives, and when these ecclesial communities are based on biblical study and the active faith of their own people, this becomes a dynamic option for resistance to oppression. When people see

25. Cadorette, *From the Heart of the People*, 18.

the church as an option for spiritual and social liberation, many will be attracted. Persecution openly publicizes the fact that such an option exists, and in this way, it acts as a positive factor in the communication of the gospel.

Again, the liberation option only acts as a positive persecution factor if an ethnic group feels oppressed and is searching for ways to resist that domination. On the other hand, if people of a society are relatively satisfied with the cultural solutions to problems, persecution will not effectively attract attention to new options. It may actually produce the inoculation effect in such cases, for it will dichotomize the traditional religion or worldview as over against the Christian threat to it. Thus, persecution's effect, whether positive or negative, will depend on a culture's openness or desire to change.

When people are open and searching for answers to their struggles, persecution presents a public witness to new options and new solutions and innovations. In this case, persecution can have positive results in the growth of the church.

The Unity of the Church

Another positive result that has often been attributed to persecution is the unity of the church. The church usually joins in oneness and cooperation when it is under the threat of persecution. When believers in Christ are under attack in the form of persecution and oppression, the natural means of defense is to seek out others who will unite with them in an attempt to gain enough strength to survive the onslaught. As people unite for worship and fellowship in a community of believers, they are also forced by persecution to join in a common cause that is similar to a nation uniting in battle against a common enemy.

The Zinacanteco *evangélicos* were an example of a unity that was formed from the threats of persecution. They united against the threats of expulsion and all agreed to stand up for each other if anyone was taken to trial. When a few of the believers were to be assassinated, others risked their lives to prevent those killings. When expulsion did take place, the *evangélicos* gathered all of their salvaged possessions and lived together and shared food and life in common for several months. A united effort to purchase land where they could relocate was successful. Much like Acts 2:44, "all the believers were together and had everything in common."

Expelled Christians shared food and life together.

Internal unity in a congregation or church will develop out of responses to persecution such as those listed in Colossians 3:12: "compassion, kindness, humility, gentleness and patience." It will be bound together with the virtues of forgiveness and love (v. 13, 14), and out of that love will emerge a unity that is a positive factor in church growth.

Others have pointed to times of persecution as opportunities for all believers in Christ to show their support for those who are suffering. The unity expressed by national and international assistance for those undergoing persecution is encouraging and impressive. Especially in instances in which Zinacanteco and Chamula *evangélicos* have undergone violent expulsions and needed emergency relief and loans to purchase new land, Christian relief agencies such as Church World Service responded generously. It must be recognized that emergency relief efforts to help believers in Christ facing persecution are positive expressions that play a role in the unity and growth of the church.

Summary

What then, would be our conclusions? Are the results of persecution mainly positive, or are they predominantly negative? We must first agree with Lesbaupin:

> Persecution, then, is a two-edged sword. It perfects Christians in their option, strengthens them in their witness, enables them to deepen their life in God. At the same time, others are vanquished. They fail the test. They retreat.[26]

This chapter does show that persecution itself carries serious negative effects such as inoculation and immunity, disruption and dislocation, and even the division and weakening of the church. The additional negative factors of the reversion of weak believers in Christ and the overall halting of the growth of the church seem to provide overwhelming evidence that the results of persecution in Chiapas have been predominantly negative, and both our preparation and response to persecution should take this into account.

There are also some positive results of persecution. Aspects such as the purification of the church, a greater reliance on God, and a public awareness of the new options available through the gospel all indicate some positive results. The unity of the church may also be a positive factor under certain circumstances. However, whether these elements of persecution will have lasting positive results on society and growth of the church depends much more on the Christian's response to persecution than on the existence of persecution itself.

I have observed, however, that the results of persecution are overwhelmingly negative. Thus, we should continue our study on how to avoid, delay, or stop persecution in every way possible. In the next chapters of this study, our concern will be to seek a response to persecution that would achieve the growth of the church in spite of persecution.

26. Lesbaupin, *Blessed are the Persecuted*, 78.

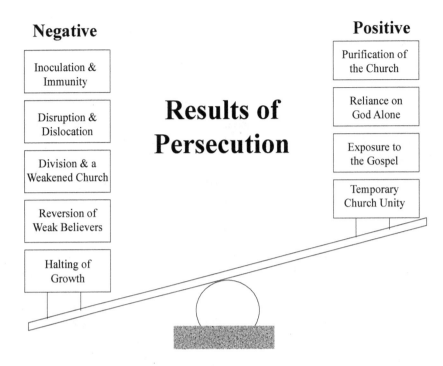

The negative results of Tzotzil persecution outweighed the positive.

Chapter 8

The Persecuted Christian's Response to Persecution

IT IS NOT PERSECUTION itself that causes the growth of the church, but the response to persecution that is determinative. This chapter weighs the validity of various reactions to persecution, giving special attention to how the missionary and indigenous church leaders might counsel persecuted Christians to respond.

Persecuted believers in Christ will respond in some way to hostility. They should not, however, merely resign themselves to the position of redemptive suffering, and assume that there is some redeeming purpose in the experience of enduring pain, derision, grief, and despair. The response will be to either seek the protection of the law, to use counter-violence, or to respond in Christian love.

It is how the individual believer in Christ, his or her family, and the local congregation of believers react to persecution that will determine the positive or negative results of persecution. If we are prepared to give a Christian response in the face of persecution, we can have a positive effect on society and culture and on the growth of the church. If the response to persecution is inadequate, it can nullify the effect of evangelism and even result in the ultimate downfall and destruction of the church.

Response #1: Claim the Protection of the Law

One natural reaction to persecution is to defend oneself and one's property and rights. Often our first response to persecution is to seek justice and defend those who are being abused and mistreated. In most countries of the world, there are specific laws or constitutional agreements that protect people from persecution and harassment on the basis of religious beliefs. In such cases, those who are persecuted feel that there is some legal recourse with which they can respond to persecution. The Christian often feels that he or she has the right and the duty to fight back, to claim legal rights, and to point out the injustice of the persecutors.

In Mexico, Article 24 in the National Constitution guarantees religious freedom: "All people are free to profess the religious belief of their choice, and are free to practice ceremonies, devotionals or respective acts of worship in church buildings and in private homes, as long as these do not constitute any violation punishable by law."[1]

Such legal guarantees certainly provide an option for Christians to respond to persecution. The New Testament encourages Christians to respect and submit themselves to the care and protection of legal authorities. Romans 13:1–7 shows that since civil authorities and laws are ordained by God, Christians must submit to them. Titus 3:1–2 reminds us to be subject to legal authorities. First Peter 2:13–15 indicates that the government authorities and laws are there to protect those who do right and to punish those who do wrong.

The New Testament writers obviously were aware that not all authorities were going to enact just laws. Many of the rulers of their time were the very ones who persecuted the Christians. However, the New Testament recognizes the fact that God has actually established laws to ensure justice and rulers to carry out the laws. Thus, Christians can and should see the legal option as one of their defenses against unjust persecution. This is true, at least, in countries or in ethnic groups where the law guarantees religious freedom or freedom of conscience.

However, the question for persecuted Christians often is not whether laws guaranteeing religious rights exist; rather, it is a question of whether those laws are enforced or respected. The Christian's response to persecution will depend greatly on the application of the laws against persecution.

1. Rabasa and Caballero, *Mexicano*, 66.

Enforcement of Laws

When laws against persecution are enforced, persecution is usually restrained quite rapidly, and Christians find that the protection of the law is a valid and helpful option. In the indigenous tribes of Mexico there are examples of persecution being impeded by enforcement of the law. The history of the Tzeltal Presbyterian Church notes that persecution was impeded in that tribe in the early 1950s when the persecutors were jailed.[2] During the years of 1965–95 the persecutors in the Tzotzil tribes were not punished and persecution became violent.

> *Observation: If laws guaranteeing religious freedom exist, and more importantly if they are enforced or respected, then legal action against persecutors does prove effective in halting or discouraging persecution.*

Clearly, if legal guarantees are enforced and respected, response #1 is a viable option for Christians suffering persecution. The missionary and the church should not only encourage persecuted Christians to claim the protection of the law, but also establish specific Christian legal defense organizations. The formation and participation in human rights organizations is another important aspect in which both missionary and church should be involved. In this way, local persecuted groups can find both legal counsel and representation and also effectively continue to keep pressure on the government for enforcement of laws.

Results of the Appeal to Legal Defense

Our concern at this point is not only if it is a viable Christian option to restrain persecution through legal channels. We must also ask the question: What is the effect on the growth of the church when the reaction to persecution is to claim legal defense? If the laws are enforced and persecution is halted by the use of the legal option, does the church grow as a result?

Chapter 1 notes several clear examples of Protestant Christians appealing to Mexican law to stop persecution threats. In the Tzeltal case, we noted that an official statement of the law by government authorities led to the first rapid growth in that tribe. When the effective enforcement of the law put the brakes on persecution violence in another area of the Tzeltal

2. Esponda, *Historia de la Iglesia*, 288.

tribe, the result was a remarkable story of the growth of the church. In the Chenalhó tribe, when legal guarantees were carried out at the tribal level, and when killers were actually sentenced to long prison terms, the church grew in a few years to over three thousand believers. In both the Chamula and Zinacanteco tribes the church grew rapidly at times when legal guarantees or law enforcement caused a lull in the persecution and expulsions.

> *Observation: When persecution is slowed or halted as a result of enforcement of the laws of religious freedom, the church is allowed to grow at a maximum rate.*

This does not mean that when law enforcement is able to halt persecution that the growth of the church is guaranteed. An example of slow growth can be seen in the Huixteco tribe in which the persecution was met with immediate legal protection from the Bureau of Indigenous Affairs (see story in chapter 1). Federal police arrested those who carried out the violent persecution, and police guarantees were granted to the Protestant evangelicals. Under this kind of government-sponsored legal protection and defense, the *evangélicos* never suffered more than a very short time of persecution, and no expulsions took place. For a period of approximately fifteen years, the Huixteco Protestant evangelicals lived in relative peace. Persecution was limited to a few instances of local threats and warnings. During this period there was very limited church growth of less than three hundred new believers in Christ. While the application of the law to stop persecution allowed the church to grow, it did not cause it to grow. Tolerance brought about by legal guarantees does not guarantee the spread of the gospel. It must be combined with the responses of love and spiritual warfare to bring the growth of the church.

> *Observation: When the legal option is the only response used to halt persecution against Christians, it can hinder the growth of the church.*

Failure of Law Enforcement

In many cases of religious persecution, the response of seeking legal protection is simply inconsequential. The fact is that, in many countries of the world, the laws that guarantee religious freedom either do not exist, or more commonly, are not enforced. This has been the case in many communist countries. Michael Bourdeaux points out that in Russia the communist constitution guaranteed freedom of religion and separation of church and state. But he tells how Stalin simply made new laws that prevented that freedom from being applied.[3] Although Mexico has clear constitutional guarantees, since 1970 certain factors have prevented them from being enforced. For many years in Chiapas, the legal option has been attempted again and again by persecuted Protestant evangelicals. The underlying assumption was that since the Mexican constitution established clear human and religious rights, halting the unjust persecution was a matter of claiming those rights through the legal or justice system. That assumption, however, has been proven invalid in case after case, since those constitutional rights were not enforced.

Reasons for the Lack of Law Enforcement

In Chiapas and in other areas of the world there are basically three reasons why laws that prohibit persecution are not enforced:

1. When powerful *cacique* systems and tribal mafias promote their own political and financial control, tribal law takes precedence over the country's guarantees for religious freedom. When national or state laws conflict with the tribal laws, all constitutional guarantees are nullified because justice officials do not intervene in these internal tribal affairs.

2. Judicial and governmental officials are willing to accept bribes and payoffs from wealthy mafias in turn for political favors and votes. Thus, the legal-justice system denies all responsibility for religious conflict or persecution. This is a widespread problem throughout much of Latin America.

3. Legal authorities justify their failure to apply the law in cases of religious conflict. They claim that persecution is not within the scope of legal and governmental responsibility since Mexico maintains a strict division of church and state. Some legal authorities attribute all of the religious conflict to foreign influence and interests that threaten traditional values. Other government authorities believe that since Mexico unofficially identifies one religious entity, in this case Catholicism, as the historical and cultural religion of a country, it is a breach of national identity and ethnic pride to grant justice and human rights to anyone who is not a part of that one religious entity.

3. Bourdeaux, *Land of Crosses*, 268.

Christian Response to Ineffective Legal System

Does this mean that when there is a breakdown in the legal system that we should not seek justice for persecuted Christians and that we should not use the legal and governmental protections that are afforded Christians in many situations? The answer to this question has been a highly controversial issue among the leaders of the Tzotzil church. Many of them feel that it is not only a useless response to seek legal help when government authorities fail to enforce the law; they also feel that it is wrong for Christians to place their confidence and invest their time and efforts in corrupt and irresponsible government officials. Many Christian leaders feel strongly that to act as if the solutions to the persecution problems lie in the hands of legal authorities is a denial of the power of God to defend the rights of the church. This issue became so controversial during the Chamula persecution that it led to the major division in the Chamula Presbyterian groups. The two largest Chamula Presbyterian churches split into different presbyteries as a result of this serious conflict of opinion over the response to persecution. After several years of deliberations, the leaders of the Tzotzil Presbytery of Chiapas concluded that while we cannot put our trust in legal solutions, we must respect the legal processes that are stipulated in the constitutional laws.

> *Observation: Christian leaders facing a decision to seek legal options in the face of persecution should report the situation to the government and legal authorities, but not rely solely on legal action in searching for justice.*

The Bible counsels us to submit to the governing authorities (Rom 13:1; Titus 3:1; 1 Pet 2:13); thus it is imperative to respect the laws. This is accomplished by presenting the infraction of laws to the corresponding authorities. The action to be taken will be the responsibility of the authorities themselves. When there is a breakdown of the legal system, Christians will not find legal justice at the local level. In the context of political corruption, they also cannot afford, both morally and financially, to become involved in competing for political favor.

It was noted in chapter 5 that during the threats and warnings stage, when legal rights or actions were demanded and were perceived as a direct challenge to the ethnic group, seeking legal action only heightened the conflict. When such is the case, the legal option is counterproductive. It simply draws the battle lines and increases the tensions of persecution. When Protestant evangelicals went outside tribal limits to solicit help from other authorities, it communicated the message that they were ready to fight against their own people and culture. The ensuing political and/or legal battle simply served to completely alienate all *evangélicos* from their tribal and cultural roots. Such a declaration of war neither helps those being persecuted nor serves the purposes of the communication of the gospel.

> *Observation: At a time when the legal system is inadequate, persecuted Christians should not invest inordinate time and money in seeking legal help.*

However, this does not mean that the legal response is not a part of the solution to expulsion and violence. In a newspaper editorial on January 29, 1991, Concepción Villafuerte dealt with the question, "What do we do about the expulsions [of Christians]?" She listed a few examples of the effective application of legal guarantees that had been carried out through jailing the *caciques* and demanding restitution for those who had been expelled. She pointed out how this kind of governmental action had brought the cessation of specific waves of persecution in the past. The clear statement in this article was: "The answer is very simple: jail for the *cacique* expellers."[4]

That important newspaper article made a clear public statement on how response #1 could have been a solution to the religious expulsions in Chiapas. It also drew attention to the need for the church to be organized in order to make public denouncements and demonstrations to decry the government's lack of responsibility in resolving injustice and persecution. Local Protestant evangelicals working alone will not often receive a just legal response to persecution. For this reason, the national and international church must work with the local *evangélicos* in this way. National and international pressure is a way of compelling state legal systems to apply the law to illegal *cacique* and tribal systems. A unified approach by the church to confront structures that allow and encourage persecution can make the appeal to legal defense a valid Christian response to an ineffective legal system.

Response #2: Counter-Violence and Self-Defense

When all hope for legal defense and government justice is frustrated, and when persecution increases in intensity and violence, the subsequent response is sometimes that of self-defense or counter-violence against the perpetrators of persecution. Christians who suffer prolonged injustice and

---

4. Villafuerte, "Editorial," Jan 29.

persecution and experience years of unresponsive government agencies will at least entertain this response as an option.

On various occasions the persecuted Protestant evangelicals in Chiapas have considered the possible use of self-defense as a viable reaction or response to violent persecution. When the violent expulsions in Chamula were met with deaf ears by government officials, and when the anarchy created in the Chamula tribe exposed the *evangélicos* to robbery, beatings, rape, and even kidnapping and murder, the Chamula believers began to talk of the need to arm themselves in self-defense.

When corrupt government officials refused to arrest or punish any of the *cacique* leaders who had openly committed crimes against Protestant evangelicals in the Mitontic and Chamula areas, some of the *evangélico* leaders actually developed plans to kidnap and hold captive a few of the main *cacique* mafia leaders. One of the local newspapers in San Cristóbal, *Tiempo*, published the news that the expelled Protestants "were organizing themselves to kidnap the *caciques* responsible for the recent expulsions. Since these *caciques* must come to San Cristóbal to carry out their activities, their kidnapping would bring an end to the expulsions: tooth for tooth. Only in this way will the government start to worry about its role in guaranteeing the constitutional rights of Article 24.[5]

The option of responding to persecution with self-defense or counterviolence was officially suggested to the Tzotzil Presbyterians in 1988 when a Christian lawyer from Mexico City, Lic. Jonas Flores, came to offer his help and advice in the difficult Mitontic persecution. He had formed a Christian political action group called El Grupo Lerdo, which was offering its services as a Christian political and legal defense organization. However, after a couple of years of disillusionment in finding all political and government doors closed to justice for persecuted Protestant evangelicals, Jonas Flores concluded that the only solution for the injustice in the indigenous tribal areas was to arm Protestant evangelicals in their own homes and villages so that they could defend themselves. His argument was that the Mexican constitutional law allowed citizens to defend with arms their private property and homes against the illegal confiscations, expulsions, and crimes of the tribal mafias.

On yet another occasion in 1989, the angry and frustrated Chenalhó Protestant evangelicals actually discussed the idea of capturing and holding prisoner one or two of the ring-leaders responsible for the persecution problems in the Chenalhó tribal area. This forced all of us to struggle with

5. Villafuerte, "Editorial," Nov 6.

the question: Is the use of violence, either in the form of self-defense or kidnappings, a valid response for Christians, to pressure for justice?

Biblical Guidelines for the Response of Violence

Although the temptation was great for the Tzotzil Protestant Christians to fight fire with fire and to defend themselves against the aggression of persecution, they realized that such actions would be nothing more than a response of anger and revenge. Even though the use of counter-violence and self-defense might attract national and international government attention, it appeared that such offensive action would be counterproductive for Christians and for the church.

In the first place, the biblical guidelines indicate that this response would be inappropriate. Although the Old Testament lists various examples of God's people defending themselves with armed action against foreign invasions (Judg 7) and against injustice (Esth 9:5-17), and even though examples such as David killing Goliath (1 Sam 17:45–54) certainly illustrate the use of counter-violence and self-defense, it is clear that the purpose was to reveal God's power and protection, not the power of the sword. David himself said that it was so that all would "know that it is not by sword or spear that the Lord saves" (1 Sam 17:47).

Moreover, the use of violence is discouraged in the following Old Testament examples: "Do not say, 'I'll pay you back for this wrong!' Wait for the Lord, and he will deliver you" (Prov 20:22). "Do not say, 'I'll do to him as he has done to me; I'll pay that man back for what he did'" (Prov 24:29). Leviticus 19:18 teaches: "Do not seek revenge or bear a grudge against one of your people, but love your neighbor as yourself. I am the Lord."

However, in looking to the Old Testament we must remember that it is not dealing specifically with a response in the cases of persecution. Thus, we must clarify our position by looking at the New Testament, where we find a clear statement that we are not only to show non-vengeance-seeking love to our neighbors but also to "Love your enemies and pray for those who persecute you" (Matt 5:44). Paul made an even stronger statement in speaking specifically about our response to persecution: "Bless those who persecute you; bless and do not curse" (Rom 12:14). Then he concludes the same chapter with what would clearly refer to those who persecute us:

> Do not repay anyone evil for evil. Be careful to do what is right in the eyes of everybody. If it is possible, as far as it depends on you, live at peace with everyone. Do not take revenge, my friends, but leave room for God's wrath, for it is written: "It is

mine to avenge; I will repay," says the Lord. On the contrary: "If your enemy is hungry, feed him; if he is thirsty, give him something to drink. In doing this, you will heap burning coals on his head." Do not be overcome by evil but overcome evil with good. (Rom 12:17–21)

Immediately following this passage is the Romans 13 counsel to submit to governing authorities. Paul surely is not urging us to respond in self-defense or counter-violence when he says: "When we are cursed, we bless; when we are persecuted, we endure it; when we are slandered, we answer kindly. Up to this moment we have become the scum of the earth, the refuse of the world" (1 Cor 4:12–13). It is obvious in verse 9 that Paul is saying this in the very context of persecution.

> *Observation: Both the Old and New Testaments discourage the use of counter-violence as a response to persecution.*

Practical Results of Use of Violence

Not only do the biblical guidelines indicate that the response of violence and self-defense would yield negative results; the practical results also confirm this response as counterproductive.

An Escalation of the Conflict

As the Tzotzil Presbytery leaders discussed the consequences of a violent response to persecution, they realized that it would not lead to a reduction of persecution but rather to an escalation of the conflict. An offensive attack of any kind against the *caciques* would only invite a more violent attack on all Protestant evangelicals. Even though the holding of hostages or some violent attack against the persecutors might afford a short lull in the hostilities and even attract government attention, the eventual result would be a heightening of the confrontation. The Tzotzil Protestant evangelicals well understood the kind of retribution that brought on persecution in the initial stages, and they knew that the tribal leaders would retaliate with even greater violence if they were threatened with counter-violence. Thus, the result would be even more persecution and suffering for the *evangélicos*.

> *Observation: The use of counter-violence in response to persecution will escalate the conflict rather than minimize persecution.*

Revolution and War

The Tzotzil Protestant evangelicals were keenly aware that in their culture the response of counter-violence would lead to an escalation of violence, and ultimately to war and revolution. The first fear that the Tzotzil *evangélicos* had of entering into such a war was that it would result in much destruction and many deaths. Since the Tzotzils knew that the tribal *caciques* were well equipped with machine-guns and automatic weapons, to think about armed confrontation would have been a deadly affair. As they heard about the Central American conflict, there were no real winners, only death. For this same reason, Jesus himself never encouraged the use of arms. As Enrique Dussel says in his discussion of subversive armed violence: "Jesus had no desire to enter into the dialectic of mutual annihilation: 'Put your sword back, for all who draw the sword will die by the sword' (Matt 26:52)."[6]

The second fear for the Tzotzil Protestant Christians was that violent revolution against their oppressors would not have accomplished the goals of freedom from oppression and persecution, even if they had the arms and weapons to win. Andrew J. Kirk, in *Theology Encounters Revolution*, quotes from Paul Lehman: "No revolution has been able to fulfill adequately its promise of freedom and equality."[7] Kirk shows that Dussel clarifies the problem of involvement in revolution and war: "Subversive armed violence prepares one for domination. The dominator, however, is always eliminated, and his place is occupied by a new dominator."[8] The Tzotzil Protestant evangelicals would have liked to eliminate those *caciques* that oppressed and dominated them, but they also knew from their own cultural history that other mafia groups would replace them.

The subversive armed movement of the Zapatista Army for National Liberation, EZLN, that emerged in Chiapas in 1994 attempted to convince all of the indigenous people of Chiapas that armed insurrection was that answer to the deep social and political problems in Mexico. The overwhelming majority of Protestant evangelicals in Chiapas rejected the armed movement because they knew that this would be counterproductive. While most agreed with the fight for justice and indigenous rights, they disagreed with use of arms because of tribal precedents and biblical criterion.

Only two times in Chiapas have the indigenous Christians used self-defense. In 1995, some of the Chamula Christians who returned to the tribal areas from which they had been expelled used arms and two-way

6. Dussel, *History of the Church*, 174.

7. Kirk, *Theology Encounters Revolution*, 89.

8. Kirk, *Theology Encounters Revolution*, 175.

radios to defend their families against their persecutors. While these armed confrontations resulted in numerous injuries and deaths, some observers believe that this armed stand against the *caciques* did help the Christians gain respect. Some Chamula Christians believe this was the only way to communicate with the persecutors that Christians are not cowards who can just be pushed around.

The second incident took place in March 1996, in the Amatenango village of El Puerto. Following several years of expulsions and violence against these new *evangélicos*, a lay missionary used arms to rescue some of the believers from physical harm. In this case the persecutors backed down when confronted with an armed threat from the Protestants. In both cases the use of arms for self-defense came at times of anger and frustration with the blatant injustice, the lack of legal recourse, and the human pain and suffering caused by persecutors. While these actions were understandable, no clear conclusions can be drawn from them.

It is precisely at the point of greatest frustration that we must turn back to the biblical counsel, which helps us realize that our goal in facing persecution is not to crush the persecutors. Christians in the midst of conflict in their culture must be interested in renewing that culture, not destroying it. We must always be conscious that the intention of the church of Jesus Christ is not to damage a culture but rather to affirm and fulfill it through the gospel. Just as we are not called to destroy people but to combat the evil that destroys them, so we are not called to dismantle cultures and peoples but to bring spiritual and social revitalization.[9] This will not be brought about by legal or physical might; it will come through the power of unconditional love.

Response #3: Love towards Persecutors

The New Testament gives very clear guidance for how we are to respond to persecutors. Romans 12:14 says it plainly: "Bless those who persecute you." Matthew 5:44 tells us: "Love your enemies and pray for those who persecute you." The emphasis of the New Testament is that we are to respond in love to those who persecute us. We are to pray that they, too, may respond to the message of Jesus Christ.

However, while it is easy to acknowledge that the New Testament speaks of loving those who persecute us, this certainly is not the normal human response to persecution. As one Tzotzil *evangélico* said after being humiliated, beaten, jailed, and expelled from his tribe: "How can I ever love

---

9. Hallie, *Lest Innocent Blood*, 11.

those who did that to my family and to me?" The answer to that comes in 1 John 4:19: "We love because he [God] first loved us." We are not called to love what persecutors do to us, but we are commanded both in the Old and New Testaments (Lev 19:18, 34; Deut 10:19; Matt 19:19; John 13:34) to love them whether they are neighbors or strangers.

> *Observation: Scripture teaches us that love should be our primary response to persecution.*

Powerful Love

There is no more powerful response than the kind of love that can return good for evil, love for hate. It is powerful because it is the only response that has the potential to transform culture and society in a way that will revitalize it rather than destroy it.

Protestant Christians in Chiapas are beaten, imprisoned, thrown from their homes, robbed of their possessions and land, and sometimes killed. Occasionally, the immediate human response is anger and revenge. Some want to strike back and use violence (response #2). Others who are persecuted in a democracy like Mexico want to look to the law to seek justice against the persecutors (response #1). However, the most effective Christian response to persecution is not to seek revenge or to demand justice but to respond in love. It should be noted here that this is the significant difference in response when the source of the persecution is internal. When the source is internal, from one's own ethnic group and people, the most effective response is love.

When Pedro Ac'obal, the Chamula tribal leader who planned and carried out the kidnapping and brutal torture and murder of the leader of the Chamula Protestant evangelicals, was captured and put in jail, the *evangélicos* in due time responded by reaching out to the killer with forgiveness and love. After the believers visited him and shared the gospel message with him, the killer cried: "Incredible! Those same *evangélicos* that I wanted to kill just kept on loving me!"

The Christian response to those who violently persecute should be: "No matter what you do to me, I'm going to keep on loving you!" That is powerful love, and Satan has no defense against it! It is the kind of love that was exemplified by the first-century Christians. It was this love for those who persecuted them that made a dramatic effect upon all of the people around them.

The effort to follow Christ and respond in love to those who persecute them can put Christians in danger of additional violence and pain.
Christians must consciously make a decision to risk loving those who abuse
them. When Tzotzil Protestant evangelicals hear news of sickness, demon
possession, death, or despair out in the non-Christian tribal villages from
which they have been expelled, they courageously send gifted witnesses to
share this powerful love. They often send their best people into the most
difficult situations. They don't say: "Wait, that's a dangerous village; we can't
risk our best preachers and evangelists!" No, they send out their best people
to pray for divine healing, to tell of freedom from fear and demonic oppression. They give their church offerings to help the poor and to buy medicine
for the sick. They risk their best leaders to share salvation in Christ. They
respond to persecutors by saying: "No matter what you do to us, we are
going to keep on loving you."

This love could also be called persistent love. To respond in this way
requires the gift of the Holy Spirit (Acts 1:8). It calls for a strong belief in the
truth of the gospel message. It demands a powerful faith in God's protection. It requires a clear trust in the promise of blessings in facing persecution. This response of love in the face of hostile situations seldom emerges
as a spontaneous, automatic reaction. Rather, this response must be taught
to Christians. This kind of persistent love usually results from a conscious
decision of the community of believers in Christ. The leaders of a specific
church must teach its people that their first and most important response to
persecution is love and forgiveness. It is not only a fruit of the Spirit, but also
an intentional response of believers to persecution and to the persecutors.
It must be emphasized, planned, and taught as an intentional strategy of the
corporate body of Christ.

The church can also use the natural springboard of ethnic cohesion
to promote the response of love. Those who have been persecuted and/or
expelled will have parents, brothers and sisters, and other extended family
and relatives from whom they have been cut off. It only takes encouragement from the Christian group to reignite feelings of love and concern for
these family members. Persecuted Christians will readily show interest in
making contact with their close kinship groups who have persecuted them,
but in order for these contacts to exemplify powerful love, Christians must
consciously decide on the basis of Scripture to reach out in love to those
who have treated them so unlovingly.

> *Observation: Powerful love is a response that must be intentionally
> taught to and planned by persecuted Christians.*

Forgiveness

When Christians do respond in love, the first part of that response will need to be forgiveness. In chapter 3 we noted that Jesus (Luke 23:34) and Stephen (Acts 7:60) are our best examples of this unconditional forgiveness.

The Tzotzil *evangélicos* admit that this is the most difficult element of the Christian response. Forgiveness seems to be an especially scarce commodity in the Tzotzil worldview. It is traditionally never given without the proper sacrifice or gift offered by the person who has wronged another. Thus, it is hard for Christians to come to the point of offering forgiveness to those who have wronged them. However, many of the Tzotzil *evangélicos* have learned that forgiveness is an essential ingredient in their response to persecution, even in very violent cases.

Only two months after Shtumina Coltesh's husband, Shalic, became a Protestant evangelical, their whole family was expelled from Chamula. A few months later Shalic, a former shaman, returned to his tribal village because he had left behind a cornfield. His wife didn't find out until three days later that when he entered his native village, he was beaten to death and thrown into a shallow stream. The family sought justice, but the governmental authorities declared the cause of death was accidental drowning.

Shtumina Coltesh was left with eight young children and a lot of anger in her heart. But she later shared that anger only made her more miserable; it didn't hurt the killers. They didn't care if they were forgiven or not. God slowly convinced her that she could only go on living if she forgave her own villagers for killing her husband. It was only after she was willing to forgive that the burden of anger and hate was lifted from her heart. Later, when serious sickness struck the families of the murderers, the Protestant evangelicals responded by praying for them and helping them. Because of this, the men who killed her husband became *evangélicos* and were forced to move to the same relocation village where she lived. So, forgiveness not only changed her, it also eventually changed them.

> Observation: It is the response of love and forgiveness that consequently brings the continued growth of the church in spite of persecution.

Power Healing

Responding in love to persecution must also address the felt needs of those who have persecuted the believers in Christ. Otherwise, it will not be

recognized as a response of love, but only as a gimmick of Protestant proselytism. The response must also fit within the boundaries that are allowable
in the culture's worldview. In the Tzotzil culture, power healing satisfies
both of those requirements and has proven to be the primary witness of the
evangélicos in hostile situations.

Tzotzil Protestant evangelicals were often invited back into their tribal
villages at night, under the cover of darkness, to pray for the healing of
someone who was seriously ill. In the face of possible beatings and death
if they were caught, these lay leaders dared to call on the power of God,
and they were rewarded with miraculous healing of diseases. As the power
of God was revealed through healing, the number of invitations increased,
which in turn caused more persecution threats and more conflict. But the
Tzotzil *evangélicos* did not believe that they should fear the threats of their
persecutors or that their all-pervasive goal should be to seek peace. They
would agree with Arthur Glasser: "The church will not grow if our most
important priority is to keep peace."[10] Therefore, the Tzotzil believers continued to accept invitations to return to their tribal villages to answer pleas
for help.

It is this response—that included offering prayers and giving financial
help for medical aid—which was the Tzotzil believers' powerful demonstration of love to their persecutors. In other cultures and situations, very different felt needs could open the doors for reaching back with love into hostile
areas. However, since physical illness was rampant in most Tzotzil villages,
the need for healing was the number one necessity. The Tzotzil worldview,
which views illness as having spiritual causes and cures, readily accepted
divine healing rather than a medical approach.

Evangelism that was done with an emphasis on evangelism through
divine healing became the natural focus of communicating the message of
Jesus Christ to the Tzotzils. Even before any incidence of persecution, we
realized that the Tzotzil worldview demanded a holistic approach to healing. The secular anthropologists who have studied the Tzotzil culture also
saw the worldview "as espousing an integrated or unified view of illness."[11]
At the same time, these anthropologists readily confirmed that, for the
Tzotzils, this holistic healing takes place principally through supernatural
forces. While they acknowledged that the exorcists or seers in the Tzotzil
culture use some natural remedies, like herbs and liquor, they also admitted

10. Arthur Glasser, interview by Vernon Sterk, Fuller Theological Seminary, Pasadena, CA, Jan 30, 1989.

11. Fabrega and Silver, *Illness and Shamanistic Curing*, 82.

that even the use of such treatments has "its origin in supernatural revelation rather than empirical observation."[12]

Therefore, since supernatural healing is such a core element in the Tzotzil worldview, it follows that power healing would provide the window for reintroduction of the powerful love of Christ into areas where the door had been slammed shut by persecution. Only spiritual power and power encounter can crack open these closed doors. C. Peter Wagner, in *Spiritual Power and Church Growth*, has correctly observed that in most of Latin America we are communicating the gospel in cultures that view the source of power over life and death as supernatural. In breaking down the barriers of persecution "this power cannot be broken with logical arguments. It can only be broken with greater power."[13]

Power healing is probably the only method that has the impact to penetrate the hostile areas of the Tzotzil tribes and demonstrate powerful love. Most other forms of evangelism require long periods of time to restore valid contact in tribal areas, since they basically present "the word aspect of the gospel message without much of the power aspect (1 Cor 4:20)."[14] Although the word aspect of the gospel is important in sharing love in response to persecution, it will not impact felt needs. As Kraft says, "Though it provides abundant *knowledge about* the things of God, there is not a corresponding demonstration of the works of God."[15]

Most Tzotzils who were struggling with serious illness were mainly concerned with who has the power to help them. For years they have trusted tribal shamans to make healing power accessible to them when they needed it. Christianity presented a demonstration of the works of God that was more powerful and more accessible than anything they had ever known. Even though persecution has placed a monumental obstacle in the path of evangelization, the Tzotzils found ways around that obstruction in order to have access to God's healing power.

> *Observation: Love shown through power healing carries the worldview and spiritual impact that opens doors that have been closed by persecution.*

A Zinacanteco woman from the village of Va'alton had been sick for fifteen years. Her husband had spent most of their meager income on

12. Fabrega and Silver, *Illness and Shamanistic Curing*, 82.

13. Wagner, *Spiritual Power*, 41.

14. Kraft, *Christianity with Power*, xi.

15. Kraft, *Christianity with Power*, xii.

animistic shamans in search of a cure. Even though they knew that contact with the persecuted expelled Protestant evangelicals might bring a similar persecution to them, they were interested in the power that these *evangélicos* supposedly had to pray for healing and cast out evil spirits. So, when this woman's brother-in-law told her that he had talked to one of the expelled believers who could pray to God for her healing, she responded. In a few weeks, through the prayers of the persecuted Protestant evangelicals, this woman became an *evangélico* and was healed completely. As the word soon passed through family lines, a neighboring family also called on the believers to pray for someone in their family who was sick. Again, the result was healing and a decision to become believers in Christ.

It has become clear to the Tzotzils that to communicate the gospel message of love in the midst of hostility and persecution, they must be aware of the focus on power healing in evangelism. C. Peter Wagner says it well: "For people in close touch with the spirit world, a style of evangelism that involves a power encounter is usually more effective than other ways of focusing the gospel message."[16]

> Observation: *The response of love towards persecutors demonstrated through power healing causes the growth of the church in spite of the obstacles of persecution.*

The above story of healing in the Tzotzil tribes could be told over with slight variations hundreds of times. When I questioned a sampling of new Zinacanteco Protestant evangelicals about what had attracted them to the gospel despite the threat of persecution, the overwhelming majority stated that it was the power of God to heal. Much the same attraction was a factor in the growth of the early church. In his book *Martyrdom and Persecution in the Early Church*, W. H. C. Frend says: "The Christians possessed strong means of attracting their fellows, especially the underprivileged members of classical society. Their claim to overthrow demons, or in other words free men from the overwhelming power of Fate was one factor."[17]

Cultural Respect

Although we often do not include it in our list of responses, to show love in the face of persecution should also be reflected in an overt respect for the

16. Wagner, *How to Have a Healing Ministry*, 149.

17. Frend, *Martyrdom and Persecution*, 257.

traditional indigenous culture. This should be expressed in a careful consideration for the indigenous worldview as well as in an obvious attempt to maintain the cultural respect for forms and functions within the biblical context.

Much of the burden for careful attention to maintaining cultural respect in times of persecution falls on the missionary and mature indigenous Christian leaders. New believers in Christ who are undergoing persecution are suffering both great emotional trauma and also resentment toward the culture that has caused them this pain and persecution. Therefore, their immediate response, especially following violent expulsion, is to reject all traditional and cultural norms and replace them with what they would assume to be Christian ones.

It is precisely at this point that the missionary or a church leader must take an active role to ensure that the indigenous Christians do not lose all love and respect for their cultural heritage. There are specific areas that must be approached with the indigenous Christians and leaders: decision-making patterns; community structures; traditional dress; worship forms; and music. Someone must encourage them to maintain cultural forms, and not just adopt the missionary or dominant culture's patterns. Someone who is culturally sensitive must be available to counsel them to be proud of their cultural heritage, to strive to maintain their cultural identity, to be fully indigenous and fully Christian, and to avoid in every way possible cutting themselves off from their tribe and people.

Vern encouraged Christian leaders to respect their culture.

When expelled Zinacanteco Protestant evangelicals moved out of their animistic villages to the new relocation community of Vida Nueva, their goal was to form a truly Christian community, but they weren't sure what that meant. They asked if traditional instruments were permissible in worship. They wondered if there were certain Christian music and tunes that they had to use for writing hymns. When the first couple was to be married, they sought counsel on what dress, symbols, and forms could be maintained from their culture and incorporated into a Christian wedding. When the first believer died, they again had to make decisions on what aspects of their culture could be included in a Christian funeral. These new Protestant evangelicals made a conscious attempt to respect their culture and maintain as many forms and symbols from their traditional customs as Scripture allows.

The *evangélicos* were constantly thinking of how they could have a positive influence on their traditional culture even while wounds were being inflicted on them in the battle between the kingdom of Satan and the kingdom of God. Because the Christians had made this their goal, their non-Christian relatives could respond to invitations to visit and they felt comfortable attending weddings and funerals in the relocation communities. If cultural respect attracts people to the gospel and opens tribal doors to evangelism, then we have the ultimate measure of whether the response of love toward persecutors is effective. This response of love will also result in church growth.

> *Observation: Love shown through cultural respect attracts people to the gospel and opens tribal doors to evangelism.*

Summary

I have reviewed three responses of individual Christians toward persecution. The first is an appeal to legal defense and a claim for protection by the law, the second is the use of counter-violence, and the third is the response of love toward persecutors. Whether individual believers in Christ choose to remain in their villages and become underground believers or make the decision to escape persecution and join a relocation community, they will ultimately choose one or a combination of the three responses discussed in this chapter. The response of love is central to the growth of the church in facing persecution.

Chapter 9

National and International Church Response to Persecution

IT IS THE RESPONSIBILITY of the organized church to respond to persecution. The organized church should be involved in giving spiritual support along with material assistance and aid. Its participation is especially important when persecution finds its roots in political and legal injustice. As already noted in chapter 8, the church can play an important role in giving persecuted Christians necessary legal counsel and representation as well as in pressuring governments to respect laws and human rights.

National Church Response

When persecuted Christians at the local (congregational or presbyterial) level find that all of their attempts to seek solutions to continued injustice, violence, and expulsion are repeatedly disregarded, they have no other recourse but to appeal to the national church. The actual organization that would be identified as the national church within a particular country depends on the particular denomination or affiliation to which the local group has become associated. In countries where a national church structure does exist, the importance of the participation and response of this national organization cannot be ignored.

For twenty years (1970–90) the Tzotzil churches attempted to face persecution conflicts with little help from the national church. Even though pleas were made to the National Presbyterian Church of Mexico during the time of the Chamula expulsions of 1972, no organized response was made. Although missionary Gerald Van Engen and I became involved in relief and relocation efforts to help expelled Presbyterian Tzotzils, these efforts were carried out through the Chiapas Mission of the Reformed Church in America. There was almost no national participation.

The fact that the persecuted Presbyterians in Chiapas found no significant support or solidarity from the national church during the early years of persecution seemed to be due to the following factors: First, the National Presbyterian Church felt that the persecution was only occurring in isolated incidents on local levels and in indigenous tribal areas. Second, the assumption was that national involvement would accomplish very little. It was thought that these conflicts must be resolved at the local and tribal levels. Third, the National Presbyterian Church of Mexico had no experience in dealing with persecution, and it was not organized to respond to these needs. Fourth, it was assumed that the missionaries who were working closely with the local churches should be the most capable of meeting persecution needs.

Legal and Governmental Representation

Persecuted Christians soon realized that expatriate missionaries were not allowed to represent them in both legal and governmental relations. For most of the monolingual indigenous *evangélicos* the complicated legal maneuvering, as well as the language barriers, made it indispensable to search for legal counsel. However, non-Christian Mexican lawyers from private and government sectors were part of the general breakdown of the legal system. It became apparent that an honest Mexican Christian lawyer was needed.

In the early 1980s, my good Christian friend, lawyer Pablo Salazar M., volunteered his professional services in several of the persecution cases. While his representation was of great value for almost ten years, he faced almost insurmountable obstacles. First, he lived and practiced law in Tuxtla Gutiérrez, which meant that he was located too far away to deal with the government Indigenous Affairs Bureau in San Cristóbal. Second, he could not dedicate sufficient time to meet the needs, since he was volunteering his time apart from his private practice. Third, he was not a member of the Presbyterian Church of Mexico, nor was he officially recognized as a legal representative for the National Presbyterian Church.

Although Lic. Pablo Salazar made faithful and concerted efforts to defend persecuted Presbyterians in legal and governmental negotiations for the return of expelled *evangélicos* (most notably in the Mitontic persecutions), the breakdown of the justice system caused all of his attempts to end in frustration. The lesson that was learned through his disappointed efforts was that, unless there are relationships and pressure at the national level, local appeals for justice will fail.

> *Observation: Persecuted Christians need legal assistance that is coordinated at the national church level.*

Need for National Church Involvement

On January 24, 1990, the leaders of the Tzotzil Presbytery attended a meeting that was the first of its kind. The president and secretary of the National Presbyterian Church of Mexico called for a gathering of the representatives of persecuted Christians from the Tojolabal and Tzotzil tribes. It was held in Tuxtla Gutiérrez, the capital city of Chiapas. The purpose of the interchange was for the National Church leaders to express their interest in helping meet emergency needs of the growing number of persecuted Presbyterians in Chiapas. The outcome of the gathering was that the leaders of the Tzotzil Presbytery gained a new vision of the possibilities for National Presbyterian Church involvement in resolving persecution problems.

The Tzotzils followed up the formal meeting by formulating a document that they sent to the National Church. Their suggestions were that the General Assembly of the National Presbyterian Church of Mexico confront persecution on three essential levels:

1. Spiritual: that a system of communication be formed to inform all of the churches in Mexico about specific persecution cases, for the purpose of forming prayer chains and special fasts for brothers and sisters who are persecuted.

2. Political and legal: (a) that the officers of the National Church request personal interviews with state and national political authorities, in order to press for the enforcement of the laws of the Mexican Constitution; (b) that the General Assembly form a Legal Defense Committee in Chiapas, for the purpose of representation in legal and judicial cases of persecution.

3. Material aid: that a permanent monetary fund be created by the General Assembly that could be used for emergency refugee needs; in cases of necessity, this might also be used to help with the relocation needs of expelled Christians.[1]

---

1. Tzotzil Presbytery of Chiapas, "Letter."

The document was mailed to the National Presbyterian Church of Mexico, and it received an immediate positive response. Ignacio Castaneda, who was president of the General Assembly of the Presbyterian Church at that time, made a personal visit to some of the relocation and refugee communities in February 1990. He was especially touched by the needs of the newly arrived refugees from the Mitontic persecution. He promised that the national church would respond to the persecution in Chiapas with a new attitude of solidarity.

> *Observation: Persecuted Christians need national church involvement and solidarity in spiritual, legal-political, and material aid.*

Political Action

In February 1990, Rev. Jorge López Pérez, who was then secretary of the General Assembly of the National Presbyterian Church of Mexico, reported that there had been recent outbursts of persecution in various parts of Mexico, including one large and violent incident in Mexico City. This incident marked the first open persecution of Presbyterians in Mexico City for over thirty years.[2] The General Assembly planned to take organized action. Their plan was comprised of three parts:

1. Organized protests were made to federal and state offices and authorities, demanding that the laws of Mexico be enforced and applied in persecution cases.

2. Communication was opened with international organizations on the subject of political and religious freedom. The goal was to put pressure on Mexican political parties to respond to the demand for human rights through the international church organizations and human rights organizations.

3. Communication was disseminated to all Mexican Presbyterian churches to plan spiritual warfare against the forces of persecution by scheduling a week of prayer and other spiritual and prayer offensives.[3]

The intentions for involvement of the national church matched the vision of the persecuted Tzotzils. The goal was to show solidarity and united political action in the National Presbyterian Church of Mexico so that national pressure might bring pressure for justice and human rights at the

2. *World*, "Violent Attack."

3. Jorge López Pérez, interview by Vernon Sterk, Feb 7, 1990.

local levels where persecution is encountered. In March 1990, responses were forthcoming from the federal government in Mexico City. On March 6, 1990, the leaders of three of the major Protestant churches in Mexico (including the National Presbyterian Church) were invited for a personal interview with the president of Mexico, Carlos Salinas de Gortari, in the presidential palace. This represented the first time in the history of Mexico that leaders of Protestant churches had been received on an official basis by any president of Mexico. Along with the opening of dialogue between church and state officials, the opportunity was presented to request justice and human rights for persecuted Protestant evangelicals who are also Mexican citizens. The president promised to work through *Gobernación* (National Department of Internal Affairs) to put an end to all religious persecution in Mexico during his term in office.[4] A special religious rights poster published by the national circulation newspaper, *Excelsior*, was distributed to all of the national churches involved in the dialogue.[5] In Chiapas, all of the Presbyterian congregations in persecuted areas began to display this poster in their church buildings.

On March 25, 1990, lawyer Pablo Salazar informed me that a new human rights group formed by the state senators in Chiapas had called him asking for information that could help them start to work against the many abuses of human rights and religious persecution in Chiapas.[6] On June 6, 1990, a presidential decree in the federal government's *Diario Oficial* announced the creation of a new National Commission of Human Rights.[7] Also, in the month of March 1990, announcements began appearing on the Chiapas state radio station XERA. This radio transmitter reaches to all of the Indian areas of Chiapas. *Evangélicos* came to us reporting that the Chiapas state governor had declared on the radio news that anyone perpetrating persecution against Protestants or Catholics in the tribal areas would be put in jail.

> *Observation: Political action by national churches and Christian defense organizations can affect a response from government organizations.*

4. *Novedades*, "Reportaje Especial."

5. Poster on Presidential Statement to Protestants in Mexico, in *Excelsior* (Mar 8, 1990).

6. Pablo Salazar Mendiguchia, interview by Vernon Sterk, Tuxtla Gutiérrez, Chiapas, Mar 25, 1990.

7. *Tiempo*, "A la Opinión Pública."

Legal Defense Organization

Along with political action, another area in which the national church can offer crucial help to those suffering persecutions is through the formation of a nationally sponsored Legal Defense Organization. Many obstacles confronted Christian lawyer Pablo Salazar when he attempted to wage an individual and local battle in legal defense of specific cases. When he received threats of violence against himself and his family if he continued to represent the *evangélicos* in Chiapas, Lawyer Salazar felt that he could no longer continue. The threats reportedly came directly from a high state government official. The National Presbyterian Church responded by officially forming a Legal Defense Organization under the auspices of the General Assembly of the Presbyterian Church in Mexico. This organization was given the title of CEDECH (State Committee for Evangelical Defense in Chiapas).

On October 31, 1990, in coordination with the synods and presbyteries that were involved in the principle areas of persecution in Chiapas, Presbyterian lawyer Abdías Tovilla Jaime presented the formal plan for this persecution defense. The local newspaper in San Cristóbal recognized this move as an important step in resolving future persecution conflicts at both the local and national levels. This was seen as an attempt "to create a link between national and state committees so that the problems in the state, in relation to expulsions, would have national diffusion. Also . . . strengthening the legal representation of the Presbyterian church in Chiapas."[8]

In connection with CEDECH, the National Presbyterian Church set up an administrative board made up of Chiapas church leaders. Emergency funds were provided to this board to handle specific persecution and refugee needs as well as costs for office and travel. As the legal committee and the administrative board coordinated their work with the local presbyteries, the organized attempt to meet persecution needs began to function. Ten years of CEDECH's service to the persecuted church resulted in gaining justice for many of the Protestant Christians in Chiapas, and CEDECH brought pressure to bear on judicial and political institutions of the government that ultimately played a part in breaking down the walls of persecution.

> *Observation: The establishment of a legal defense organization at the local level is an essential part of the effort to bring relief to persecuted Christians.*

8. Sierra Martínez, "Los evangélicos," 4.

Positive Effects of the Persecution Defense Effort

The immediate effect of the work of a local defense organization was a shift in the Mexican government's attitude toward persecution. The General Assembly of the National Presbyterian Church was afforded direct access to *Gobernación* in order to communicate any future cases of persecution. Promises were made that there would be investigations of injustice in persecution cases in Chiapas. Although this did not result in instant respite for persecuted Protestant evangelicals, it did begin to affect public opinion, and a change in attitude was reflected in the national press.[9] The state and local press publications also began to publish articles that related the facts about the government's embarrassing record in cases of persecution and human rights.[10]

While this change of attitude may seem quite inconsequential in actual solutions to persecution problems, it did eventually swing public opinion in Mexico and Chiapas. When public opinion began to demand a halt to expulsions and human rights abuses in the Indian tribes, the pressure on all levels of political entities was vital. Especially in a time of expanding political plurality in Mexico, the PRI party became very sensitive to press and public criticism. While many factors must be taken into account, the amazing reduction in persecution in the decade of the 1990s could be clearly seen.

> Observation: *The involvement of the national Christian defense organizations is effective in the search for long-term solutions to the persecution conflict.*

Even at the local and tribal levels, where the persecution battles were fierce, the evangelical defense effort exerted its effect. The public declarations and radio announcements that result from national church pressure became powerful factors in the growth of the church in persecuted areas at the local level.

The persecuted Presbyterians in the Zinacanteco tribe reported that many were joining their church because they had heard the governor's publicity campaign against religious persecution. Many of them were hearing for the first time that they did have constitutional guarantees for freedom of worship. Several requested the pamphlet on Article 24 of the Mexican Constitution that was published by IMLIR, Mexican Institute for Religious

9. Martinez García, "Existe," 2; and "Indígenas protestantes," 2.

10. Villafuerte, "Editorial" Jun 19.

Liberty.[11] Indigenous people were made aware of the laws regarding individual religious profession and the rights of corporate worship. Many of them had never heard that indigenous people had the legal right to hold home worship services and construct church buildings.

**Church buildings, constructed by indigenous Christians,
are now permitted in most villages.**

They certainly had never been told that they had the legal right to refuse to participate in traditional religious duties such as the *cargo* positions.

Indigenous tribal leaders and *caciques* had been successful in convincing their people that no laws allowed freedom to practice any religion other than the traditional animistic folk religion. When the national church response to persecution reached into the tribal areas, it became a factor in breaking down the power of the *caciques* and their resolve to use persecution as a means of political control. When the winds of freedom began to sweep over the tribal areas and create a ground swell of resistance to the mafia control among the grass-roots people, the potential for moving toward persecution solutions was greatly increased.

11. Flores, "El Artículo 24 Constitucional," 1–2.

A Temporary Lull in the Conflict

The most observable extended effect of the national church involvement was the temporary interval in persecution hostilities. The shock waves of government declarations caused the mafia leaders to take some time to re-group. It took the *caciques* some time to test out the seriousness of the government declarations about the enforcement of laws concerning religious freedom in the indigenous tribes.

During the 1990s, the *evangélicos* enjoyed a time of relative peace. Some of the Tzequemtic Presbyterians were even convinced that the expulsions and violent persecution were over, and that these freedoms were theirs to claim. In a six-month interim in which there was a relaxation of hostility, the Protestant evangelicals found that the number attending their house churches nearly doubled. They even started a second house church group to accommodate the growing number of believers in Christ. A lull in persecution allowed an increase in church growth.

> *Observation: When the fear of persecution abates, the church may grow at a greatly increased rate.*

While a lull in hostilities did allow for growth among the *evangélicos*, the pause in persecution was usually temporary. The first successful attempts in pressuring for legal and political guarantees did not assure a lasting peace or permanent justice in persecution situations. *Cacique* leaders eventually tested the threat to their political power by renewing persecution or expulsions. If the local government agencies then reneged on the promises that were made at a state or national level, persecution often resumed with even greater intensity.

Because government promises were not enacted, I witnessed renewed persecution problems in the Mitontic, Chamula, Zinacanteco, and Amatenango tribes. The local Indigenous Affairs Bureau attempted to make the renewed expulsions in the Zinacanteco tribe appear to be voluntary departures of Presbyterians. The state governor, Patrocinio Gonzalez Garrido, failed to honor his promises of justice because of the political implications, explaining that the solution to the expulsions was not in "a cold application of the law."[12] But this did not invalidate the endeavor of the national church defense organizations to put an end to religious persecution in Mexico. The effects were slow in reaching the grass-roots level. Governments worked very slowly in turning around the corruption and injustice at the

12. Henriquez Tobar, "Las Expulsiones," 4.

state and local levels. But the pressure had to be continued, and the unity of the church had to be maintained in encountering persecution issues. It was this kind of national and internal pressure that finally brought about the dramatic changes that were seen in the Soviet Union and other Eastern Bloc countries. In Chiapas, the pressure created at the national level by the National Presbyterian Church of Mexico was effective in tipping the scales of justice to bring a cessation of persecution. By the year 2000, persecution in Chiapas had almost been eliminated.

Solidarity—Unity of the Church

Not only does the participation of the national church positively affect legal and political sectors, it also builds solidarity in the church itself. In chapter 7, the unity of the church is discussed as one of the potential positive results of persecution. This unity is greatly enhanced when the national church is involved in showing solidarity with persecuted Christians. This was one of the points of strength of the early church:

> "See how these Christians love each other" could be echoed from one end of the Mediterranean to the other. The Romans in particular sent alms and money to other churches, to the needy and to confessors condemned to the mines. The egalitarianism of the early church seems to have been maintained. Slaves, widows and paupers were fed out of the savings of the faithful, and *solidarity* [emphasis mine] was often carried to fantastic lengths.[13]

The solidarity of the church shown at the national level accomplished much more than just lending spiritual and moral support to local Christians; it provided organization and strength that had immediate effects on the local waves of persecution. The persecution of Presbyterians in the Ch'ol village of La Arena followed the normal stages. After the Presbyterians did not flee at the first threats and warnings, the homes of three believers in Christ were destroyed in February 1990. Since it was at the same time that the National Presbyterian Church of Mexico was initiating its involvement in the persecution in Chiapas, there was an organized attempt to coordinate all of the efforts of the church from local to national levels.

Missionary Bill DeBoer, who coordinated the efforts of the Ch'ol Presbytery and the National Presbyterian Church, gave a preliminary report of the effect of this solidarity: "The efforts of the National Presbyterian Church

13. Frend, *Martyrdom and Persecution*, 257.

at the national level have brought no tangible results as far as government actions are concerned, but the efforts of all of these people at all the levels has been a great comfort to the persecuted families. The importance of their feeling of unity with the larger Body of Christ cannot be overemphasized."[14]

The national church organizations also responded with economic aid, especially in the form of emergency food and supplies to be sent to the persecuted Presbyterians who continued to resist expulsion. When large shipments of food from the organized church arrived in support of the *evangélicos* in that village, the strength of the persecution was defeated. The result was that the persecutors realized that they were up against a highly organized national church, and as DeBoer reported: "Six of the persecuting families, including the strongest anti-Protestant person, have left [the village]. The Protestant evangelical families now make up the majority (13 to 11 families). People tell me that what seemed to break the back of the opposition was the arrival of the first big load of donated food."[15]

Food offerings of corn helped the persecuted church survive.

Some of the unbelieving families in the village started showing new interest in the gospel, and possibilities for evangelism and church growth began to increase in the surrounding area.

14. Letter from Bill DeBoer to author on Ch'ol Persecution, from Palenque, 2. Chiapas, Jun 22, 1990.

15. Letter from Bill DeBoer to author on Ch'ol Persecution, from Palenque, 2. Chiapas, Jun 22, 1990.

> *Observation: National church support and participation can play a prominent role in both halting persecution and in encouraging the growth of the church.*

Although we cannot expect that all persecution cases are going to present the same circumstances or produce such immediate and positive reactions, DeBoer's final comments are noteworthy: "If it turns out as well as it seems to be going, it would clearly be the result of the Lord's working, of the firmness of the believers in showing resistance to persecution without hatred and violence, and of the support of the larger Christian community. Not much credit can go to the government."[16]

Credit for an effective response to persecution, at least in this case, must be given to the efforts of the national church in combination with the Ch'ol Presbytery. The involvement of the national church defense organizations can have even wider effect if it can combine its efforts with those of other national churches and organizations.

Combined Efforts of National Churches

To achieve the greatest effect, the efforts of the National Presbyterian Church of Mexico must work in relation with other national church groups and denominations. Such solidarity was demonstrated in the March 8, 1990, meeting with Lic. Carlos Salinas de Gortari, the President of the Republic of Mexico. In a combined effort to halt persecution, the Presbyterians were joined by the National Baptist Convention of Mexico and also by the Methodist Church of Mexico.[17] In the document presented to President Carlos Salinas de Gortari, the second sentence declares the unity of other Protestant churches of Mexico, such as "Congregational, Episcopal, Mennonite, and Calvinist Reformed churches."[18] The churches demonstrated their solidarity in purpose with the country of Mexico, and they declared their unity in the Christian faith. They made clear statements that they are recognized, officially registered churches according to the laws of Mexico.

In times of persecution, it is also important for this unity to be expressed at the state level. As early as 1987, the joint Ministerial Alliance of Tuxtla Gutiérrez that represents churches from all over the state of Chiapas

---

16. Letter from Bill DeBoer to author on Ch'ol Persecution, from Palenque, 2. Chiapas, Jun 22, 1990.

17. *Novedades*, "Reportaje Especial," A4.

18. *Novedades*, "Reportaje Especial," A4.

held a large demonstration march through the streets of the capital city. In this display of Christian unity, forty churches marched in support of persecuted Chiapas Christians.[19]

On February 20, 1989, nearly three hundred pastors from eight denominations from all over the state of Chiapas attended a historic meeting with the governor of Chiapas. Included in the group were pastors from the indigenous areas where persecution had been rampant. In the official document presented to the Governor, Patrocinio Gonzalez Garrido, the pastors made a united plea, demanding that the constitutional laws be applied and that persecution against Protestant Christians be halted.[20] The document was presented and signed by eight different denominations, including Nazarene, Pentecostal, Baptist, Presbyterian, and Independent Gospel churches.[21] Such combined efforts have a powerful effect on both public opinion and on government actions related to the cessation of persecution and expulsions. The unified front presented by various national churches at the state level in combination with the national level endeavors were effective in pushing for long-term solutions to the persecution conflict.

The International Church Response

While the national church's involvement was irreplaceable, without the backing and support of the international church the force of the national church efforts were often dissipated through legal and political subterfuge. National church involvement can be effective in initiating changes in public and government opinion, but it will often fail to succeed in implementing the enforcement of laws and guarantees for human rights at the local level. Especially where tribal *cacique* systems are strong and local government corruption allows persecution and human rights abuses to continue, international church involvement can be the decisive factor.

When there is an increasing emphasis on international trade and relations, the role of the international church in lending strength to the cause of the particular national church or churches is indispensable. Mexico opened new doors to international trade in 1990. The Gortari administration invested great amounts of time and effort to attract international investment in the Mexican economy. On February 6, 1991, a trilateral free-trade agreement was signed by Mexico with the United States and Canada.[22] The

19. *La República en Chiapas*, "Marcha de Pastores."
20. "Credo y Compromiso," 5.
21. "Credo y Compromiso," 6.
22. *El Nacional*, "Deciden México," 23.

historic defensiveness to anything foreign was changing, especially in the political-economic realms, to an attitude of openly courting outside interests. The Mexican government desired an upbeat, modernization image to attract foreign capital and technology. Any negative reports about Mexico in the foreign press were unwelcomed, especially if they exposed poor government records in the area of human rights.

International Church Involvement in Human Rights

The theme of human rights became a major issue in Mexico and in world politics. In June of 1990, the report of the non-governmental New York based organization, America's Watch, was published in newspapers in Mexico. In relation to human rights violations in Chiapas, the report was extremely critical of the government's role in human rights. After a detailed description of actual cases of violence and unjust expulsions of families by police and authorities in Chiapas, the report expressed a note of concern that all of the incidents had been carried out by local PRI (ruling party) affiliates. "It suggests that the police forces in Chiapas are at the service of local political forces. Their subsequent conduct that includes violations of constitutional procedures indicates that they are simply carrying out the orders of *caciques* and local [mafia] chiefs."[23]

The America's Watch report goes on to note that the new element in Mexico is their concern for favorable international opinion about their human rights record.

> The Mexican government is very sensitive in relation to protecting its national and international image of Human Rights. It has created an exterior illusion of being a nation very respectful of Human Rights, promoting them in international forums, and it judiciously forms an image of being a country that gives safe asylum to political adversaries of repressive governments. Countries like the United States of America refuse to criticize Human Rights abuses in Mexico.[24]

It was encouraging that human rights organizations called attention to the abuses of human rights in Mexico as well as China, since an improvement in human rights will also bring some improvement in situations for persecuted Christians. However, the church cannot depend on human rights organizations to affect pressure for the cessation of persecution.

23. America's Watch, "Los Derechos Humanos," 82–87.
24. America's Watch, "Los Derechos Humanos," 1–13.

Human rights groups are secular organizations that usually don't want to be perceived as giving support to Protestant evangelical groups. Thus, in Chiapas it was interesting to note that all human rights reports seemed to deliberately ignore the mention of the abuse of human rights that were connected to supposed religious persecution. Even the most violent and well-publicized cases of persecution and massive expulsions were ignored in the reports of the human rights organizations.

Therefore, the role of the international church in keeping the pressure on national governments to ensure justice for persecuted Christians was indispensable. Because governments close their eyes to persecution and to human rights abuses if no one draws their attention to these abuses, the role of the international church is to bring such injustice into the international spotlight. Governments often play games with international politics and economics, but the international church must draw attention to human rights and religious freedom abuses through the national and international press. It must use all the means at its disposal to assist the national church and local people that are suffering persecution and human rights abuses in maintaining pressure on abusive and permissive governments. Since most of these governments are susceptible to international opinion and pressure, the international church has a distinct opportunity to make a difference in situations of persecution and human rights abuses.

> Observation: The international church can use international opinion and pressure to influence governments in the area of human rights, and thus push for international political solutions to persecution conflicts.

While some would argue that the church should not be involved in international politics and human rights, I believe that it is a part of its mission responsibility. In a conference held in Switzerland on the church and human rights, it was stated: "Human rights is not a matter of practicality, economics, politics, or laws. It is a matter of basic human dignity, and this is a matter for the Church."[25] If the church is willing to send its missionaries to fulfill the evangelistic mandate, then it must also be responsible to support the indigenous believers in Christ who are persecuted when they respond to that evangelism. The international church is obligated both to the evangelistic mandate and to the "prophetic mandate,"[26] which demands that we seek justice in an unjust world.

25. Glasser, *Church in a Hostile Environment*, 201.
26. Aigbe, "Cultural Mandate," 38–39.

The strategy of the international church in dealing with persecution must include the prophetic mandate of both spiritual responsibilities to Christians in other countries as well as the sociopolitical obligations of justice and human rights for persecuted Christians. When national churches cry for international pressure to implement justice for persecuted Christians, the international church must respond with all of its spiritual and sociopolitical resources.

In procuring justice and human rights, the international church can also promote the growth of the church by helping national churches limit persecution. It is noted numerous times in this book that when hostility to the gospel is minimized, the potential for the growth of the church is maximized. Therefore, pressure by the international church for a cessation of persecution can contribute to the growth of the church.

> The prophetic mandate affirms the reality that socio-cultural and politico-economic factors can and do help a church to grow by providing a positive contextual atmosphere favorable to church growth, and that the same external factors can and do stifle or dramatically slow down church growth if they (socio-cultural and politico-economic factors) turn out to create a hostile and negative environment unfavorable to church growth.[27]

The international church, including all denominational and ecumenical organizations, can fulfill its prophetic role in mission by using international opinion and pressure to influence governments to guarantee the rights of persecuted Christians. It is this international church pressure that can have the greatest effect in bringing a reduction in persecution conflicts.

In the Central American country of El Salvador, the deaths of the Jesuit priests on November 16, 1989, gained international attention and world awareness for the preferential option for the poor. These priests were killed because they had denounced the crimes and injustice of the military. Any church or group of Christians that challenges the injustice and oppression of the government can be subjected to hostility and violence.

A Christian lawyer, Lic. Salvador Ibarra, of the Lutheran Church in El Salvador noted that the persecution was almost unbearable until international pressure was brought to bear on the situation. When international groups, churches, and the US Senate took the role of pressuring the repressive government, there were no further incidents of church bombings or shooting of innocent Christians. But he added: "If the international pressure is reduced, then the cycle of violence returns. Pressure must be constant for the punishment of crimes of murder and torture, to uphold the law, to

---

27. Aigbe, "Cultural Mandate," 42.

guarantee justice and human rights. The U.S. Christians must be the eyes and ears of our world to encourage and promote the defense of human rights. In this, the unity of the body of Christ is essential."[28]

This lawyer admitted that local Christians and Christian lawyers can make legal denouncements of injustice and persecution within the local and national contexts. These are valid, and some battles will be won at this level. However, he pointed out: "Work in international denouncements . . . this is the most effective way to bring a halt to persecution."[29] Coming from a lawyer who was imprisoned for over six months for his legal defense of Christians, this emphatic statement carries great validity.

While the kind of persecution and hostility that was experienced in El Salvador and Nicaragua was different from that which was seen in Chiapas, the effective role of the international church was much the same. The commitment of Christians and churches from other countries to press for justice and human rights for suffering Christians in Central America and Mexico was a key factor. In almost every oppressed and persecuted village and church that we visited in Central America, they expressed much the same idea: "Every time a group like yours comes, we feel protected. Whether human rights are respected in our country depends a lot on the work you do in your country. Peace in our country depends a lot on you."[30]

I was amazed at the sense of hope and protection that the Central American Christians felt in our presence and in our promise to carry their cause to the United States. Their confidence in the help afforded by the international church resulted from their experience that when a group of Christians from the United States visited them, the army and other oppressors were hesitant to use violence against them for fear it would be published in the foreign press. The Christians in Central America trusted that Christians from the US would unite with other international Christians to pressure the United States government to demand justice and human rights in El Salvador and Nicaragua.

> Observation: International pressure is necessary for local Christians to find protection and help in combating oppression and persecution.

28. Salvador Ibarra, interview by Vernon Sterk, San Salvador Lutheran Church, May 27, 1990.

29. Salvador Ibarra, interview by Vernon Sterk, San Salvador Lutheran Church, May 27, 1990.

30. Paarlberg, "War Makes Us Lose Hope," 4.

International Church Involvement
in Chiapas Persecution

Mexican National Presbyterian leaders did not, at first, recognize the importance of the international church involvement in Chiapas. Not until 1990 could they admit in *Presbyterian Survey*: "Since the political situation in Mexico makes it very unlikely that the government will confront the tribal mafias with law enforcement at this time, the only pressure that we believe can be effective is international pressure."[31] Yet, even though national and Chiapas church leaders were aware that very little was being accomplished without international pressure, the question was whether such involvement was worth the risk.

Principally, involvement of the international church could put the work of expatriate missionaries in jeopardy since they could be accused of subversive activities against the government. This was confirmed by Benjamin F. Gutiérrez, associate for South America and Mexico in the Global Mission Ministry Units, when he met with leaders of the National Presbyterian Church of Mexico in late October 1990. Gutiérrez reported that "the Mexican Presbyterians did not speak out sooner because they were afraid of inflaming the situation and endangering the work of North American missionaries in Mexico."[32] With the government's sensitivity to international criticism, any negative press that would cause pressure from the North American church or government could be attributed to missionaries from the United States. The possibility of missionaries becoming scapegoats for the Mexican government was real. It was conceivable that missionaries working with the persecuted Protestant evangelicals in Chiapas would be expelled in a retaliatory action.

In 1986, leaders of the North American Presbyterians offered to help the persecuted Presbyterian Christians in Chiapas by writing to both United States and Mexican officials in an effort to apply some pressure on local authorities. However, the President of the National Presbyterian Church of Mexico, at that time, explained that the situation was very delicate and that "letters from the United States would exacerbate the problem."[33]

In 1989, following the expulsion of six hundred indigenous Presbyterians from the Mitontic tribe, the Presbyterian Church USA offered to go directly to the US Senate to demand justice. One United States senator, who is a member of the Presbyterian Church USA, volunteered to make official

---

31. Stimson, "Mexican Protestants Ask Help," 43.
32. Stimson, "Mexican Protestants Ask Help," 42.
33. Schlossberg "Religious Liberty Alert," 40.

excursions to both Chiapas and Mexico City to put pressure on government officials. However, the National Presbyterian Church of Mexico discouraged such involvement for fear that "reprisals would be undertaken against missionaries in the area who are affiliated with the Reformed Church in America."[34] The Chiapas Mission of the Reformed Church in America agreed with the assessment of the national church at that time.

Concern for the continued presence of missionary staff is often the reason that international denouncement is not used. However, should the primary concern of expatriate missionaries be to protect their own existence? Is international pressure, a major tool in confronting persecution and injustice, to become completely unusable for the sake of missionary self-preservation? If this is the case, then something is seriously wrong. Can missionaries justify ignoring their prophetic role of denouncing injustice and persecution and in exposing human rights abuses on the basis that to do so might prejudice their presence?

It is imperative for missionaries to be involved in facing the risks of international involvement for the sake of persecuted Christians. My position on the questions raised in the previous paragraph is best summarized in what Henry Venn told missionaries in 1680: "Although the missionary is primarily a minister of the gospel, that ministry inevitably has consequences. *In the face of injustice, the missionary has no choice but to cry out against it, whatever the cost*" (emphasis mine).[35]

If the fear of international denouncement of persecution arises only out of a desire to protect missionary presence or a mission program, then missionaries should be willing to risk that presence and program. Missionaries and mission organizations should respond to the needs of the growing indigenous church. If the persecuted Protestant evangelicals and the leaders of the church in Chiapas feel that international pressure is necessary to resolve mounting persecution problems, they need to weigh the risks to missionaries who work with them. While it is essential that missionaries use great wisdom and never become directly involved in politics, they have an obligation to maintain a prophetic role in spite of the risks.

> *Observation: In spite of the risks, the international church and its missionaries must fulfill their prophetic mandate in pressing for solutions to help persecuted Christians.*

34. Schlossberg "Religious Liberty Alert," 40.
35. Shenk, "Authoritarian Governments and Mission," 305.

The International Church and the Zapatista Rebellion

Unfortunately, the international church did not play a major role in Chiapas persecution until after the Zapatista rebellion in 1994. The sad part of the story is that even after 1994, many international church organizations did little to support the persecuted church, but enthusiastically backed the insurgency Zapatista political movement. From 1994 until 1998 a massive and well-organized propaganda war in the news media and over the Internet seduced many Christian organizations into the Zapatista camp. The Zapatista rebel movement attracted world-wide attention. Many Catholics and Protestants in numerous countries sent both physical and financial support for these self-declared freedom fighters. Such massive support from Christian churches seemed inappropriate to the persecuted Christians in Chiapas, who had failed to receive this kind of support and attention during thirty years of violence against evangelical Protestants and Catholics. Amazingly, many Christian denominations will blindly support and give full credence to insurgency political movements, yet many of these Christian social justice organizations turn a blind eye to the incredible waves of persecution of Christians around the world.

In October 1999, *Christian Century* published an article by Mark Taylor, professor of theology at Princeton Theological Seminary and an ordained minister in the Presbyterian Church USA, in which he said: "Churches should cast their lot with the Zapatista effort." He concluded his plea: "The struggle in Chiapas presents churches with a chance to make a stand for the dignity of indigenous peoples."[36] Mark Taylor traveled around the United States promoting financial support and personal visits to the Zapatistas. This contributed to an incredible backing of the Zapatista political movement in Chiapas, while the cause of the persecuted Christians was again ignored. The international church proved that it is a powerful force in effecting public opinion and government action but did not effectively use its influence to support the persecuted church.

International Church Involvement through the Media

One effective method that the national and international church can use to gain justice for persecuted Christians is the international press and the Internet. Such interdenominational religious news services such as *Open Doors*, *Church in Chains*, and *The Voice of the Martyrs* provide excellent worldwide communication to the international church about persecution

36. Taylor, "Zapatista Church," 1031.

and civil rights abuses. These enterprises are well organized with international reporters located in specific areas of the world to provide the communication link to specific church publications around the world. Reports from religious news services eventually reach major radio and television networks and national news sources. The Internet and e-mail provide communication tools that can enhance the rapid diffusion of persecution events. The Zapatista movement in Chiapas has used the Internet media with great success, and the persecuted church should be equipped to publicize information and prayer requests to churches around the world. The changing world situation in international trade relations and human rights interests makes the news media and the Internet essential tools in fighting for justice in persecuted areas. It will be through these communication resources that political pressure can be exerted by the international church.

A Proposed Response to Persecution

If a missionary or indigenous church is faced with threats of hostilities against Christians in a specific area of the world, a suggested plan of action could be helpful. The following represents a ten-point strategy for an organized response to persecution.

1. Notify all church leaders and pastors in a specific country by means of their presidents and secretaries, and notify the directors of Christian defense and human rights organizations of the national church. In this way, prayer chains and circles of fasting can be organized throughout the nation. The battle is a spiritual one, so we must start there. Also, offerings for financial assistance should be initiated in order to be ready to meet inevitable needs when persecution moves to other stages.

2. Counsel must be given to the persecuted Christians so they will negotiate for acceptable options so that expulsions might be avoided or delayed. Use the affirm and fulfill model to affirm worldview concepts wherever possible. Do not attack or become defensive; do not escalate the conflict by making accusations or demands before legal authorities if the persecution has only taken the form of threats and warnings or scare tactics. Trust the Lord for protection, and do not abandon homes and tribal lands on the basis of threats and warnings. Counsel Christians to avoid signing illegal documents that demand voluntary withdrawal from land or property.

3. Distribute study materials on the biblical teaching about persecution so that Christians gain a scriptural perspective on persecution.

4. Encourage Christian leaders to identify and battle the spiritual forces that are behind the persecutors. In this way, they can follow the biblical directive to love their persecutors, while waging spiritual warfare against Satan and his emissaries.

5. Establish a Christian legal defense organization that would channel all necessary reports to legal and government authorities. Refer persecuted Christians to this church-related defense organization. Remind Christians not to place their trust solely in legal solutions.

6. Make official reports to legal and government officials when: people have suffered from physical abuse or imprisonment in which violence is used as a means of intimidation; property such as homes or church buildings have been vandalized or destroyed; actual expulsions have taken place; there has been any loss of life related to persecution.

7. When expulsion by forced removal has occurred: Organize local churches to meet emergency needs of expelled Christians. Encourage Christians to seek the possibility of a calculated return. Stress the importance of maintaining contact with ethnic or family groups still living in the tribal area.

8. Following expulsions, organize Christian community. Establish worship groups and congregations. Don't betray or reject hidden Christians; provide prayer and teaching for them. Establish residential relocation communities when all other options have been exhausted, but beware of the premature purchase of land for relocation of persecuted Christians.

9. Respond in love to the persecutors. Remind persecuted Christians that forgiveness and power healing outreach are basic keys to the growth of the church. Encourage cultural respect and maintenance of cultural forms and patterns. Worship in house churches if the building of churches is strongly opposed.

10. When persecution becomes increasingly violent and persistent: Use local and state level newspapers to publish as much of the actual persecution events as possible. Ask the national church to pressure state and federal government authorities. Appeal to the international church for solidarity, support, political denouncements and political action. Facilitate international publicity through Christian news sources and church publications along with the Internet and e-mail.

This ten-point plan for a unified response to persecution may not meet all persecution situations and needs. It is based on the Chiapas persecution model. However, the main points will be helpful in forming a constructive response to persecution in most situations.

Summary

The involvement of the national and international church is a key element in the total response that can lead to eventual solutions in the persecution conflict. This involvement holds the potential to respond with both the solidarity of the church as well as the force of political influence.

The national church can be very effective in providing solidarity in spiritual, legal-political, and material aid. Political action and pressure by the church at the national level does affect changes in government attitudes and action in dealing with persecution, and this is essential in the search for long-term solutions. Even at the local level, the involvement of the national church can play a prominent role in halting persecution and in encouraging the growth of the church.

The importance of international church involvement in pressing for justice for persecuted Christians has increased with the change in international government relations. The international church must be willing to fulfill its prophetic mandate in using all of its resources to push for a cessation of unjust persecution. The example of Central America shows that international involvement is an essential key in the response to persecution. In spite of the risks, international pressure must be applied in response to the pleas of persecuted Christians.

Epilogue

I BEGAN STUDYING PERSECUTION more than forty years ago. My original goal was to discover an anthropological model that would help new Christians avoid persecution. The affirm and fulfill model was developed out of my desire to present the gospel message in a positive, non-confrontational way. However, while this model was successful in avoiding premature persecution, it became painfully clear that the gospel itself would bring eventual confrontation. I was encouraged to see the Mayans respond positively to the gospel in my first decade of living with them, but with that growth came the pain of seeing new believers in Christ being ostracized, beaten, jailed, and some martyred. When the expulsion of Christians in the Tzotzil tribes increased dramatically during my second decade of working with them, I felt an urgency to begin an analysis of persecution which eventually resulted in this book.

The most rewarding part of my experience in studying the dynamics of persecution has been seeing the results of the approaches and insights that are presented in this book. Fifty years have passed since we began working with the Tzotzil people of Chiapas, Mexico, so it is time to reflect on how God, in his grace, has chosen to bring about a decrease in persecution and an increase in the numbers of Christians there.

As I look back to 1969 when my wife and I began living in a Zinacanteco village, there were no evangelical Protestant Christians in Zinacantan and only a few small clusters of believers in Christ in each of the other Tzotzil tribes. In our initial years, I personally experienced some threats of persecution, but as the church began to grow, the new believers in Christ became the real targets. By the mid-1980s, more than twenty-five thousand Tzotzil Christians had been expelled from their tribal lands, and many endured violent persecution. I praise the Lord, however, that by the year 2000, the Christian defense organization in Chiapas reported that persecution incidents had almost ceased. I have observed that each time there was a respite from persecution, the church was allowed to grow at a rapid rate. Thus, by the year 2019, the Tzotzil churches have increased so significantly, that an indigenous pastor recently reported that there is an evangelical church or worshiping group in every village of both the Zinacanteco and Chamula tribes. Since these two Tzotzil tribes were the most resistant to the gospel message, and persecution and expulsions were most prevalent in these tribal areas, this is amazing news! Yet, even more amazing are the statistics that I am receiving that the number of evangelical Christians in the indigenous tribes of the Tzotzil-speaking people is estimated to be nearly two hundred thousand.

The amazing growth of the Tzotzil church was not only positively affected by a decrease in persecution, but also by the Zapatista insurgency movement in the 1990s. This movement brought international attention to the Mayan people of Chiapas. National news sources and the federal government of Mexico channeled massive efforts and resources into the indigenous tribal areas. The tribal *caciques* and other persecutors turned their attention to the threats of the armed Zapatistas, and the incidents of persecution and expulsions decreased.

The inter-confessional translation of the first full Tzotzil Bible also had a positive effect on the spread of the gospel. The translation team that my wife and I coordinated was made up of both Presbyterian and Roman Catholic indigenous translators. After ten years of working together on this translation project, the tensions between Catholics and Protestants were significantly reduced. When this Bible, which contains not only the Old and New Testaments, but also the intertestamental books, was dedicated by both evangelical and Catholic indigenous leaders, most Tzotzil people claimed this translation as their own. The unity that was created by the joint translation of this Tzotzil Bible also brought a reduction in persecution. The transformation brought about by the Word of God in the language of the indigenous people not only helped stem the tide of persecution in Chiapas, it also caused new waves of evangelism and church growth. Once persecution was nearly halted in the Chiapas highlands, and the Mayan Christians felt free to focus their efforts on outreach, they organized the first mission agency of Chiapas, called AMICH. It not only offered training for indigenous missionaries to reach beyond their own tribal areas, but selected candidates to be sent beyond the borders of Mexico.

I praise God for the work of his Holy Spirit in the Tzotzil Mayan tribes of Chiapas. I believe that the concepts and insights in this book were used by God to limit the damaging effects of persecution and to communicate the good news to the unreached Tzotzil Mayans. Persecution and hostility against Christians have become prevalent in so many areas of the world today. I trust that the observations and suggestions shared in this book will help persecuted churches around the world understand, prepare for, and respond to persecution in a way that allows them to survive and grow. I also hope that the international church will realize its essential role in advocating for the persecuted church. On the other hand, I realize that not all of the principles and guidelines in this book are applicable to every persecution context. I would be the first to recognize that many of the cases of persecution in other parts of the world may present different causes and challenges. Yet, I do believe that there are many similarities and that most of the principles that have been learned in my Chiapas experience can be applied wherever the threat of persecution arises.

Finally, I pray that valuable insights might be gained by all who read this book, who are attempting to understand and survive persecution, and who endeavor to give direction to the persecuted church around the world.

Bibliography

Aigbe, Sunday. "Cultural Mandate, Evangelistic Mandate, Prophetic Mandate: Of These Three the Greatest Is . . . ?" *Missiology* 19 (1991) 31–43.

America's Watch. "Los Derechos Humanos en México." *Tiempo* (Jun 27, 1990) 82-7.

Avante. "Denuncia a la Procuraduria de la Repùblica." San Cristóbal de Las Casas, Chiapas, (Jul, 1985) 3.

"The Basil Letter." International Congress on World Evangelism, Lausanne, Jul 1974. Located in Arthur Glasser's files, Fuller Theological Seminary, Pasadena, CA, 1974.

Beeson, Trevor. *Discretion and Valour.* Philadelphia: Fortress, 1982.

Bosch, David J. "Mission in the 1990s: Three Views." *International Bulletin of Missionary Research* 14 (1990) 150.

Bourdeaux, Michael. *Land of Crosses: The Struggle for Religious Freedom in Lithuania.* Chulmleugh, Devon: Augustine, 1979.

Cadorette, Curt. *From the Heart of the People: The Theology of Gustavo Gutierrez.* Louisville, KY: Meyer-Stone, 1987.

Cancian, Frank. *Economics and Prestige in a Maya Community.* Stanford: Stanford University Press, 1965.

Canfield, Leon H. *The Early Persecutions of the Christians.* New York: AMS, 1968.

Chao, Jonathan, and Ralph Covell. "Questions most frequently asked about the Christian church in China." *Theology, News and Notes* 31 (1984) 9.

Cooksey, J. J. *The Land of the Vanished Church: A Survey of North Africa.* London: World Dominion, 1926.

Crary, David. "Government Restrictions on Religion Increasing Worldwide." AP News. https://www.apnews.com/3f554ea6fe6a42c08c0618745eee8c2b.

"Credo y Compromiso de La Iglesia Evangélica en Chiapas." Tuxtla Gutiérrez, Chiapas: Unpublished document presented to Governor Patricinio González Garrido, Feb 20, 1989.

Deyneka, Peter, Jr., and Anita Deyneka. *A Song in Siberia.* Elgin: David C. Cook, 1977.

Dussel, Enrique. *History and the Theology of Liberation.* Maryknoll, NY: Orbis, 1976.

———. *A History of the Church in Latin America.* Grand Rapids: Eerdmans, 1981.

Earle, Duncan. "Appropriating the Enemy: Maya Religious Organization and Community Survival." In *The Politics of Popular Religion*, edited by Lynn Stephen and James Dow. Unpublished manuscript, 1987, 19–20.

El Nacional. "Deciden México, EU y Canadá dar inicio al acuerdo trilateral." Feb 6, 1991, 23.

Elison, George. *Deus Destroyed: The Image of Christianity in Early Modern Japan.* Cambridge: Harvard University Press, 1973.

Esponda, Hugo. *Historia de la Iglesia Presbiteriana de Chiapas.* Mexico City: El Faro, 1986.

Fabrega, Horacio, Jr., and Daniel B. Silver. *Illness and Shamanistic Curing in Zinacantan.* Stanford: Stanford University Press, 1973.

Flores, Jonas. "El Artículo 24 Constitucional." Mexico City: IMLIR, nd.

Foster, George M. *Traditional Societies and Technological Change.* New York: Harper & Row, 1973.

Frend, W. H. C. *Martyrdom and Persecution in the Early Church.* Oxford: Basil Blackwell, 1965.

"From Pain to Promise." *Voice of the Martyrs.* February 11, 2019. www.persecution. com.

Glasser, Arthur F. *The Church in a Hostile Environment.* Unpublished collection of case studies, Fuller Theological Seminary, Pasadena, CA, n.d.

Goff, James E. *The Persecution of Protestant Christians in Colombia, 1948–1958: With an Investigation of Its Background and Causes.* Cuernavaca: CIDOC, 1968.

Gonzalez, Miguel. "Autoridades y Religiosos Expulsan a 154 Indígenas Protestantes de la Comunidad de Aldama, Chiapas." *Excelsior* (Nov 11, 1989) A-2.

Grossu, Sergiu. "Methods of Degradation and Brainwashing." Located in Arthur Glasser's files, Fuller Theological Seminary, Pasadena, CA (1975) 60.

Hallie, Philip. *Lest Innocent Blood Be Shed.* New York: Harper & Row, 1979.

Henríquez Tobar, Elio. "44 Personas de Zinacantán expulsadas por ser evangélicas." *Tiempo* (Sep 11, 1990) 1, 4.

———. "Las Expulsiones 'no es un problema estrictamente religioso': Patrocinio." *Tiempo* (Sep 13, 1990) 1, 4.

———. "Todos los expulsados de Aldama regresan hoy." *Tiempo* (Nov 15, 1989) 1.

Hernández, Erisel. "Freno a Caciques Indígenas Demandan Evangelistas." *Diario Popular* (Jul 26, 1989) 1, 4.

Hesselgrave, David J. *Communicating Christ Cross-Culturally.* Grand Rapids: Zondervan, 1978.

Hiebert, Paul G. *Anthropological Insights for Missionaries.* Grand Rapids: Baker, 1985.

Hofman, J. Samuel. "Enforcing Village Solidarity." *Missionary Monthly* (Jun 1990) 6.

———. "Liberty Comes to La Libertad." *Missionary Monthly* (August, 1988) 3.

Holme, Leonard R. *The Extinction of the Christian Churches in North Africa.* New York: Burt Franklin, 1989.

Huie Balay, Diane. "Mexican Methodists Seek Help to Halt Catholic Attacks." *The United Methodist Review* (Sep 28, 1990).

Kirk, Andrew J. *Theology Encounters Revolution.* Downers Grove: InterVarsity, 1980.

Kraft, Charles H. *Christianity in Culture.* Maryknoll, NY: Orbis, 1979.

———. *Christianity with Power.* Ann Arbor: Servant, 1989.

La República en Chiapas. "Marcha de Pastores Evangélicos se Efectuará hoy en Esta Capital." Mar 21, 1987.

Lam, Wing-hung. *Chinese Theology in Construction.* Pasadena: William Carey Library, 1983.

Laman, Gordon D. "Our Nagasaki Legacy: An Examination of the Period of Persecution of Christianity and Its Impact on Subsequent Christian Mission in Japan." *The Northeast Asia Journal of Theology* (Mar/Sep, 1982) 108–17.

Las Casas, Bartolomé de. *The Devastation of the Indies: A Brief Account*. New York: Seabury, 1974.

Latourette, Kenneth Scott. *Christianity through the Ages*. New York: Harper & Row, 1965.

———. *A History of Christianity*. New York: Harper & Row, 1953.

Lesbaupin, Ivo. *Blessed are the Persecuted*. Maryknoll, NY: Orbis, 1987.

"A Letter to the Churches in Asia." Evangelical Fellowship of Asia Consultation Participants. *Asia Theological News* 14 (1988) 1–4.

López Pérez, Jorge. "Interview by Vernon Sterk." Feb 7, 1990.

Marocco, James. "Territorial Spirits." PhD diss., School of World Mission, Fuller Theological Seminary, Pasadena, CA, 1988, 5.

Martinez García, Carlos. "Indígenas protestantes: ¿agentes del imperialismo?" *Uno Más Uno* (Oct 18, 1990) 2.

———. "¿Existe persecución religiosa en México?" *Uno Más Uno* (Oct 11, 1990) 2.

Mayers, Marvin K. *Christianity Confronts Culture*. Grand Rapids: Academie, 1987.

McGavran, Donald A. *The Bridges of God*. New York: Friendship, 1955.

———. *Understanding Church Growth*. Grand Rapids: Eerdmans, 1970.

———. *Understanding Church Growth*. 3rd ed. Edited by Peter Wagner. Grand Rapids: Eerdmans, 1990.

McHenry, J. Patrick. *A Short History of Mexico*. New York: Doubleday, 1962.

Miller, Frank C. "Cultural Change as Decision-Making: A Tzotzil Example." *Ethnology* 4 (1965) 61.

Moffett, Matt. "Mexicans Convert as a Matter of Politics." *Wall Street Journal* (Jun 1, 1988) 20.

Moore, Art. "Ugandan church leader urges African Christians to prepare for persecution." *Pulse* (Mar 9, 1990) 4.

Nash, Manning. "Political Relations in Guatemala." *Social and Economic Studies* (As quoted from Cancian) 7 (1958) 65–75.

Neill, Stephen. *A History of Christian Missions*. Grand Rapids: Eerdmans, 1965.

Nida, Eugene A. *Customs and Cultures*. New York: Harper & Row, 1954.

———. *Message and Mission*. New York: Harper & Row, 1960.

Novedades. "Reportaje Especial." (Mar 8, 1990) A4.

Número Uno. "Editorial." (Mar 14, 1987) 2.

Open Doors News Service. "Persecuted Mexican Christians Seek Protection." *Missionary Monthly* (1987).

Open Doors USA. "Standing Strong through the Storm." Daily devotional, December 14, 2018, 14.

Outerbridge, Leonard M. *The Lost Churches of China*. Philadelphia: Westminster, 1952.

Paarlberg, John. "War Makes Us Lose Hope, but Not Our Hope in You." *The City Gate*, Office of Social Witness, Reformed Church in America (1990) 4.

Palacios, Oscar. "Mitontic: Caciquismo, no choques religiosos." *Semanal Ambar* (Jul 17, 1989) 1–3.

Parkes, Henry Bamford. *A History of Mexico*. Boston: Houghton Mifflin, 1966.

Pascal, Pierre. *The Religion of the Russian People*. Translated by Rowan Williams. London: Mowbrays, 1976.

Pérez U., Matilde. "No puede haber indigenismo sin apoyo gobernamental decidido." *Tiempo* (May 10, 1990) 2–3.

Rabasa, Emilio O., and Gloria Caballero. *Méxicano: Ésta es tu Constitución.* Mexico City: Cámara de Deputados, 1982.

Richards, Cole. "The Price of Leaving Islam to Embrace Christ." *Voice of the Martyrs* (Jan 2019).

Richardson, Don. *Peace Child.* Glendale, CA: Regal, 1974.

Rogers, Everett M. *Diffusion of Innovations.* 3rd ed. New York: Free Press, 1983.

Rus, Jan. "Managing Mexico's Indians: The Historical Context and Consequences of Indigenismo." Unpublished paper in author's file (1976) 11–13.

————. "Social Change and the Power of Bilinguals in a Community of Highland Chiapas." Unpublished working paper in author's files (1975) 16–20.

Samayoa Arce, Amet. "Mitontic, Pueblo Sin Ley." *Diario El Dia* (Jul 16, 1989) 4.

Sanchez, Saldinu. "Mas de 600 Tzotziles Echados, tras Violación de un Acuerdo." *Número Uno* (Jul 28, 1989).

Schlossberg, Herbert. "Religious Liberty Alert: Who'll Help Presbyterians Persecuted in Mexico?" *Presbyterian Survey* (Oct 1990) 40.

Shenk, Wilbert T., ed. "Authoritarian Governments and Mission." *Mission Focus: Current Issues* (1980) 305.

Sierra Martínez, Luis. "Chiapas es un Estado de Caciques: Jaime Sabines." *Tiempo* (Nov 14, 1989).

————. "En Zequentic no Aceptaron el Regreso de 10 Familias Evangélicas Ayer." *Tiempo* (Oct 24, 1990) 4.

————. "Los evangélicos llevan al plano nacional el problema de las expulsiones." *Tiempo* (Dec 1, 1990).

Sobrino, Jon. *The True Church and the Poor.* Maryknoll, NY: Orbis, 1984.

Steven, Hugh. "Night of the Long Knives." *Christian Times* 2 (1968) 4–7.

————. *They Dared to be Different.* Irvine, CA: Harvest House, 1976.

Stimson, Eva. "Mexican Protestants Ask Help." *Presbyterian Survey* (Jan 1990) 42–44.

Taylor, Mark. "A Zapatista Church: Presbyterians in Chiapas; Displaced and Abandoned." *Christian Century* (Oct 27, 1999) 1031.

Tiempo. "A la Opinión Pública." (Jun 13, 1990) 3.

Tucker, Ruth A. *From Jerusalem to Irian Jaya: A Bibliographical History of Christian Missions.* Grand Rapids: Academie, 1983.

Tzotzil Presbytery of Chiapas. "Letter to General Assembly, National Presbyterian Church of Mexico." Jan 24, 1990.

Van Engen, Charles Edward. *The Growth of the True Church: An Analysis of the Ecclesiology of Church Growth Theory.* Amsterdam: Rodopi, 1981.

Villafuerte, Concepción. "Editorial." *Tiempo* (Jun 19, 1990) 2.

————. "Editorial." *Tiempo* (Nov 6, 1990) 2.

————. "Editorial." *Tiempo* (Jan 29, 1991) 2.

Vogt, Evon Z. *Zinacantan: A Maya Community in the Highlands of Chiapas.* Cambridge: Belknap, 1969.

Von Hagen, Victor W. *World of the Maya.* New York: Mentor, 1960.

Wagner, Charles Peter. *How to Have a Healing Ministry without Making Your Church Sick!* Ventura: Regal, 1988.

————. *Spiritual Power and Church Growth.* Altamonte Springs, FL: Strang, 1986.

Woehr, Chris. "Mexican Governor Pledges to Halt Persecution in Chiapas." *Christian Informer* (Sep 1989) 8.

Wolff, Hans Walter. "Masters and Slaves: On Overcoming Class-Struggle in the Old Testament." *Interpretation* 27 (1973) 259.

Workman, Herbert B. *Persecution in the Early Church.* London: William Clowes and Sons, 1906.

World. "Violent Attack Breaks up Mexico City Prayer Meeting." Feb 17, 1990.

Yaker, Henri M., ed. *The Future of Time.* Garden City, NY: Doubleday, 1971.

CPSIA information can be obtained
at www.ICGtesting.com
Printed in the USA
BVHW042317180120
569257BV00004B/4